THE OLD TESTAMENT
AND THE SIGNIFICANCE OF JESUS

The Old Testament and the Significance of Jesus

EMBRACING CHANGE — MAINTAINING
CHRISTIAN IDENTITY

• •

*The Emerging Center
in Biblical Scholarship*

Fredrick C. Holmgren

WILLIAM B. EERDMANS PUBLISHING COMPANY
GRAND RAPIDS, MICHIGAN / CAMBRIDGE, U.K.

© 1999 Wm. B. Eerdmans Publishing Co.
255 Jefferson Ave. S.E., Grand Rapids, Michigan 49503 /
P.O. Box 163, Cambridge CB3 9PU U.K.

Printed in the United States of America

04 03 02 01 00 99   7 6 5 4 3 2 1

Library of Congress Cataloging-in-Publication Data

Holmgren, Fredrick Carlson, 1926-
The Old Testament and the significance of Jesus:
embracing change — maintaining Christian identity:
the emerging center in biblical scholarship /
Fredrick C. Holmgren.
p.   cm.
Includes bibliographical references.
ISBN 0-8028-4453-7 (pbk.: alk. paper)
1. Bible. N.T. — Relation to Old Testament.
2. Christianity and other religions — Judaism.
3. Judaism — Relations — Christianity.
4. Jesus Christ — Person and offices.
5. Bible O.T. — Hermeneutics.
I. Title.
BS2387.H55   1999
230'.0411 — dc21   98-50025
CIP

TO BETTY
in whom
candor and caring love
are finely woven together

Contents

Contents

Foreword

Political domination by the Christian West has gone hand in hand with religious intolerance, and that for many centuries. None has been more the object and victim of that political domination/religious intolerance than the Jewish community, especially as the Jewish community has insisted on its own legitimate textual-theological-interpretive claims. It is an astonishing fact that it has taken the barbarism of the Holocaust for us to notice the systemic abuse of the Jewish community by the Christian West. Indeed, much of the theological tradition of the Christian West has been venomous toward Jews, right up until World War II; only since that time has an elemental rethinking been undertaken of that sorry, shameful history, an elemental rethinking that now can hardly be avoided.

It has become clear, moreover, that that sorry history is not only one of political domination, but that the horrendous political habits are deeply rooted in interpretive practices of supersessionism that have been wholesale and almost completely unexamined in the Christian community. Indeed, Kendall Soulen *(The God of Israel and Christian Theology)* has made a powerful case that classic Christian formulation from the outset is intrinsically anti-Semitic and assumes supersessionism at its core. Soulen is front and center among those who call for a radical rethinking of Christian claims from the ground up.

Slowly, and very much in our own time, Christians have begun to make a response to this long, abusive history of anti-Semitism. The first response of redress has been what I would call a "political" one, which

sees the hurt inflicted by conventional Christian assumptions and is de-
termined that it must cease. There has emerged almost a "lobby" of
such political insistence that continues to perform an important service
among us, and the present book is fully appreciative of that effort.

But if the failure of Christianity toward Judaism is not only political
but also interpretive, then a frontal political response by itself is not fully
adequate. Along with it is required the close, careful, patient work of
exegesis, the rereading of texts that reconsiders the long, habituated mis-
reading by Christian supersessionism. The present book by Fredrick
Holmgren is a major contribution to this more demanding redress that
the church must now make, given its long history of abusive interpretation. Indeed, I know of no study that is as careful and delicate and "down
under" about specific texts as is this study of Holmgren, that is bound to
make a decisive impact upon future study. Holmgren's study will lead
most readers (certainly this one) to an entirely new scholarly literature
that has yet not received great attention. Beyond that, he shows himself to
be a sensitive reader of texts, thoroughly grounded in the primary claims
of Christian faith but able to move with freedom and imagination so that
we see texts afresh.

His study is rich with new suggestion, and the book will be a semi-
nal source for much subsequent scholarship. Here I will identify three
areas of study that strike me as especially important:

First, Holmgren spends a great deal of time considering what he
calls "creative/depth" exegesis, whereby ongoing interpretation fits
"earlier texts to later times." He reviews the way in which the New Testament community, the community of rabbinic interpretation, and the
Qumran community all engage in imaginative interpretation of texts
well beyond any possible "authorial intent," in order to serve subsequent communal claims. Holmgren shows that the text is immensely
open to such reading and that all three communities engage in the same
sort of reading, thus making clear that as the method is legitimate and
congruent with the text, all such readings are in principle legitimate, including those of Judaism.

The effect of the argument is to insist that Christianity, which
reads the text toward Jesus, has no monopoly on imaginative interpretation and cannot deny the legitimacy of the same enterprise in Judaism.
This most important recognition moves against Christian monopolistic
tendencies. Regina Schwartz, *The Mark of Cain,* has recently argued
that the "myth of scarcity," rooted in monotheism, produces violence.

Holmgren suggests to me that it is a monotheistic myth of *interpretive scarcity* that produces exclusionary Christian interpretation that in the end does violence to Judaism. But, as Holmgren makes clear, there is no scarcity of reading in these texts. There is a plenitude of interpretive futures that neither requires nor permits exclusionary reading. Thus Christians practice "believers" exegesis, but so do the parallel communities of Judaism. The implications of this argument about "creative/depth" exegesis are enormous for future interpretive respect and cooperation between Jews and Christians.

Second, Holmgren provides an extended exegetical reflection on Jeremiah 31:31-34 and the assertion of the new covenant. The text is important both because it has provided the formula "New Testament" and because, as in the letter to the Hebrews, it has served the interests of supersessionism. Holmgren shows the rich and diverse ways in which the "new covenant" passage can be understood. He pays close attention to Norbert Lohfink's notion of "never revoked." His own major contribution, however, is to suggest that the rejection of the "old covenant" in the passage is to be understood ironically, for the "new covenant" is in fact the "old covenant" reaffirmed. While the text clearly can be read toward Jesus, there is no necessary requirement in that direction, thus making a *mandated* move toward Jesus impossible.

Third, the final discussion, "Jesus in the Creeds," is, in my judgment, a contribution of major significance. It is no small matter to have a scripture scholar move into a consideration of the creeds, but Holmgren does so with authority and sensitivity. He knows what is at stake as he takes them up. His judgment is that in the creedal development of the early church, Jesus is cast as "the Wisdom of God" but is presented in "Greek dress." Holmgren, however, is not content simply to reduce "Wisdom" to a slogan about which to argue, but probes the several formulations that variously refer to the wisdom of God and focuses upon the "wonder" of God discerned in Jesus. He observes, moreover, that the "divinity" of Jesus is not flatly given but is the "upper limit" of the textual claim (Hengel). He makes much of Calvin's observation that the creed is "a song to be sung." The formulations of the creeds are not to be flattened to substantive, rationalistic discourse, but must be kept in the range of exuberance that refuses precision. The church "apparently did not intend to affirm that Jesus equals God," but Holmgren observes that it is that affirmation that reduces *doxology* to *rational formula,* an incredible stumbling block for the way ahead with

Judaism. The importance of Holmgren's argument can hardly be over-stated, for it opens the way to think back to the church's formula and back behind those formulations to where there is common ground with the forms of emerging Judaism.

It is to be stressed that Holmgren is not "soft" on Christian claims. Rather, he wants to attend to what is in fact claimed, without all of the careless, cultural, uncritical accouterments that have come to accompany those claims.

It is a special delight to celebrate this book from my longtime, cherished friend Fred Holmgren. He and I shared graduate study in ancient days under James Muilenburg at Union Seminary in New York. In those days, Muilenburg talked much of Martin Buber and was greatly engaged with Abraham Heschel, who was just across the street at Jewish Theological Seminary. The largeness of Muilenburg's vision and his sense of commonality and solidarity with the Judaism of Heschel are a rich bequest to those of us who were his students. That largeness of vision is now well voiced by Holmgren. Beyond that, in our cadre of graduate students, Holmgren was the most quiet and the most irenic. This book proceeds in that same quiet and irenic spirit, in confidence of the truth of Christian claims. It is, however, a truth not given in idolatrous form, ready to "leap over" its own absolutes to where the text yet insists that we might go. Holmgren gets at hard questions, the answers to which make redress of barbaric domination a task to be undertaken with resolute, joyous determination. There is so much to unlearn and then to relearn. Holmgren teaches us along the way.

Columbia Theological Seminary   Walter Brueggemann
July 24, 1997

Preface

A sabbatical period in 1991 at the Albert-Ludwigs-Universität, Freiburg, Germany, served to initiate this volume. Here I experienced the warm welcome of Prof. Dr. Lothar Ruppert, Professor of Old Testament, Institut für Biblische und Historische Theologie, who sponsored my research at the university and made available to me office space, computers, and the enviable resources of the University Library. I am deeply grateful for his embracing friendship and continuing encouragement. Further, the friendly thoughtfulness of Frau Rhodika Matasariu, Secretary to Professor Ruppert, are well remembered.

A *Deutscher Akademischer Austausch Dienst* award and a grant from North Park Theological Seminary funded the research of the above-mentioned sabbatical period. In the years following, research and writing have been supported by the latter institution and by long-term colleagues and friends, Dr. Glenn and Sharon Palmberg, who, in their engagement of people and issues, reflect the central concerns of Scripture.

Since 1991 Betty and I have spent three months of every year in Freiburg, where we lived in a pleasant apartment at the home of Herr Josef and Frau Arntraud Huber. They have blessed us with family kindness which increased in great measure the enjoyment of living and working in this beautiful city.

This volume is an attempt to contribute both to the world of scholarship and to the preaching, teaching ministry of clergy. For this reason, I sought the assistance of a number of pastors who agreed, along with Dr. Paul Koptak, Assistant Professor of Communication and Biblical Interpretation at North Park Theological Seminary, to read the first draft of the complete manuscript; namely, Steven Elde, Stacey Littlefield, James Sundholm, and James Widboom. For their willingness to do so and especially for the influential critique offered, I am thankful. The final and longest chapter in the book concentrates on the crucial theme of Christology. In addition to readers listed above, I passed it under the critical eyes of faculty colleagues who work in this area. To them I am indebted for sharing with me their expert knowledge; namely, Dr. Philip Anderson (Church History), Dr. Donald Frisk (Theology; emeritus), Dr. Klyne Snodgrass (New Testament), Dr. John Weborg (Theology). I have profited immeasurably from all who have read and commented on the manuscript and express to them, at least, "a thousand thanks."

The exceptional contributions that Dr. Walter Brueggemann has made to the world of scholarship and the church are widely known and richly appreciated. I am delighted and honored that he, a fellow classmate of some years ago at Union Theological Seminary (N.Y.), is writing the foreword to this volume.

North Park Theological Seminary
Chicago, Illinois
Advent: December 10, 1997

INTRODUCTION

Jews and Christians

SEEING MATTERS AS THEY REALLY ARE

The Old Testament and Jesus:
The Emerging Center in Scholarship

The character of the Old Testament and its relationship to Jesus Christ are ancient and continuing themes within the Christian church. They have always been important subjects of discussion because they relate directly to Christian identity as well as to the teaching and preaching ministry of the church. In recent years, however, the above themes have been the subject of renewed activity on the part of biblical scholars.

An important and encouraging aspect of this new emphasis is that it consists of contributions from both conservative/evangelical and mainline scholars.[1] Their publications witness of a growing movement toward the "center" in biblical interpretation — a stance which embraces change while holding to the importance of maintaining Christian identity. Areas of agreement are substantial, and where there is difference of opinion, discussion of the divergent viewpoints takes place increasingly in an irenic context. Such a development, in which respect and generosity are expressed, is a welcome change from earlier hurtful exchanges when scholars viewed one another as opponents to be defeated. Before beginning the research for this volume, I was not fully aware of the present-day "gathering around the

---

1. These designations are not fully satisfying, but they indicate in a general manner what is happening in our day.

center." It was one of the delightful surprises resulting from this undertaking.

Jews and Christians in Conversation

The new activity regarding the relationship of the Old Testament to the New Testament's proclamation of Jesus occurs in the context of serious discussions between Christian and Jewish leaders which have been brought about mainly by the Shoah (Holocaust). Christianity and Judaism hold many beliefs in common, but it is evident also that foundational differences exist between the two faiths. These differences have created a deep and enduring chasm of estrangement. For both Christians and Jews, the differences are bound up with the character of the New Testament proclamation and its interpretation of the Old Testament. In the midst of the present dialogue then, and in light of modern scholarship, the church needs to address (1) the manner in which Christians approach the Old Testament scripture, which, with a different arrangement of books, is also the Jewish Bible; (2) areas of commonality with and differences from Judaism; (3) the New Testament's witness concerning Jesus Christ, who is the church's reason for existence. In the present volume, *The Old Testament and the Significance of Jesus,* we intend to discuss these and associated issues.

The Bible is the touchstone for the church's witness. In the changing circumstances of life (e.g., racism, sexism, war, abortion), the Christian community has had to return again and again to this scripture to discover direction and authenticity. Today, as the church stands in conversation with the Jewish tradition and the contemporary Jewish community, it needs to wrestle again with the Bible. Much of the focus today is on the Old Testament (Hebrew Bible), out of which both rabbinic Judaism and Christianity draw life. As one confronts the interpretations of this scripture by Jews and Christians, it becomes apparent that there are important similarities and differences.

To be sure, fairness requires Christians to recognize and value the similarities that exist between the two faith communities, but as David Tracy has remarked, focus on similarities may be an escape from the demand of facing the other as "other." Not to confront the "otherness" of the other community is to show disrespect for the integrity of that faith community. Tracy suggests that when we speak of similarities between two communities, we should speak (and think) of "similarities-in-difference."[2] Krister Stendahl recognizes also that similarities are important, but he declares: "But the time has come for us to avoid constructing special Christianities in order to smooth the way for dialogues with various other religious traditions." On the other hand, Stendahl asks:

> Does Christianity *have* to identify itself as that which is *over and against* Judaism? Indeed, is this really the case? Are there models of living together instead of over and against each other that do more essential justice to both our faiths? We must somehow modify our symbol systems so that we do not continuously engender trends of demonization and contempt.[3]

A healthy and helpful dialogue takes place when both differences and similarities are held in view. To overemphasize the one or the other aspect creates distorted images of both communities.[4]

On the following pages we hope to be guided by the wise words of David Tracy and Krister Stendahl. We understand that difficult issues are being addressed in this volume and that within the church there are differing, conflicting responses. All of the voices need to be heard. Every Christian is responsible to speak as clearly and as truthfully as possible about matters that touch on Christian life and thought. This we

2. David Tracy, *Dialogue with the Other: The Interreligious Dialogue* (Grand Rapids: Wm. B. Eerdmans Publishing Co., 1990), pp. 41-42. See also p. 6. Recognizing the other as "other" does not mean recognizing the other as alien, but rather: "To recognize the other *as* other, the different *as* different is also to acknowledge that other world of meaning as, in some manner, a possible option for myself." Martin E. Marty, in a foreword to Jacob Neusner's volume, *Telling Tales: The Urgency and Basis for Judeo-Christian Dialogue* (Louisville: Westminster/John Knox, 1993), p. 4, alludes to something similar when he says: "If they [i.e., the people in dialogue] are realistic, frank, aware of their own stories, they can further such dialogue. If they keep making up soft versions of their own traditions, they will produce mush or hypocrisy. They will waste everyone's time and create nothing but illusions."

3. Krister Stendahl, "Anti-Semitism and the New Testament," *Explorations* 7, no. 2 (1993): 7.

4. See the wise comments of Michael Wyschogrod, "The Impact of Dialogue with Christianity on My Self-Understanding as a Jew," in *Die Hebräische Bibel und ihre zweifache Nachgeschichte*, ed. E. Blum et al. (Neukirchen: Neukirchener Verlag, 1990), p. 726.

have attempted to do, admittedly from our point of view,[5] in discussion with many contemporary scholars of varied theological traditions.

This book arises out of a desire to speak to the needs of college and seminary students, and it represents a continuing interest to provide resources for Christian pastors and priests in their preaching and teaching ministry.[6] We offer this study to the Christian community with the hope that it will increase appreciation for the Old Testament and the Jewish tradition(s) as well as revitalize commitment to the church's proclamation of God's redeeming presence in Jesus Christ.

5. See Walter Brueggemann's important article, "Biblical Theology Appropriately Postmodern," *Biblical Theology Bulletin* 27 (1997): 4-9 (esp. p. 8). Brueggemann speaks a hard but necessary word to all who wish to interpret scripture for other communities. He reminds us that all interpreters read from their own point of view (i.e., "locally"). One need not apologize for such local interpretations, he declares, but "apology is to be made for cultural seduction of forgetting that our reading is local, provisional, and imagining that it is total and settled. That seduction, very strong in hegemonic Christianity, leads me to read only in isolation or in the company of other readers like myself. Precisely because the text advocates, sponsors, and insists upon many readings, my local provisional reading must perforce be done in the presence of other serious readings . . . which endlessly subvert my own preferred readings."

6. For other contributions, see recently: Fredrick Holmgren and Herman Schaalman, eds., *Preaching Biblical Texts: Expositions by Jewish and Christian Scholars* (Grand Rapids: Wm. B. Eerdmans Publishing Co., 1995). See also Fredrick Holmgren, "Mount Zion or Armageddon: Isaiah 2:1-5," *Interpretation* 51 (1997): 61-64; "Israel, the Prophets, and the Book of Jonah. The Rest of the Story: The Formation of the Canon," *Currents in Theology and Mission* 21 (1994): 126-32; "The Pharisee and the Tax Collector: Luke 18:9-14 and Deuteronomy 26:1-15," *Interpretation* 48 (1994): 252-61; "Holding Your Own against God (Genesis 32:22-32)," *Interpretation* 44 (1990): 5-17.

CHAPTER 1

The Prophetic
Denunciations of Israel

SELF-CRITICISM, NOT DIVINE REJECTION

Synopsis

In the past, the church has taken over many of the teachings and the promises of the Old Testament and left the denunciations to the Israelites and Jews. Often these denunciations have been viewed as evidence for the unusual wickedness of the Israelites which is seen as the ground for God's rejection of Israel. This same wickedness, so it is held, is the reason why so many Jews refused to believe in Jesus.

We agree that these reproaches are addressed to Israel (as are all the teachings and promises) but believe that the above interpretation of their presence in the Old Testament is mistaken. The accusations of the prophets speak of Israel's ability to practice and endure self-criticism, a virtue that every religious community must possess if it is to remain honest before God and neighbors. The fact that Jews preserved the severe accusations of the prophets as well as the castigating caricatures of the book of Jonah — canonizing them as holy scripture (!) — reflects a remarkable spiritual maturity.

1

The Accusations of the Prophets

Many fierce denunciations of the Israelites are embedded in the Old Testament. Amos castigates the people of his day because they "trample on the poor . . . afflict the righteous" (5:11-12). Hosea adds that "their heart is false" (10:2). Isaiah speaks of Israelites who are a "sinful nation, . . . laden with iniquity . . . who have despised [God] . . . who are utterly estranged" (1:4) and whose "hands are full of blood" (1:15). Jeremiah questions whether it is possible to find in Jerusalem even "one person who acts justly and seeks truth" (5:1), and Ezekiel effectively depicts the depth of Israelite rebellion when he accuses Judah of exceeding the wickedness of Sodom (16:46-48)! Ezra continues the accusatory stance of the prophets when he declares in prayer that "'our [Jewish] iniquities have risen higher than our heads, and our guilt has mounted up to the heavens'" (9:6).

Traditional Interpretation of Prophetic Accusations

If these words are to be taken literalistically, then the early church founders were right when they portrayed Jews as a people who were extraordinary sinners, in league with the devil and rejected by God. Although many church scholars directed fierce words against the Israelites and Jews, no doubt the most savage accusations were spoken by Chrysostom:[1] "As an animal, when it has been fattened by getting all it wants to eat, gets stubborn and hard to manage, so it was with the Jewish people. Reduced by gluttony and drunkenness to a state of utter depravity, they frisked about and would not accept Christ's yoke." Or again: "Nowadays everything among the Jews is a game, and a sport and a disgrace and a piece of huckstering, replete with inordinate wickedness."[2] Were the church founders right? Did they read the Bible cor-

---

1. Marc Hirshman maintains that Chrysostom would not have directed such fierce attacks against the Jews had not a number of people within the church revealed an appreciation for the Jewish tradition. See his comments in *A Rivalry of Genius: Jewish and Christian Biblical Interpretation in Late Antiquity* (Albany: State University of New York, 1996), pp. 113-16. Likewise, the sharpness of Paul's attack in Galatians probably had to do with the fact that a significant number of Christians in that community were attracted to Jewish practices.

2. For the two citations above, as well as a discussion of the views of the

rectly? Were the Israelites and Jews so sinful? The early church leaders appear to be reflecting the thought of the ancient prophets whose incendiary words abound in scripture. Nowhere else in the ancient Near East did prophets denounce so severely their own communities. Are we then to conclude that of all the peoples in the ancient world, the Israelites were the worst sinners? Seemingly so!

Hearing the Whole Story:
Another View of Prophetic Accusations

But before we read the Old Testament's accusations in this manner, we should, as Paul Harvey says, "hear the rest of the story." And what is the full story? Before a response may be given, a question must be asked: What does it mean that in Israel there existed a strong prophetic movement that was very critical of Israelite society, especially of the king, people of wealth and influence, as well as religious leaders? Let us note again: elsewhere in the ancient Near East there were also prophetic communities, but in none of these communities do we find a critique of society comparable to that of the Israelite prophets. Does this mean that the people in these other societies were more moral than the Israelites — not in need of this critique? No! The evidence, if it points in any direction at all, points in the opposite direction! Responding to the accusation that the Israelites were unusually evil, Walter Harrelson declares:

> Christian scholars know well that this is a theological judgment. Compared with its neighbors, Israel was certainly not such a reprehensible community. Quite the contrary is indicated by the legal material that is known from ancient times, the narratives portraying the restrictions on kingship, the overall concern for public righteousness,

church fathers, see Rosemary Radford Ruether, *Faith and Fratricide: The Theological Roots of Anti-Semitism* (New York: Seabury, 1974), pp. 117-82, esp. pp. 127 and 177 for the above citations. See further the words of Martin Luther in "Concerning the Jews and Their Lies," published in *Disputation and Dialogue: Readings in the Jewish-Christian Encounter*, ed. F. E. Talmage (New York: KTAV, 1975), p. 34: "What then shall we Christians do with this damned, rejected race of Jews? Since they live among us and we know about their lying and blasphemy and cursing, we can not tolerate them if we do not wish to share in their lies, curses and blasphemy. In this way we cannot quench the inextinguishable fire of divine rage (as the prophets say) nor convert the Jews."

and the fact that *the prophets had a forum within the community from which to speak.*

Harrelson continues:

> Empirically, the ancient Israelite community was not a bad community, and we know without doubt that the prophets were too sweeping in their indictments, if we think of the mere facts in the case. They spoke in such sweeping terms because they had such an exalted notion of the vocation of God's people in the world.[3]

The strong prophetic denunciations of Israelite society reflected and eloquently articulated the criticism of Israelite life that was simmering in circles devoted to God and the divine teachings. The prophets did not stand alone in their indictment of society; significant numbers of people shared their concerns. For example, the divine oracle addressed to the despairing Elijah declares that at least seven thousand Israelites remained faithful to God (1 Kings 19:18). This announcement makes us aware of the existence of a *prophetic community which stood behind the prophet.* This community support was crucial in preserving the life of Jeremiah (Jer. 26:16-19). Due to the existence of this prophetic community in Israel, the prophets had the freedom to address society's wrongs and to call for repentance. Without strong, influential popular support, the prophetic movement could not have found root in Israel — a truth that present-day "prophetic" pastors, rabbis, and priests can well appreciate. True, we know that *some* prophets were persecuted and killed. But the opposition and persecution of the Israelite prophet was probably not all that different from the experience of prophetic persons in other societies. In fact, the prophets who proclaimed "Thus saith the Lord" in Israel probably lived longer than would have been the case if they had announced their message elsewhere in the ancient Near East. Furthermore, the "prophets" in the United States have not fared much better than those who served in Israel. Such people have been ignored, harassed, persecuted, and killed (e.g., Martin Luther

---

3. Walter Harrelson, "Christian Misreadings of Basic Themes in the Hebrew Scriptures," *Quarterly Review,* summer 1982, p. 59, emphasis mine. A further statement on p. 60 points in the same direction. See also comments on the confession of sin in Ezra 9:13 and a comparison of this passage with the confession of the lost son in Luke 15:21 and that of the tax collector in Luke 18:9-14 in Fredrick Holmgren, *Ezra and Nehemiah: Israel Alive Again* (Grand Rapids: Wm. B. Eerdmans Publishing Co., 1987), pp. 78-79.

King, Jr., as well as others who worked for racial justice in the 1960s). A survey of other nations would tell the same story.

What are we to say then about those passages that so uncompromisingly criticize Israelite society? First, Israelite society was not a perfect community. As in any society, secular or religious, there was enough injustice, corruption, and falseness to warrant condemnation. The *prophetic denunciations* should be taken *seriously* but not *literalistically.* The prophets, as preachers today, used exaggerated speech to bring their point home. So also Jesus. Such speech is used frequently in order to startle the ears of those who are accustomed to and comfortable with their sins. Second, we must admire this Israelite society in which rigorous criticism could be voiced. Such fierce critique of the king and people of power probably would not have been tolerated in Israel's neighboring cultures. Further, in the present day, we can think of families, communities, and institutions where serious dissent is not allowed. This was not the case in Israel.

In this remarkable society, harsh words of criticism were permitted to be voiced by a succession of prophets (the few we know and the many unknown) for a period of over five hundred years! This could take place because in Israelite society there was general respect for the Torah tradition; the authority of the Sinai teaching (Torah) was generally recognized. Such respect made for an open society in which prophets had a rightful place as interpreters and proclaimers of the divine will.

The Unexpected: The Prophetic Attacks Honored as Holy Scripture!

The real wonder of the Israelite/Jewish society is the preservation of these fierce prophetic oracles and their later elevation to the status of holy scripture. The severe pronouncements of the prophets were not cast aside, forgotten, or subjected to paraphrased moderation, but were preserved to be read as the Word of God. What kind of people subjects itself to this kind of continuing self-criticism? Certainly not a people who are unusually wicked or close their ears to the divine teaching.

This is not to say, as indicated above, that the prophetic attack on Israelite society lacked basis in fact. On the contrary, the prophets pointed to serious wrongs present in the Israelite community. Nevertheless, one should remember that these are the wrongs that afflict every community, including present-day Christian society. In fact, it is precisely because the sins of Israel are so similar to the sins of our day that Christian preachers use the Old Testament prophetic texts to address the evils of our time. The sins of Israelite society were real and serious, but they were not peculiar to the Israelites.

Contrary to the judgment of some of the church founders, the Israelites were not especially or unusually evil. *Their sins are our sins.* The prophetic word endures and speaks to human beings throughout the ages. The language is Hebrew but the message is universal. The prophetic message heard in ancient Israel is never out of date or irrelevant because the wrongs of the past are alive wherever and whenever people live in society. On this planet there exists no perfect community. However, we learn from the Israelites that if a community opens itself to critical review and takes part in self-criticism, it can be a place, despite its flaws, where people can live and find blessing.[4]

Self-Criticism Is Sometimes Misinterpreted

But to be open and to subject oneself to self-criticism is dangerous. From experience we know that if we speak critically of ourselves or admit too candidly the criticism made of us, we become vulnerable to people who do not know or like us. We learn therefore not to be *too* honest or explicit when acknowledging our faults to the general religious community. *This was Israel's failing; Israel was* too *honest about her sins.* This people realized that there were great wrongs in their society — wrongs that continued on and needed to be addressed. Therefore the prophetic accusations were preserved and held for all to read as holy scripture.

Israel would not hide the passionate attacks of the prophets, would not pretend that the wrongs did not exist — would not moderate the prophet's scream. No, the accusations, "trample the poor . . . afflict

---

4. Such self-criticism is not absent from Christian congregations. One may compare the confession of Ezra cited above (Ezra 9:6) to a recent communal confession at my home church, North Park Covenant, in Chicago: "Gracious God, our sins are too heavy to carry, too real to hide, and too deep to undo. Forgive what our lips tremble to name, what our hearts can no longer bear, and what has become a consuming fire of judgment." One could conclude from this prayer that one should avoid such a wicked congregation! But it is especially in this kind of self-critical community that one may find blessing and hope for the future.

the righteous . . . the heart is false . . . the hands full of blood . . . no one acts justly" — these words *must* be included in Israel's scripture. Are there many other examples in the world of a people taking up accusations made by prophetic persons and including them in holy scripture?

The Book of Jonah: Jews Struggling to Survive Are Cartooned

Prophetic criticism knifed painfully under the Israelite skin; it hurt, but it was retained for the benefit of future generations. But what are we to say about the inclusion of the book of Jonah as a part of holy scripture? It is one thing to be fiercely criticized by prophetic oracles, it is something else to be caricatured and cartooned[5] by a prophet such as the author of the book of Jonah. Caricature and cartooning makes one look foolish — and its seeming unfairness often creates both deep hurt and rage. The author's caricature of Jonah, and by extension the whole Jewish community, as an uncaring nationalist showed little sympathy for this community's struggle to survive (probably in the time of Ezra-Nehemiah). Communities striving to hang on do not very often have an outward look to others. For example, behind the books of Daniel and Revelation stand communities under pressure. In these books one finds many threats against the enemy; there is no hint of a gracious mission to them. One might wish for a different kind of response, but we all know that when one is struggling to survive, it is extremely difficult to preserve a generous heart. The communities standing behind Daniel and Revelation, together with the postexilic community reflected in the book of Jonah, needed assurance that, with the help of God, they would survive. What they did *not* need was someone making fun of them for their inability to open up to the world at the very moment when their community was threatened with extinction. Certainly some people in

---

5. I have used the term "cartoon" in the following paragraphs in order to assist the reader in understanding how repugnant the author's representation of Jonah must have been to some in the Jewish community. The word "caricature," often used, does not in my opinion convey the sharpness of the author's criticism of Jonah and of those in the Jewish community who thought as did Jonah. The author of the book of Jonah cartooned Jonah — made fun of him and those sharing his outlook — but still, Jews preserved this book as scripture. A cartoon held as scripture! Truly exceptional!

the postexilic community must have judged the author of Jonah as one without any sense or feeling for the danger threatening the community.

The Book of Jonah: Why?

Why did the Jewish author of Jonah choose this "unreal and unfair" story as a means of addressing his community? Did it not have enough problems facing the threat of the surrounding countries? Was this story-sermon necessary? The story appears to be out of balance, one-sided; it characterizes Jonah (and the Jews of his day) as uncaring, focused only on themselves. The author shows no awareness of the threatening situation in which Jews found themselves; that is, newly returned to a ruined land and surrounded by powerful non-Jews who seemed none too friendly.

Judging from the author's depiction of Jonah, one is left looking at a rebel against God, a person who has absolutely no sensitivity for other people. Before God can use him to carry out his will, God must catch him and then — by means of a storm, being thrown overboard and swallowed by a fish — redirect him. But, one asks, why did Jonah attempt to escape from God in the first place? The surprising answer reveals the stone heart of this worshiper of the LORD (Jonah 1:9): he fled because he feared that God would not follow through on his promise to destroy Nineveh (4:1-2)! Do those who think as he does belong to the people of God?

Are Jews So Bad and Gentiles So Good?

But there are other aspects of this story that surprise the reader. Not only do we find out that Jonah's Jewish heart is selfish and crusted hard, but the Gentiles that Jonah meets are all sincere, generous, and ready to obey the divine will. Even the capital city of Assyria (Nineveh), Israel's ancient enemy, seems to be inhabited by the kind of people that would please the God of Israel. In this foreign city everyone immediately repents: people, king, and animals! And they do so even though there is no promise that repentance will save the city. One is astounded that a Jewish author could depict Gentiles in such a positive manner, especially these Assyrian Gentiles who had brought North Israel to its end in 721. Can we believe that the Jewish community (represented by Jonah) is so bad and the Gentile community so good?

The Book of Jonah: Written by a Jew!!

Against the background of non-Jews responding quickly to the call for repentance, the author concludes this book. He depicts Jonah as angry over God's decision to spare Nineveh. Jonah is more concerned about a small tree (and Jonah's comfort under it!) than for the many citizens of Nineveh! *If* the author of Jonah had been a Gentile, then one could understand why the citizens of Nineveh are depicted as sincere and repentant people. Further, the unattractive picture painted of Jonah, the Hebrew, would also be readily explained. *But* the author was a Hebrew, a member of the Jewish community. Why would a Jewish author cartoon a Jewish "prophet" and in so doing make fun of the community that he represented? No one likes to be portrayed as foolish.

The Book of Jonah: Held in Honor by Jews!

Hurt and anger had to be the response of a number of Jews who heard or read the story of Jonah. Certainly the book must have been the object of much discussion within the community, but of the community's early reaction we know nothing. No doubt some members of the Jewish community wanted to trash this "unfair" report. However, remarkably it survived and was included in the canon of holy scripture. Jews had hesitations about the inclusion of some other books as sacred scripture (e.g., Proverbs, Job, Ecclesiastes, and Ezekiel), but apparently there was no big controversy over the story of Jonah. *The Jewish community preserved this author's cartooned portrayal and held it as the Word of God.* Such a decision is not the usual response of a community subjected to caricatured critique!

Still today the book of Jonah has an important place in the liturgy of Judaism. It is read at one of the most sacred festivals of the Jewish year, Yom Kippur. Here, at a festival that calls the Jewish community to repentance, the comic, cartoon story of Jonah serves as a reminder that God expects and respects repentance. Even though Jews have suffered at the hands of Gentiles, still they have retained the book of Jonah in the liturgy; it is a book in which the Gentile citizens of Nineveh become the model of repentance for the Jewish community! In this story, written by a Jew, the Gentile "outsiders" do the repentance that God asks from Jewish "insiders."

Jews: Listening Even When It Hurts

Those who have selected this book for reading at Yom Kippur have probed underneath the caricatured representation of Gentile repentant-piety and of Jonah's hardness of heart. The story is seen to point to a central element of religious life and thought that tends ever to be slighted. That central element is repentance: the broken heart and contrite spirit. This passionate tract, made scalpel-sharp by cartooned humor, is received (along with the attacks of the prophets) by the Jewish community as God's own word.

Some Christians, past and present, have taken the book of Jonah literally and have used it to illustrate Jewish nationalism and hardness of heart. However, the presence of the book in the Jewish canon of scripture points to the spiritual sensitivity of the later Jewish community which accepted this book as a holy book that speaks a continuing message to later generations. Self-criticism, sharply done, is in short supply in our world. People are sometimes reluctant to expose themselves to self-criticism for fear that others will use it against them while pretending to have no such serious sins themselves. Jews have experienced this perverse response to their honesty of soul. *Israelite-Jewish self-criticism has been taken up, literalized, and used to demonize this community.* Those who do that overlook the fact that the story of Jonah is a message to every community in every age. Jonah's foolish and insensitive behavior constitutes a spirit in the faith community that must ever be held up for criticism.

The decision of the Jewish community, spread over hundreds of years, to include the prophetic writings and the book of Jonah in the canon speaks a word of encouragement to the human situation. The acceptance of these books as scripture reminds us that people are capable of listening attentively to the divine voice even when it speaks sharp, accusing words regarding wrongs that have been done. Without denying the human capacity for terrible evil, the courageous decision of the Jewish community to adopt these books as holy scripture speaks of that "other" aspect of humankind that is sometimes forgotten: the ability to respond to God with exceptional sensitivity and sincerity. Such people are present in every community and every age; they nourish hope in the midst of a world that often gives reason for despair.

But, for our purposes, it needs to be underscored here that the people who exhibited this impressive openness to the divine voice by selecting the prophets and Jonah as holy scripture were Jews. It was precisely in the Israelite-Jewish community that the prophets had the freedom to speak their severe oracles. It was among Jews that the author of Jonah found the support to launch an unprecedented satirical cartoon story criticizing the Jews![6] How different would have been Jewish-Christian relationships had the church founders been capable of appreciating Israel's ability to engage in and support self-criticism — even to the extent of preserving denunciations against it as holy scripture.

Discovering Jesus and the Rejection of the Jews in the Old Testament

In the following chapters, we will see that early Christians, following their experience with Jesus, looked back to the Old Testament and discovered texts that pointed to him. Unfortunately, there were those also who found texts in the Old Testament that supported their claim that God had rejected the Israelites and Jews because of their willful blindness to God's teaching. This theme was taken up and strengthened by the early church founders, as we noted at the beginning of this chapter. For centuries, God's rejection of the Jews has been a prominent motif in Christian preaching. The joyful Christian proclamation of Jesus as Savior and Lord was accompanied, frequently, by reproaches against nonbelieving Jews for their rebellion.

Very often it was thought that the willful blindness of Jews was proven by the fact that they did not believe their own scripture (the Hebrew Bible/Old Testament), which Christians thought "spoke" of Jesus. The following chapters will examine the relationship of the Old Testament to the New Testament proclamation of Jesus. In chapter 2 we will look at the manner in which both Jews and Christians interpreted the Hebrew Bible/Old Testament. In chapter 3 various texts in the New Testament that cite the Old Testament will be surveyed with references to contemporary interpretation undertaken by conservative and mainline biblical scholars. It is clear that change is taking place. It is the kind

6. Some of the material in this chapter represents a revised form of material previously published. See, e.g., "Israel, the Prophets, and the Book of Jonah. The Rest of the Story: The Formation of the Canon," *Currents in Theology and Mission* 21 (1994): 126-32, and "Preaching the Gospel without Anti-Judaism," *Christian Ministry* 26 (1995): 11-14.

of change that helps right the wrongs of the past while maintaining the core of Christian identity.

CHAPTER 2

Finding Jesus in the Depth
of the Old Testament

APPROACHING THE SCRIPTURE
AS JEWISH CHRISTIANS

Synopsis

Traditionally the church has viewed the relationship of the Old Testament to the New Testament to be one of promise and fulfillment. Recently, however, evangelical and mainline scholars have cautioned against a rigid application of this formula because it undercuts the integrity of the earlier scripture. Further, they point out that early Christians did not discover Jesus as the result of an initial study of the Old Testament. Rather the movement was in the opposite direction; that is, from their "meeting" with Jesus Christians looked back to the Old Testament, their scripture, in order to gain understanding of what took place.

Jews and early Christians employed a "believer" or "depth" interpretation of scripture as a way of giving it voice for a new time and situation. Using this approach, Jews were able to find in the Hebrew Bible the basic beliefs of their day, whether those of the Qumran community or of rabbinic Judaism. Employing this same approach, the first Christians (mostly Jews) discovered texts in the Old Testament that pointed to Jesus, his death and resurrection. Christians "knew" by experience who Jesus was, but they needed the words and imagery of the scripture common to both Jews and Christians to articulate this "knowing."

13

Paul's interpretations of two Old Testament passages in 1 Corinthians 10:4 and Ephesians 4:8 provide examples of Christian "creative/depth" exegesis which offered insight into the significance of Jesus.

Promise and Fulfillment?

A traditional approach to the relationship of the Old to the New Testament has been expressed in terms of "promise and fulfillment": the Old Testament is viewed as "promise" and the New Testament is considered to be "fulfillment." This estimate of the two scriptures has been an axiomatic truth in the church from early times to the present.[1] Evangelical scholars of a few years past tended to emphasize the predictive aspect of the so-called "promise" character of the Old Testament. For example, the evangelist Billy Graham used to declare that there were many direct predictions of Jesus Christ in the Old Testament.[2] So clear and direct were these predictions, implied Graham, that they left no excuse to those who did not believe in Jesus. In more recent years, however, evangelical scholars have, for the most part, avoided the term "prediction" in favor of the more open term "promise."[3]

1. In modern times, see statements made by various church bodies compiled in *The Theology of the Churches and the Jewish People: Statements by the World Council of Churches and Its Member Churches,* ed. Allan Brockway et al. (Geneva: WCC Publications, 1988). For example, see the First Assembly of the World Council of Churches (1948), p. 6, and the General Convention of the American Lutheran Church (1974), p. 70.

2. For a similar view today, see Walter Kaiser, Jr., *The Messiah in the Old Testament* (Grand Rapids: Zondervan, 1995). Kaiser declares that if one accepts "supernaturalism" (p. 235), then the obstacle against believing in such predictions and fulfillments falls away. He believes that "a straightforward understanding and application of the [Old Testament] text leads one straight to the Messiah and to Jesus of Nazareth" (p. 232). See also pp. 240-42, which present a "Chart of the Progress of Sixty-five Direct Predictions of the Messiah in the Promise Doctrine."

3. See, e.g., David Baker, *Two Testaments, One Bible* (Downers Grove, Ill.: InterVarsity, 1991), pp. 212, 214.

14

The Old Testament Leans toward the New?

Both conservative and mainline scholars have found the promise/fulfill-ment model attractive. Included among the latter is the well-known Old Testament scholar Gerhard von Rad. He held that the Old Testament "leads forward" to the New Testament and declared that this is so be-cause the Old Testament could not have been "taken over by the New Testament . . . if the Old Testament writings had not themselves con-tained pointers to Christ and been hermeneutically adapted to such a merger."[4] On the other hand, in von Rad's view, Judaism leads away from what is best in Old Testament religion and carries forward what is the lowest expression of this faith, namely, the so-called rigid law reli-gion of the postexilic period (e.g., the time of Ezra-Nehemiah).

Von Rad thought that with the arrival of Ezra, something "new" took place in Israel: "This new thing is usually called Judaism." In his opinion, this "new" religion of Judaism lost contact with the old, gra-cious Torah faith that brought delight and strength to the Israelite com-munity and moved to a religion of rigid law which "Israel had to serve."[5] In recent scholarship there exists a much more positive evalua-tion of postexilic Judaism and the law. For example, Brevard Childs de-clares:

> There is no evidence of any conscious transformation of the Hebrew
> Bible's understanding of God by post-exilic Judaism. Jews did not
> lose their sense of closeness to God. The Psalter continued to provide
> an unbroken continuity with the faith of Ancient Israel. The same
> biblical tensions between God's immanence and his transcendence
> found in the Hebrew scriptures continued to be felt.[6]

The case of von Rad is interesting because, while adopting a view of Ju-daism that appeared to negate it as a healthy expression of faith, he himself stood opposed to the anti-Semitic attitudes that were present in

4. See Gerhard von Rad, *Old Testament Theology,* II (New York: Harper & Row, 1965), pp. 319-35, esp. pp. 322, 333. See Brevard Childs's rejection of the view that the Old Testament "leans toward" the New Testament in *Biblical Theol-ogy of the Old and New Testament: Theological Reflection on the Christian Bible* (Minneapolis: Fortress, 1993), p. 721.

5. See Gerhard von Rad, *Old Testament Theology,* I (New York: Harper & Row, 1962), pp. 85-92.

6. Childs, *Biblical Theology,* p. 360.

15

the church.[7] In his research and writing he intended to respect the integrity of the Old Testament.

Promise and Fulfillment: Modified

Jews have suffered under the promise/fulfillment model. The most extreme representation of this interpretation which finds direct predictions of Jesus in the Old Testament portrays Jews as rebellious sinners who have defiantly shut their eyes to obvious prophecies of Jesus in their own Bible. But even the more sophisticated statement which speaks of "promise" rather than "prediction" undercuts the integrity of the Old Testament because this ancient scripture is viewed as being in need of "Christian" fulfillment (i.e., in the New Testament). Little consideration is given to the existence of the Jewish community in which the teaching of the Old Testament/Hebrew Bible is interpreted and carried forward.[8]

The promise/fulfillment relationship between the two Testaments is maintained still in our day, but with critique and qualification. Those who hold to it in principle recognize that this model can be too simplistically interpreted. There is increasing recognition that the promise/fulfillment pattern rests on a very selective choice of Old Testament scriptures.[9] For example, as C. S. Rodd has observed, it is a curiosity that

7. See James L. Crenshaw, *Gerhard von Rad* (Waco: Word, 1978), pp. 19-21.

8. See, however, Thomas Ridenhour, "The Old Testament and Preaching," *Currents in Theology and Mission* 20 (1993): 257, who adopts the promise/fulfillment model but still affirms the validity of God's relationship to Israel: "Each fulfillment is left to God's creative and surprising way of acting so that when a promise is fulfilled such fulfillment does not close down God's relation to Israel."

9. James Charlesworth speaks a qualified good word for the promise/fulfillment model, noting that "Christians ultimately would admit that in some ways Jesus fulfills God's promises." Further, he says, it helps us understand the continuity in which the early Christian community stands regarding the Old Testament. But, Charlesworth declares, although the promise/fulfillment model gives us insight into "the dynamic enthusiasm of Jesus' early followers . . . it tends to perpetuate a selective reading of the Scriptures. It does not adequately represent the diversity either in the Old Testament or in the New Testament, or the complexities and richness of the relationship" ("What Has the Old Testament to Do with the New?" in *The Old and New Testaments,* ed. J. H. Charlesworth and W. P. Weaver (Valley Forge, Pa.: Trinity Press International, 1993), pp. 42-43. See also pp. 44-

the "one demand which is universal throughout the Old Testament and is expressed by law-giver, prophet, psalmist, and wise man, the total rejection of lending on interest," finds no place in the New Testament or in Christian interpretation.[10]

The Old Testament Fully Fulfilled in the New Testament?

The Old Testament is a multivoice scripture which addresses the diverse realities of living in this world. There are long passages and complete books in the Hebrew Bible that do not fit under the rubric of "promise." One can hardly claim that the whole Old Testament is a promise of which the whole New Testament is a fulfillment. The books of Ecclesiastes, Job, Song of Songs, Proverbs, Nahum, Obadiah do not fit readily this model of relationship between the Testaments. To affirm that the themes of injustice, suffering, and death discussed in Job, Psalms, and Ecclesiastes are fulfilled in the suffering and death of Jesus is to say too much. The New Testament's proclamation of Jesus adds a new dimension to the discussion of these themes, but it does not bring a "fulfillment" solution to them. In fact, the church needs these books in order to keep its feet on the ground of reality. Without their continuing presence as scripture, the Christian message could settle, as it sometimes does, for a spiritual answer in which Jesus' suffering and death becomes the answer for all the difficult aspects of life. To place the above books in some sort of "christological" perspective conceals their continuing validity for today.[11]

Further underscoring the inadequacy of the traditional representation of promise and fulfillment is the awareness that the Old Testament's vision of world peace remains unfulfilled. It is not fulfilled in the coming of Jesus, and, after nearly two thousand years of the church's existence, such a vision remains still far distant. In the past some schol-

---

48 for comments concerning the promise/fulfillment approaches of Walter Eichrodt and Gerhard von Rad.

10. C. S. Rodd, "New Occasions Teach New Duties? The Use of the Old Testament in Christian Ethics," *Expository Times* 105, no. 4 (1994): 100.

11. See Erich Zenger, "Die jüdische Bibel — unaufgebbare Grundlage der Kirche," in *Das Judentum — eine Wurzel des Christlichen*, ed. H. Flothkötter and B. Nacke (Würzburg: Echter Verlag, 1990), pp. 72-73.

ars attempted to account for this lack of fulfillment by distinguishing between Old Testament passages that pointed to the first coming of Jesus and those that envisioned his second coming. Such arbitrary exegesis, however, invites little support among scholars who respect the historical-theological integrity of the Old Testament. Further, regarding this theme of world peace, it is fair to say that both the Old Testament and the New Testament are books of promise. They both look forward to a time when God's rule will be complete. Isaiah 25 has a vision of a time when God will wipe away all tears. This same vision is taken up by the book of Revelation (chap. 21).[12]

The Old Testament, for the most part, addresses its own time with little indication that it is looking to the far future for a "Christian" fulfillment. For example, this scripture speaks of living a responsible life in covenant with a loving God who forgives sin and nourishes faith. In these passages there exists no hint of a look to the future for fulfillment. Touching on the same point are the comments of Robert Hubbard, Jr., who holds, in general, to the concept of promise and fulfillment, but in modified form. He declares:

> With some trajectories the NT seemingly assumes the full validity of their OT theologies and adds virtually nothing to it. The theology of justice offers an example. It seems likely that, had one asked Jesus or the apostles, "How should Christians practice social justice?" their reply would be, "Go back and read the law of Moses and prophets like Amos. We really have nothing to add." One could make a similar case for OT proverbial wisdom.[13]

12. See the discussion of Klaus-Peter Hartzsch, "Christliche Predigt über Texte aus dem Alten Testament," *Berliner Theologische Zeitschrift* 14 (1997): 3-13 (esp. pp. 9-11).

13. Robert L. Hubbard, Jr., "Doing Old Testament Theology Today," in *Studies in Old Testament Theology,* ed. Robert L. Hubbard, Jr., et al. (Dallas: Word, 1992), p. 42. Cf. p. 33. J. Gordon McConville, "Messianic Interpretation of the Old Testament in Modern Context," in *The Lord's Anointed: Interpretation of Old Testament Messianic Texts,* ed. Philip E. Satterthwaite, Richard S. Hess, and Gordon J. Wenham (Carlisle, Pa.: Paternoster; Grand Rapids: Baker, 1995), pp. 10-11, affirms that promise and fulfillment are "implicit" in the biblical texts, but he says this schema should not be viewed too simply, declaring: "The interpretation of the Old Testament is not a one-way street, but a two-way flow, in which contemporary situations were compared with the Scriptures, and the Scriptures were then brought to bear, sometimes in (to us) unexpected ways on the situations."

A recent book of essays, *The Lord's Anointed: Interpretation of Old Testament Messianic Texts,* whose editors and contributors represent the cutting edge of conservative/evangelical scholarship, gives expression to a new understanding of what has been called promise and fulfillment.[14] Philip P. Jenson, employing the expression "prophetic prediction," summarizes the varied approaches scholars have taken in understanding the New Testament's use of the Old Testament. He lists them under seven metaphors: a stone, sight, a code, a stream, a plant, a bird, and music. Cautioning interpreters against understanding prophecy and fulfillment too rigidly or simplistically, Jenson indicates that one must work with continuity and discontinuity. In his view, the last two metaphors of a bird and music provide the best insight into the prophetic character of the Old Testament: "The prophetic tradition is more helpfully compared to the freedom of a bird in flight, or the creativity of a master musician improvising on a theme. There is an openness and provisionality to biblical prophecy that calls for the kind of creative faithfulness that may be seen in Matthew's use of the Old Testament."[15] Viewing Matthew's approach to the Old Testament as one of "creative faithfulness" touches upon an understanding that is appealing to many conservative and mainline scholars. In this chapter and the one following, we will discuss this approach under such terms as "creative" or "depth" exegesis. The words "believer" or "faith" interpretation point in the same direction.

Fulfillment to Promise: From Jesus to the Old Testament

Today, many Christian biblical scholars representing diverse traditions within the church are pulling away from the promise/fulfillment approach to scripture because they believe it is a misrepresentation of the relationship existing between the Old and New Testaments. John Goldingay, for example, observes: "It is not self-evident that Christ is

14. Philip E. Satterthwaite, Richard S. Hess, and Gordon J. Wenham, eds., *The Lord's Anointed: Interpretation of Old Testament Messianic Texts* (Carlisle, Pa.: Paternoster; Grand Rapids: Baker, 1995).

15. Philip P. Jenson, "Models of Prophetic Prediction and Matthew's Quotation of Micah 5:2," in *The Lord's Anointed,* p. 212. See also McConville, esp. pp. 15-16.

the fulfilment of OT hopes. Whether one recognizes him as such will be dependent on whether one is willing to acknowledge him for his own sake."[16] Similarly, the authors of *Old Testament Survey* observe:

> By simply picking verses from the prophets and pasting them together to give . . . "Jesus Christ in prophecy," one creates the impression that prophecy is "history written in advance." However, when one studies the prophets, this glamorous concept suddenly disappears. It is necessary to plow through chapters that have nothing to do with the future to find a single verse, or even part of a verse, that is "prophecy."[17]

Brevard Childs, who has led the way in bringing about a new approach to the Bible and is insistent upon the basic unity of the Old and New Testaments, shares, in general, the views expressed above. He indicates that when the New Testament authors make use of the Old Testament, they do not move from the Old Testament text to the reality of Jesus; rather they move from this reality to the text of the Old Testament. New Testament authors, together with the Christians who followed them, read the scripture through the glasses of their experience. In so doing, Childs declares, the New Testament writers "transformed" the Old Testament text, and their interpretation of this older text created considerable "tension" with its "original" meaning. Commenting on Isaiah 53, Professor Childs declares: "Each evangelist [in the New Testament] did his theological redaction in different ways, but all came from an encounter with the reality of Christ and brought that understanding to bear on the scriptures [i.e., on the Old Testament]."[18]

16. John Goldingay, *Approaches to Old Testament Interpretation* (Downers Grove, Ill.: InterVarsity, 1981), p. 119. Rolf Rendtorff agrees. In *Hat denn Gott sein Volk verstossen?* (Munich: Kaiser, 1989), pp. 121-22, he observes that the Jesus whom Christians know from the pages of the New Testament is unknown to the Old Testament scripture. So similarly Erich Zenger, *Das Erste Testament: Die jüdische Bibel und die Christen* (Düsseldorf: Patmos, 1991), pp. 123-32.

17. William LaSor, David Hubbard, and Frederic Bush, *Old Testament Survey: The Message, Form, and Background of the Old Testament* (Grand Rapids: Wm. B. Eerdmans Publishing Co., 1982), pp. 304-5.

18. Childs, *Biblical Theology*, p. 382. Further, Childs observes (p. 65) that "the New Testament pattern of prophecy-fulfilment frequently functions only in terms of the Greek text [as opposed to the Hebrew text]." For a more recent statement of Childs's general view, see his article "Toward Recovering Theological Exegesis," *Pro Ecclesia* 6 (1997): 16-26 (esp. p. 24). In a recent article, Lothar

Alden Thompson, addressing the matter of promise and fulfillment, stands in agreement with the above views. He observes that Matthew does not think of predictions in the Old Testament which are fulfilled but of words that "are filled full of fresh new meaning, meaning which, quite literally, had never been thought of before."[19] As early Christians looked back on the Old Testament following their meeting with Jesus — in whom they discerned the activity and presence of the God of Israel — they came to a new and different reading of this scripture.[20]

Judaism and New Testament: Making the Ancient Text Contemporary

It is apparent, as will be seen from the paragraphs that follow, that the New Testament citations of the Old Testament do not reflect the plain sense of these texts. Rather, by relating an Old Testament text to Jesus, they transform and change its meaning. No doubt the New Testament writers were aware of the plain sense of the Old Testament text, but being Jewish themselves, they treasured the "depth" (or "creative") approach to this scripture which was practiced in the Jewish tradition. Jewish interpreters held the scripture to be divinely inspired, and this being so, they considered its words to be alive with meaning and meanings. The noted Jewish scholar Nahum Sarna concludes: "Rabbinic exegesis is firmly grounded in the cardinal principle that embedded in the sacred text is a multiplicity of meanings. . . . the intrinsic, endless variety of interpretation, even if, or perhaps especially because, it may be internally contradictory and replete with antinomies, reinforced the reality of the divine inspiration behind the text."[21] Following are some ex-

---

Ruppert alludes to the way in which the New Testament extends or interprets the primary meaning of an Old Testament text: "'Mein Knecht, der gerechte, macht die Vielen gerecht, und ihre Verschuldungen — er trägt sie' (Jes 53:11)," *Biblische Zeitschrift* (1996): 16-17.

19. Alden Thompson, *Who's Afraid of the Old Testament God?* (Grand Rapids: Zondervan, 1989), p. 154.

20. See also Horst D. Preuss, *Das Alte Testament in christlicher Predigt* (Stuttgart: Kohlhammer, 1984), pp. 20, 21, 24, 28.

21. Nahum Sarna, "The Authority and Interpretation of Scripture in Jewish Tradition," in *Understanding Scripture,* ed. C. Thoma and M. Wyschogrod (New York: Paulist, 1987), p. 10. In a recent article written by Rabbi Sanford Shudnow for his column "Discovering Torah" (in the *Chicago Jewish Star* news-

amples of a deeper, nonliteral meaning the rabbis found in some texts of the Hebrew Bible:

1. Exodus 21:24 declares that in any physical conflict one should exact an "eye for an eye." The plain, literal meaning (Heb. *peshat*) of the text in its context speaks of physical violence: one exacts from an opponent what was done to oneself. The rabbis, however, applied a "depth" interpretation (Heb. *derash*) to this text and understood the meaning to be that money should be paid to the one who was injured.[22] But in the biblical text there is no hint of money serving as a payment. The rabbis, as David Halivni observes, "read in" the idea of money compensation.[23]

2. Exodus 17:9 occurs in the context of a battle between Israel and Amalek. To the modern objective interpreter, the references here are of an historical nature. No doubt many early Jewish interpreters understood this text to be interpreted literally; however, a certain Rabbi Elazar ha-Modal saw a "deeper" meaning in the following phrase: "tomorrow I will stand on top of the hill." Commenting on this brief declaration, he states: "Tomorrow we shall declare a fast and be ready, relying on the deeds of the patriarchs. 'Top' — these are the deeds of the patriarchs; 'hill' — these are the deeds of the matriarchs."[24] We do not know how many agreed with this rabbi's interpretation, but the fact that

---

paper, October 25, 1997), it is said: "What typifies our [the Jewish] approach to everything in Holy writ is the non-literal interpretation — the allegorical, the homiletical, anything but the literal. Even the *peshat* (simple) meaning in traditional hermeneutics is non-literal. It is often the sense of the text and not what the words actually say which is deemed important."

22. See Mekhilta de-R. Yishmael, Nezikin 8, p. 277, cited by Rimon Kasher, "The Interpretation of Scripture in Rabbinic Literature," in *Mikra*, I, ed. M. J. Mulder (Philadelphia: Fortress, 1988), p. 566. See also David W. Halivni, *Peshat and Derash: Plain and Applied Meaning in Rabbinic Exegesis* (New York: Oxford University Press, 1991). Pp. 4-5 and 176 n. 7 provide other examples in rabbinic literature. On pp. 8-9, Halivni speaks about the stance that the rabbis take before a biblical text: "It is my contention that the rabbis did not share our devotion to the simple literal meaning. . . . the rabbis' interpretive state of mind did not dictate to them that the simple, literal meaning was inherently superior to the applied meaning. Athough they generally began their interpretations of the Bible with the simple, literal meaning of the text, they did not feel committed to it. The slightest provocation, most often an apparently superfluous word or letter, moved them to abandon it."

23. Halivni, pp. 23-24.

24. See Mekhilta, Amalek 1, p. 179, cited by Kasher, pp. 553-54.

he proposed it — and that it was preserved — makes us aware that such a free understanding of the text was respected and accepted in the wider community.

3. Other examples of a "creative/depth" interpretation of scripture come from rabbis who are eager to find the hope of resurrection in the inspired texts. For example, references to the resurrection are found in Exodus 15:1, Job 10:10-11, and Deuteronomy 31:16, all of which to the present-day reader contain not the slightest glimmer of such a meaning.[25]

The Old Testament:
Fitting Earlier Texts to Later Times

The above examples of early Jewish interpretation of scripture stem from a time later than the first Christian century. However, this basic contemporizing approach roots in pre-Christian times, even in the Old Testament itself. Iain Duguid, for example, has observed how "Zechariah's prophecies frequently picked up earlier material and adapted and reused it. Similarly, his own words [i.e., the words of Zechariah] have been taken up and adapted by the New Testament writers, who saw them as being fulfilled in Jesus."[26] One may consider also the freedom exercised by the Septuagint translators who modernized the text of Isaiah 9:12 (LXX 9:11) by changing "Aramaeans" and "Philistines" to names that were contemporary for the translator (i.e., to "Syrians" and "Greeks").[27] This change may be viewed as a small one, but it illus-

---

25. See Kasher, pp. 573-74. For other examples of this "depth" reading of scriptural texts, see pp. 553-84.

26. Iain Duguid, "Messianic Themes in Zechariah 9–14," in *The Lord's Anointed*, p. 276. Many scholars would agree with the judgment of William Johnstone in his estimate that Chronicles "bears some relationship to the type of Jewish literature known as *midrash*. . . . The task of the *midrash* is not to incorporate new historical data; it is to reinterpret the given data in such a way that new insights for the edification of the community are achieved." See Johnstone, *Israel's Place among the Nations: 1 Chronicles 1–2 Chronicles 9* (at end of the introduction), which will be published by Wm. B. Eerdmans Publishing Co. in the International Theological Commentary series in 1999.

27. See E. Earle Ellis, *The Old Testament in Early Christianity: Canon and Interpretation in the Light of Modern Research* (Tübingen: J. C. B. Mohr, 1991), p. 66.

trates that early translators or editors of the text felt free to make such contemporizing changes.

Qumran: Fitting Biblical Texts to Later Events

We find, then, a beginning of the rabbinic contemporizing method already in the Bible. But it is in the scrolls from the Dead Sea community, dating from the first and second centuries before the Christian era, that we find ample evidence of this pre-Christian "creative/depth" exegesis. The practice at Qumran relates closely to the manner in which the New Testament writers interpret the Old Testament.[28] At Qumran, as Michael Fishbane and others have observed, texts from the Hebrew Bible, dating hundreds of years before the rise of this community, are often cited as "proof texts" for the correctness of the community's teaching.[29] These biblical citations are employed, as Fishbane notes, in order to "give both prestige and authority" to the declarations of the Qumran community. However, he declares, "what is of particular interest is that these citations can almost never be read according to their plain sense."[30]

The Qumran approach to the Hebrew Bible reveals similarity to biblical interpretation practiced in rabbinic literature and in the New Testament. That is, it reflects "creative/depth" interpretations of Old Testament texts. The following two examples — many more could be given — illustrate this approach:

1. The following portion of Isaiah 40:3 is taken up for interpretation at Qumran. It reads: "as it is written: 'prepare in the wilderness the

28. McConville, p. 12, observes that "we are bound to recognize that the New Testament writers belonged to the same world as the exegetes of Qumran and other Jews. Christian appropriation of the promises of a Messiah do not avoid the basic dynamics of hermeneutics." See also the comments of F. F. Bruce, *A Mind for What Matters* (Grand Rapids: Wm. B. Eerdmans Publishing Co., 1990), p. 53.

29. See the interesting contribution of W. S. LaSor, "Interpretation and Infallibility: Lessons from the Dead Sea Scrolls," in *Early Jewish and Christian Exegesis,* ed. C. Evans and W. F. Stinespring (Atlanta: Scholars Press, 1987), pp. 123-37. LaSor points to the proof-text method at Qumran (pp. 131-32) and the dangers of pursuing this method today (pp. 136-37).

30. Michael Fishbane, "Use, Authority and Interpretation of Mikra at Qumran," in *Mikra,* I, pp. 347-48.

way of [the LORD], make straight in the desert a path for our God.'" The Qumran interpreter holds to the plain sense of the first clause because it legitimizes the founding of the community in the wilderness by the Dead Sea, but gives a "depth" meaning to the second clause: "make straight in the desert a path for our God." This "path," declares the interpreter, "is the study of the Law [Torah]" which God gave to Moses and which is the central interest of the Qumran community.[31]

2. In the Qumran commentary on the seventh-century book of Habakkuk, we find another example of "depth" interpretation of scripture. The Habakkuk text reads (2:8b): "Because of the blood of men and the violence done to the land, to the city, and to all its inhabitants." The Qumran commentator declares: "Interpreted, this concerns the Wicked Priest [a person contemporary with the Qumran community] whom God delivered into the hands of his enemies because of the iniquity committed against the Teacher of Righteousness [a highly honored person of the time]."[32] Although both the text in the biblical book of Habakkuk (seventh century B.C.E.) and that of the Qumran commentary (first century B.C.E.) share the theme of violence, the commentary has taken the liberty to relate this text to two specific persons, the Wicked Priest and the Teacher of Righteousness. Most certainly these two persons were not in the mind of the prophet Habakkuk when he set down the words that are now in the Bible. The Qumran commentator contemporizes and actualizes the ancient text and does so by means of a "creative/depth" interpretation which goes beyond the plain sense of the biblical text. In so doing the interpreter is able to give authority to the Qumran teaching.

Qumran, Rabbinic Judaism, and New Testament: "Depth" Exegesis

It appears, then, that the New Testament authors, together with interpreters at Qumran and in rabbinic Judaism, make use of what may be called "creative" or "depth" interpretation. The texts from these three

31. The Qumran text (IQS 8:13-15) is taken from the translation of Geza Vermes, *The Dead Sea Scrolls in English* (Sheffield: Academic Press, 1987), p. 73. See the comments of Fishbane, pp. 349 and 361.
32. See Vermes, p. 288.

very different writings cite the Old Testament, basically, for the same reasons, that is, to justify and legitimize the teaching of the respective later communities. There is, of course, a great difference between the New Testament approach to the Old Testament and that of Qumran or rabbinic Judaism in terms of content (i.e., focus on Jesus as opposed to Torah).[33] William Klein calls attention to what he calls an "atomistic" approach to the Old Testament which is found in some rabbinic texts, but he nevertheless concludes that "NT writers interpret the OT in ways not unlike the ancient rabbis. Thus, knowledge of their methods illumines the NT use of the OT."[34] The Old Testament functions as a "depth" source that validates interpretation in the respective communities.[35]

Further observations underscoring the similarities between Qumran and the New Testament in their use of scripture are found in the comments of C. F. D. Moule: "Most of Matthew's so-called 'formula quotations' . . . seem to be doing much the same [as that done at Qumran]. Ignoring the original context and doing violence to the original meaning, the Evangelist fits the ancient words by force into a contemporary, Christian meaning."[36] As observed above, David Halivni

---

33. It should not be overlooked, however, that many "Christian" terms and images have their precursors in Qumran writings (e.g., "church of God," "works of the Law," "New creation," etc.). See the brief, excellent article of Hartmut Stegemann, "Qumran, Jesus and Early Christianity," *Theology Digest* 40, no. 3 (1993): 203-10.

34. William Klein, *Introduction to Biblical Interpretation,* ed. W. W. Klein, C. L. Blomberg, and R. L. Hubbard, Jr. (Dallas: Word, 1993), p. 25. Regarding Klein's observation concerning rabbinic exegesis, see Howard Eilberg-Schwartz, "The Puzzling Rabbis," *Religion* 23 (1993): 1-18, who comments: "Routinely, these attempts to connect a specific legal ruling to Scripture appear forced and far-fetched. Each Scriptural verse, phrase, word and sometimes even single letter is made to support numerous nuances of law which seem foreign to it" (p. 2).

35. Thompson, pp. 149-50, points to the similarity that exists between the rabbinical approach to the scripture and that of the New Testament authors, concluding: "Given this Jewish background, I can now appreciate the way in which some early Christians excitedly mined the Old Testament for fresh 'prophecies' of this Messiah . . . [which] were simply later confirmations of something his followers already believed."

36. C. F. D. Moule, *The Origin of Christology* (Cambridge: Cambridge University Press, 1977), p. 128. Moule designates this use of scripture as "vehicular." By "vehicular" he means: "the use of Scriptural words simply as a vehicle. In themselves, such words do not authenticate what they bear; they merely convey it. 'Out

has underscored the unity of Jews and Christians in approaching the scripture. He observes that it is difficult for the modern reader to appreciate rabbinic exegesis of the Hebrew Bible, because the rabbinic commentary applies a "creative, seemingly artificial interpretation" to what appears to other readers to be the "straightforward, austere sense" of the scriptural passage.[37] This is exactly the problem that many readers of the New Testament have as they reflect on the use that the New Testament makes of this older scripture. The New Testament understanding of the Old Testament is similar to that of the rabbis in that both present a nonliteral, "creative" interpretation of scripture. Donald Hagner comments on the New Testament's employment of "depth" interpretation in his discussion of Matthew's "fulfillment quotations." He observes: "These quotations represent Matthew's own creative interpretation of his narrative."[38]

---

of Egypt have I called my son' is a phrase which had no authority of its own to lend to Jesus; it is merely a vehicle of words to carry a particular understanding of one whose authority is derived from elsewhere" (p. 132). Other passages that he has in mind when he uses the term "vehicular" are Matt. 1:23; 2:6, 16, 23 (p. 128). But while admitting that the early Christians related the New Testament to the Old Testament in a somewhat arbitrary, superficial manner (pp. 129, 133), he argues that such correspondences were employed because they were aware of a deeper "organic" way in which "Jesus was . . . the fulfiller of something which is basic to the whole of Scripture" (p. 129; cf. p. 133).

37. Halivni, pp. v-vi.

38. Donald A. Hagner, *Matthew 1–13*, Word Biblical Commentary, vol. 33A (Dallas: Word, 1993), p. liv. Similarly, Klyne Snodgrass observes: "Any serious reading will show that the way the New Testament uses the Old Testament is far different from what we expected or have been led to believe. The New Testament writers have been disturbingly creative in their use of the Old Testament" ("The Use of the Old Testament in the New," in *The Right Doctrine from the Wrong Texts? Essays on the Use of the Old Testament in the New*, ed. G. K. Beale [Grand Rapids: Baker, 1994], p. 30; cf. pp. 34 and 36). In the same volume, see the discussion of Richard N. Longenecker, "'Who Is the Prophet Talking About?' Some Reflections on the New Testament's Use of the Old," pp. 379-84. James Sanders, "Habakkuk in Qumran, Paul and the Old Testament," in *Paul and the Scriptures of Israel*, ed. Craig Evans and James Sanders, JSNT Supplement Series 83 (Sheffield: JSOT, 1993), pp. 98-117, adds to the above discussion, noting: "Paul said something more than Habakkuk said" (p. 115) and in this way "modernized" a prophet who was "not consciously" looking to Christ or the Christian era (p. 114). Matitiahu Tsevat, "Theology of the Old Testament: A Jewish View," *Horizons in Biblical Theology* 8 (1986): 36, describes the similarity of rabbinical and Christian exegesis (especially that of Paul) in the following, negative, man-

It may be noted, by the way, that something similar took place in the interpretation of New Testament texts by the councils of Nicaea and Chalcedon. Raymond Brown declares, for example, that the conciliar statements of the fourth century go "beyond what is stated explicitly in the New Testament." Elsewhere he observes that conciliar formulations "have gone beyond what was clearly articulated or visibly understood in NT times, precisely because questions were being asked that had not been asked in earlier times."[39] Just so was it in the case of rabbinic Judaism and early Christianity regarding the Hebrew Bible/Old Testament: questions were being asked that had not been asked before, and "believers" probed the depth of scripture to find guidance.

In summary then, at Qumran, as also in the writings of rabbinical Judaism and the New Testament, we find that texts from the scripture are often given a "creative/depth" interpretation instead of one that holds to the plain meaning of the text. In all three of these early communities the "Old Testament" is looked to as the scripture that validates the beliefs of the respective communities.[40]

Jewish-Christian Exegesis:
Not What It Meant but What It Means

Why do the rabbis and the New Testament writers generally prefer a "depth" interpretation of the Old Testament to simply passing on the

---

ner: "To be sure, the Jews at the time of Paul and later did no less violence to the Old Testament than did he" (!).

39. Raymond Brown, *An Introduction to New Testament Christology* (New York: Paulist, 1994), pp. vi and 5 n. 4.

40. For a rich discussion that probes some issues which we have only touched here, see Bruce Chilton and Craig Evans, "Jesus and Israel's Scriptures," in *Studying the Historical Jesus: Evaluations of the State of Current Research*, ed. Chilton and Evans (New York: Brill, 1994), pp. 281-335, esp. pp. 282-83 and 333-35. See also David E. Orton, "Matthew and Other Creative Jewish Writers," in *Crossing the Boundaries* (New York: Brill, 1994), pp. 133-40. Alan Segal observes that while the Christian interpretation of the Old Testament (e.g., Ps. 110) "was new, this kind of reinterpretation was a standard procedure during the period and was absolutely justifiable from the perspective of any contemporary." See his discussion in *Rebecca's Children: Judaism and Christianity in the Roman World* (Cambridge: Harvard University Press, 1986), p. 89.

plain sense of the text? No doubt there are a variety of reasons, but one, already mentioned, seems to be preeminent: the desire to contemporize and actualize scripture. Every text has its historical, religious, and cultural context and is therefore, to a greater or lesser extent, bound by this context. In order to "live," the text must be interpreted and brought into the world of those who are looking to the text for guidance.[41] Rimon Kasher, commenting on the rabbinic approach, points out that, in general, the plain interpretation of the text speaks to what the text *meant,* whereas the "depth" interpretation concerns what the text *means.*[42] In employing this latter approach, neither the rabbis nor the New Testament writers believed that they were falsifying scripture. Both approaches to scripture (i.e., the literal and creative) existed side by side in Judaism and in early Christianity. For the most part, however, the rabbinic literature and the New Testament were interested, to use Kasher's words, in what the scripture *means* as opposed to what it *meant.*[43] When some Jews were confronted by the extraordinary figure of Jesus — and in fact became his followers — they attempted to understand him in the context of the faith of Israel preserved in the Hebrew Bible.

Roland Murphy points out that the New Testament writers were not simply interested in a general understanding of the Old Testament; rather these authors turned to the Old Testament in order to under-

---

41. Childs, *Biblical Theology,* p. 382, suggests that the church must be involved in a "multiple-level approach to the text." One must hear the voice of the text in its historical and literary context, but "At the same time the reality of God testified to in the Bible, and experienced through the confirmation of God's Spirit, functions on a deeper level to instruct the reader toward an understanding of God that leads from faith to faith. Because of a fuller knowledge of the reality of God revealed through reading the whole corpus of scripture, the biblical texts resonate in a particular Christian fashion. . . ."

42. Kasher, p. 577. See also Clark Williamson's chapter on "The Authority of Scripture," in *A Guest in the House of Israel* (Louisville: Westminster/John Knox, 1993), pp. 139-66, esp. pp. 153-58.

43. See Roy F. Melugin's "Reading the Book of Isaiah as Christian Scripture," *Society of Biblical Literature: 1996 Seminar Papers* (Atlanta: Scholars Press, 1996), pp. 118-203. He comments: "To explain what the scriptures *meant* is insufficient. The scriptures must be used to *do* something, namely, to shape the church's relationship with God and to aid the church in creating just and loving relationships among human beings" (pp. 189-90). In general agreement with our discussion in this chapter, he further observes that the New Testament texts and their interpretations of the Old Testament "color the interpretation and use of Isaiah [and other books in the Old Testament] in the church" (p. 191).

stand Jesus.[44] Cristina Grenholm makes the issue clear as she distinguishes between the need of the New Testament authors and that of present-day Christians. She indicates that both the New Testament authors and the church founders "were anxious to show the continuity between the Old Testament and Christ in order to justify the claims made by or about Jesus. The Old Testament [the inspired Scripture] was the obvious point of departure. Christ was the one who had to be interpreted and explained." However, she continues: "To us, the problem is the contrary: the New Testament and Christ are given, the Old Testament needs to be clarified and understood."[45]

New Testament: From Jesus to the Old Testament and Back Again

The Jewish followers of Jesus moved from what they considered to be the fuller "reality" of God expressed in Jesus to the text of the Old Testament rather than from the text of scripture to Jesus.[46] The people of the New Testament community, after meeting and following Jesus, searched the scriptures and discovered him in the Old Testament.[47] These inspired texts were written centuries before the appearance of Jesus; the original, intended meaning of the texts had nothing directly to do with Jesus. The New Testament writers did what the later church fathers did, but with more restraint they "interpreted" Jesus into these ancient texts.

This appeal to Jewish scripture (whether in Hebrew or Greek form)

44. Roland Murphy, "Old Testament/Tanakh — Canon and Interpretation," in *Hebrew Bible or Old Testament?* ed. R. Brooks and J. J. Collins (Notre Dame: Notre Dame University Press, 1990), p. 19. See also Childs, *Biblical Theology,* p. 241.

45. Cristina Grenholm, "Christian Interpretation of the Old Testament in a Pluralistic Context," *Studia Theologica* 48 (1994): 98.

46. See Childs, *Biblical Theology,* pp. 381-82.

47. For similar views, see Klyne Snodgrass, who, in agreement with Brevard Childs, Cristina Grenholm, and others, indicates that the early church moved from Jesus to the Old Testament text, not from this scripture to Jesus: "The conviction about his [i.e., Jesus'] identity did not derive from the Old Testament. They did not find texts and then find Jesus. They found Jesus and then saw how the Scriptures fit with him. They were not proving his identity in the technical sense so much as they were demonstrating how Scriptures fit with him." See Snodgrass, pp. 39-40.

validated Christian preaching and possibly secured a hearing within the Jewish community. It may be that some Jews held an open ear to the Christian interpretation of Old Testament texts because these interpretations *in terms of approach* had similarities to Jewish interpretation.[48] In any case, depth interpretations of Old Testament texts nourished and instructed the faith of early believers. Today, depth interpretation is carried on within the church for the same reason. However, by focusing on the Christian understanding of the text, it is easily overlooked that the Jewish community preserved and reinterpreted the scripture because it nourished in them also a life of faithfulness. Today, as Christians are becoming more aware of the Jewish tradition, we are learning that both Jews and Christians probe the "depth" of scripture and bring it to life; in this manner they find life for themselves. We conclude this chapter by offering examples of "depth" interpretation by the apostle Paul.

Depth Interpretation and Paul: "The Rock Was Christ" (1 Cor. 10:4)

Paul in 1 Corinthians 10:4 refers to a "spiritual rock" which *followed* the Israelites in their journey through the desert. From this rock the Israelites were able to quench their thirst. Paul identifies this rolling rock from which they drank: "The rock was Christ."

In the Old Testament, it is twice mentioned that a rock spouted water to satisfy Israelite thirst (Exod. 17:6 and Num. 20:9-12). In addition, this scripture mentions wells which gave life-giving water to the Israelites (Exod. 15:23-25 and Num. 21:16-20). But nowhere in the Hebrew Bible is there a reference to a rock following them, let alone a "spiritual rock." Apparently, however, together with other Jews of his day, Paul was aware of a "depth" interpretation of these biblical texts which spoke of a *stone following* the Israelites through the desert. This interpretation reflects acquaintance with an oral form of a Jewish legend which, written down, dates from about 400 C.E.:

> And so the well which was with the Israelites in the wilderness was a
> rock, the size of a large round vessel, surging and gurgling upward, as

---

48. Some scholars are doubtful that Christian preaching was viewed as a witness to Jews. See, e.g., Hagner, p. lvi.

from the mouth of this little flask, rising with them up onto the mountains, and going down with them into the valleys. Wherever the Israelites would encamp, it made camp with them, on a high place, opposite the entry to the Tent of Meeting.[49]

Paul feels free to use this Jewish legend, based on an Old Testament text, to speak of the significance of Jesus.[50] He has committed his life to preaching Christ, and he employs every possible illustration or analogy that gives strength to his proclamation. Although his illustrations derive almost always directly from scripture, he is not embarrassed to use an apt image that comes from Jewish interpretation. He saw in this legend of the water-giving stone an image of what Christ means to the Christian community.

Depth Meaning and Paul, Continued: "Receiving," Not "Giving" (Eph. 4:8)

A further example of Paul's creative use of an Old Testament text may be found in the "exegesis" of Psalm 68:18 appearing in Ephesians 4:8. In the latter text Paul is urging Christians to consider themselves as members of one body who share one hope, one faith, one baptism, and one God. This one body is a "gifted" body and the gifts present in this community are varied. He then makes a point not to be missed: these varied gifts are given by Christ. To provide scriptural warrant for his teaching, he cites Psalm 68:18:

> Therefore it is said,
> "When he ascended on high he made captivity itself a captive;
> *he gave gifts* to his people." (emphasis mine)

49. See *The Tosefta. Second Division Moed,* trans. Jacob Neusner (New York: KTAV, 1981), Sukka 3:11.
50. For further discussion of 1 Cor. 10:4 and the biblical/rabbinic sources, consult E. Earle Ellis, *Paul's Use of the Old Testament* (Grand Rapids: Baker, 1957 [1991]), pp. 66-70. See also in the Qumran literature that the spring mentioned in Num. 21:18 is identified as the Torah (Covenant of Damascus 6:4). Paul's familiarity with Jewish interpretive traditions and his use of them is discussed by Linda L. Belleville, "Tradition or Creation? Paul's Use of the Exodus 34 Tradition in 2 Corinthians 3:7-18," in *Paul and the Scriptures of Israel,* pp. 165-86.

However, in addition to interpreting the exaltation of God in the psalm as a statement about the ascension of Jesus, Paul makes a significant change in the scriptural text. Both the Hebrew and Greek (Septuagint) texts read "*receiving* gifts from people" as opposed to Paul's citation of "he *gave* gifts to his people." The Hebrew and Greek texts did not suit Paul's purpose, therefore he cites a paraphrase of the scriptural text, namely, one from the Aramaic Targum, which reads "gives gifts." This change of the text, which reverses the direction from "receiving" to "giving," allows him to relate the Old Testament text to the contemporary issue, that is, to the matter of gifts present in the congregation.

Robert Sloan lifts up some other Pauline texts in which a free use of the Old Testament is employed; he refers to them as "surprising shifts." For example, in 1 Corinthians 15 Paul reverses the meaning of Hosea 13:14. Whereas the latter passage is "a summons to Death to come forward and do its worst," the Corinthians passage is a song of triumph over this dark power.[51]

Depth Interpretation after the Manner of Paul

That Paul appears to handle scripture in such a free manner is somewhat surprising to the reader.[52] Throughout history, however, Christian preachers have undertaken similar approaches to the scriptural text, even following Paul's example of reversing the plain meaning of texts. In this way they have been effective in engaging issues faced by their congregations. In the following paragraphs we look at two modern examples of "reversal" exegesis.

What Paul has done with the reversal of imagery in Ephesians

51. Robert Sloan, *Reclaiming the Prophetic Mantle* (Nashville: Broadman, 1992), p. 143. See also pp. 144-45 for further examples.

52. Childs, *Biblical Theology*, pp. 238-43, discusses at some length Paul's liberties with the Old Testament text. He declares that "for Paul scripture (text) and reality belong together. One cannot understand scripture apart from the reality of which it speaks, namely Christ." Further: "Paul is not interested in the Old Testament 'for its own sake'" (p. 241). Childs, however, warns that one cannot simply imitate the New Testament writers (p. 381). In a theological reading of the Old Testament, place must be given to the historical and literary contexts so that the voice of the Old Testament is not distorted or silenced.

(from "receiving" to "giving") and in 1 Corinthians (from threat to promise) may be compared to Rolf Rendtorff's treatment of the narrative in Matthew 8:24-27 which is included in his sermon on Isaiah 51:9-16.[53] The Isaiah text speaks to Jews who have been swept away by the raging waters of the Babylonian armies (the theme of water is prominent in the text). In the course of his sermon, Professor Rendtorff comments on the Matthew passage that depicts the fearful disciples in a boat with Jesus. The boat is rocking violently in the swirling waters. Professor Rendtorff provides the traditional commentary on the text; he observes that *at times* the situation of the fearful disciples *is* that of the Christian church. As the first-century disciples, so have later-born Christians found themselves in the midst of dangers and in need of the reassuring presence of Jesus.

A different time and situation, however, sometimes demands a changed understanding of the text. For example, there have been times when the church has not been a threatened community but a threat to other communities. During these periods, Christians did not sit in the

> boat, but they formed the sea — the wild, raging, angry, monsterlike sea — which without mercy or pity swept over those who sat in the boat. So it was, for example, in the time of the Crusades, when the Christian Crusaders broke [as angry waves] over the Jewish communities on the Rhein, in Köln, Mainz, Worms and Speyer and, in the name of Jesus Christ, murdered the descendants of those [Jews] who had returned from the captivity under the pagan Babylonians.

Looking at the Christian community of his time, a community under threat and pressure, the Gospel writer could not have imagined Rendtorff's interpretation of this story. Nevertheless, changed circumstances justify this reversal of understanding. One might say it is *because* of this reversal of meaning that Rendtorff's words strike the ear and heart with a wake-up call to self-criticism. Rendtorff's interpretation offers a reality check by means of which Christians may come to see that the church, especially regarding the Jews, has been the threatener and not the threatened.

A further example of "reversal" exegesis may be seen in Norbert

---

53. Rolf Rendtorff, "Der Eine Gott (Jes. 51:9-16)," preached the fourth Sunday after Epiphany, 1979, in Peterskirche in Heidelberg at a worship service of the University of Heidelberg, mimeographed copy.

Lohfink's handling of Romans 9–11.[54] He does to Paul's words what Paul himself did to the Old Testament in the above passages from 1 Corinthians and Ephesians. Lohfink believes that the "situation which he [Paul] describes in Rom 9–11 [has] been reversed." Against the background of the dismal history of the church's relationship to Jews, Lohfink holds that Christians need to read these chapters differently. They should be read, declares Lohfink, so that the minor theme (i.e., Gentile Christian pride and the sins it spawns) is heard as the major theme. After what has happened in the almost two thousand years of Jewish-Christian relations, it is impossible to read Romans 9–11 exactly as Paul wrote it. Too much has intervened between the time of Paul and our time. Paul's shocking warning that Gentile pride could be reason for God's judgment has taken on added weight as the centuries have progressed. To read Romans 9–11 exactly as Paul wrote it, Lohfink declares, is to do exegesis on a text tied to a past time and to silence its voice for our contemporary life within the church.

Common sense and good exegetical balance inform us that "reverse" interpretation is not always appropriate! However, interpretation of scripture, whether Old Testament or New Testament, is not a science; it is the contribution of one who, in addition to possessing the gift of communication, knows well the biblical text *and* the local, contemporary situation of the congregation. Richard Hays says it well: "Texts are not inert; they burn and throw fragments of flame" and their "meaning has a way of leaping over" all the scholarly hedges we place about them — "like sparks." He continues: "That is a way of saying that texts can generate readings that transcend both the conscious intention of the author and all the hermeneutical structures that we promulgate."[55]

Intentional words spoken by significant people "have their day"

---

54. Norbert Lohfink, *The Covenant Never Revoked: Biblical Reflections on Christian-Jewish Dialogue*, trans. J. J. Scullion (New York: Paulist, 1991), pp. 75-82.

55. Richard B. Hays, *Echoes of Scripture in the Letters of Paul* (New Haven: Yale University Press, 1989), p. 33. Elsewhere in the same book (p. 222 n. 1), Hays points to a rabbinic comment (Sanhedrin 34a) on a passage from Jeremiah translated by Moshe Greenberg in an unpublished article: "'Is not my word like fire, declares the Lord, and like a hammer that shatters rock' (Jer. 23:29). As a hammer [stroke] scatters many slivers/sparks so a single Scriptural passage yields many senses." The comments of Patrick Miller, "The Old Testament and Christian Faith," *Currents in Theology and Mission* 20 (1993): 249, point in the same direction.

when originally spoken — and "have their day" again and again in later periods of time when they are rediscovered. This aliveness of the biblical text that Hays speaks about spurred early Jewish and Christian interpretation; it underlies effective preaching in our own time. Just as Paul draws out the "depth" meaning of a scriptural text in order to bring forth a living word to his community, so in such manner do many preachers speak a needed "scriptural" word to the modern-day faith community. Ancient words striking the flint of new situations burst into a fire that enlightens and warms those who are later born. Walter Brueggemann, who has long been creative and imaginative in his exposition of scripture, provides insight into the New Testament's use of the Old Testament as well as encouragement for present-day teaching and preaching. He speaks of texts that originate at a certain time and then "linger" on in the community:

> Out of that lingering, from time to time, words of the text characteristically erupt into new usage. They are seized upon by someone in the community with daring. Or perhaps better, the words of the text seize someone in the community who is a candidate for daring. In that moment of reutterance, the present is freshly illuminated, reality is irreversibly transformed.[56]

To be sure, this kind of approach opens itself to arbitrary, acrobatic interpretations that strive after newness and difference. But then, no approach to scripture comes with an absolute guarantee against misuse. Almost every approach has its own perils. As usual, it is the interpreter himself (with knowledge of scripture and tradition) who is the key to right use and misuse of the scriptural text. Many approaches may be taken to a biblical text *provided* the preacher lets the congregation "in" on what is taking place. To present, for example, a "depth" interpretation *as if* it were the plain sense of scripture does violence to that text. Those who listened to the creative interpretation of the apostle Paul were hardly in the dark concerning the character of his interpretation because, as we have already indicated, such an approach was well known in his time.

---

56. Walter Brueggemann, "Texts That Linger, Words That Explode," *Theology Today* 54 (1997): 180.

Jews and Christians: Differing Depth Interpretations

Against the background of this chapter, which has underscored the use of a "creative/depth" interpretation of scripture at Qumran, among the rabbis, and in the New Testament, we offer a brief comment that will orient the reader to the next chapter. In the past, Christians have accused Jews of not believing their own scripture because they have not followed Jesus, who, it was held, fulfilled in impressive detail the prophecies of this scripture. If, however, it is true that the New Testament writers could only find "references" to Jesus in the Old Testament by reading back their experiences into these texts, then such accusations fall to the ground. Christians can hardly justify reproaching Jews for their failure to see the figure of Jesus in the New Testament's "creative" interpretation of the Old Testament. Nor can Jews denounce Gentiles for their failure to discover talmudic teaching in the "depths" of the Hebrew Bible.

Depth or creative interpretation arises out of the faith stance of the community; it is believer exegesis. Although the early Christian community stood in continuity with much that was found in the Jewish tradition, its focus on Jesus rather than on Torah created a significant difference. It was the experience of "meeting" Jesus and following him that moved the early Christians to seek and find him in the Old Testament. It is this aspect of the New Testament witness that we will take up in the next chapter. We will look at a variety of texts which reveal the way in which early Christians interpreted the Old Testament as they endeavored to understand the significance of Jesus.

CHAPTER 3

"And It Was Fulfilled"

READING THE OLD TESTAMENT
OUT OF CHRISTIAN EXPERIENCE

Synopsis

We continue and expand our comments from the previous chapter, where we observed that New Testament authors interpreted the Old Testament out of the community's experience with Jesus. Viewed against the background of this life-changing meeting, the Old Testament took on a "depth" dimension that helped Christians understand and articulate their belief in Christ. At times, however, only the Septuagint provided this kind of contact (e.g., Heb. 10:5; 2:7; Gal. 3:15-18; Matt. 1:23).

In the Gospels the term "fulfill" is repeatedly employed to express relationship to the Old Testament (e.g., Matt. 2:15, 16-18, 23; John 13:18). Frequently it has the sense of "corresponds to" or "analogous to," as, for example, the betrayal of Jesus is analogous to an earlier event in Israel (John 13:18/Ps. 41:9). The New Testament's interpretation of the Old Testament is "insider" or "believer" exegesis; it understands the older scripture in the light of faith in Jesus.[1]

---

1. See, e.g., Richard N. Longenecker, "'Who Is the Prophet Talking About?' Some Reflections on the New Testament's Use of the Old," in *The Right Doctrine from the Wrong Texts? Essays on the Use of the Old Testament in the New,* ed. G. K. Beale (Grand Rapids: Baker, 1994), pp. 376-79, who notes that the New Testament writers "began with Jesus" and then looked for "prefigurements" of him in the Old Testament texts (p. 379).

The Early Church:
Preaching the "Depth" of Scripture

Gail Ramshaw's excellent article "The First Testament [Old Testament] in Christian Lectionaries" offers examples of "depth" interpretation from early Christian preaching. She observes that the Old Testament provides the *imagery* for Christian proclamation. In such preaching there is no attempt to prove the Old Testament text to be a promise of which the New Testament is fulfillment. Rather, the appeal to the Old Testament text by these preachers is that of Christians who offer insider, "depth" interpretation. Professor Ramshaw cites a bit of such exegesis by Ambrose: "Marra was a bitter fountain. Moses cast the wood in it, and it became sweet. For water without the preaching of the cross of the Lord is no advantage for future salvation."[2] Ambrose is not engaging in promise/fulfillment interpretation. He desires only to touch the imagination of the hearer or reader. Melito of Sardis offers a similar approach to the Old Testament in his preaching on the suffering of Jesus on the cross. "It is he [Jesus] that was in Abel murdered, and in Isaac bound and in Joseph sold, and in Moses exposed, and in the lamb slain, and in David persecuted, and in the prophets dishonored."[3] In the above allusions to the earlier scripture, Melito is speaking about events that are similar or analogous to what took place with Jesus. These references have a homiletical character and do not intend to establish any kind of predictive or "prophetic" relationship to what happened later with Jesus.

New Testament: Depth Interpretation
of the Old Testament

There is general agreement among present-day conservative and mainline scholars that the Gospels reflect the preaching of the early church.[4] This preaching in the New Testament is similar to that oc-

---

2. Gail Ramshaw, "The First Testament in Christian Lectionaries," *Worship* 64 (1990): 494-510. The citation is on p. 498.

3. Ramshaw, p. 502.

4. See James R. Edwards, "'Who Do Scholars Say That I Am?'" *Christianity Today*, March 4, 1996, p. 17: "Modern scholarship has correctly shown that the Gospels are not strict biographies, but presentations of Jesus told from the

curring in the sermons cited above. For example, in the walk to Emmaus with his despairing disciples, Jesus declares that Moses and all the prophets witnessed of him (Luke 24:26-27). These portions of scripture "witness" of him in the same manner as the men mentioned by Melito of Sardis, who refers to Abel, Isaac, Joseph, David — and also to Moses and the prophets. Another example of this kind of preaching in the New Testament may be found in Acts 8:26-35, where Philip "proclaimed" to the Ethiopian eunuch "the good news about Jesus." The Ethiopian was reading the scripture and Philip began to preach, much like Melito of Sardis, and showed him how Isaiah 53 was speaking of Jesus. Dr. Klyne Snodgrass comments: "This account points both to the Christological way in which the early church interpreted the Old Testament and *to the need of guidance in understanding.*"[5]

The servant figure in Isaiah 52:12–53:13 has become so much a part of Christian thinking about Jesus that the *Christian reader* finds it very natural to see Jesus in this ancient text.[6] J. Alec Motyer has written of Isaiah 52:13-15: "It is impossible not to be reminded of the resurrection, ascension and heavenly exaltedness of the Lord Jesus."[7] This may be true for Christians who "look back" to these texts from the vantage point of a "relationship" with Jesus. For someone "looking ahead," however, without the benefit of the Christian tradition or Christian instruction, the text reflects the ambiguity which characterized the thinking of the Ethiopian man. This Ethiopian Bible reader would not have "found" Jesus in this ancient text had it not been for the persuasive

standpoint of faith and for the purpose of furthering faith. The Gospels are part of the kerygma, the proclamation of the early church, which means that Jesus can be known only through the testimony of his followers." Edwards emphasizes, however, that "the early church acted as custodian of the Jesus tradition rather than as corrupter of it."

5. Klyne Snodgrass, "The Use of the Old Testament in the New," in *The Right Doctrine from the Wrong Texts?* p. 32.

6. Christians living in developing nations complain, rightly, that the church often focuses too finely on the figure of Christ in Isaiah 53. Wong Wai Ching Angela, "Asian Realities: Oppression and Dehumanization," in *People of God, Peoples of God: A Jewish-Christian Conversation in Asia,* ed. Hans Ucko (Geneva: WCC Publications, 1996), p. 40, sees other figures in this text: "I see here a vivid portrayal of the sufferings of the marginalized communities in Asia."

7. J. Alec Motyer, *The Prophecy of Isaiah: An Introduction and Commentary* (Downers Grove, Ill.: InterVarsity, 1993), p. 424.

preaching of Philip.[8] Acts 8:35 indicates that Philip *began* his preaching "with this scripture." We can well imagine that he, as Melito of Sardis, continued by citing other passages from the Old Testament that "pointed to" Jesus and his sufferings.[9]

Brevard Childs cautions that the Christian interpreter today "cannot merely imitate the approach of the Apostles" but then observes that "this caution does not rule out the right, indeed necessity, of reading the Bible in the light of the further knowledge of God's reality gained from the entire Bible." But, he asks, how is this to be done? He then illustrates his view with the following comments on the famous servant passage in Isaiah:

> The Old Testament voice of Isaiah 53 cannot be correctly heard if this witness is directly identified with the passion of Jesus Christ. . . . Yet to know the will of God in Jesus Christ opens up a profoundly new vista on this prophetic testimony to God who "laid on him the iniquity of us all." . . . For those who confess the Lordship of Jesus Christ there is an immediate morphological fit.[10]

In numerous passages from the Old Testament, the Christian believer can find Jesus "present." In the above passages, including those alluded to by Melito of Sardis, we see that Jesus walks the same difficult path that others before him walked. He "fulfills" Old Testament texts not because these texts had him in mind, but because what happened earlier was somewhat analogous to what happened to him.

This kind of analogous reasoning is not limited to Jesus in the New Testament. In some cases early Christians saw themselves or their

8. John Sawyer remarks concerning Isa. 52:13–53:12: "Like the Isaianic verses which have been taken to refer to the nativity (1:3; 7:14) and the early ministry of Jesus (9:1-2), this is a poem that has been removed from its context in the life of ancient Israel and brilliantly used to enrich and interpret the response of Christians to the life, death and resurrection of Jesus Christ" (*Isaiah*, vol. 2 [Philadelphia: Westminster, 1986], p. 149).

9. See the comments of Erich Zenger, who underscores also the preaching character of these two texts in *Das Erste Testament: Die jüdische Bibel und die Christen* (Düsseldorf: Patmos, 1991), pp. 127-28.

10. Brevard Childs, *Biblical Theology of the Old and New Testament: Theological Reflection on the Christian Bible* (Minneapolis: Fortress, 1993), pp. 381-82. Further (p. 379), Childs declares: "To read back into the story [the Old Testament] the person of Jesus Christ . . . is to distort the witness and to drown out the Old Testament's own voice."

situation addressed in ancient scripture. For example, Paul and Barnabas see themselves and their Gentile mission (Acts 13:47) alluded to in Isaiah 49:6, which declares that the servant will be "a light to the nations." In Luke 2:32, however, this Isaian text is used to speak of the mission of Jesus. The extraordinary passage in 1 Corinthians 9:1-10 exhibits also this free use of scripture. Here Paul refers to Deuteronomy 25:4 (one should not muzzle an ox treading grain) in order to justify requesting financial support for himself and Barnabas. Paul asks: "Is it for oxen that God is concerned? Or does he not speak entirely for our sake? It was indeed written for our sake. . . ." But, of course, the plain meaning of Deuteronomy 25:4 indicates that God *was* concerned for the oxen!

Paul does not use the term "fulfillment" in the above passage, but when he declares that Deuteronomy 25:4 was "indeed written for our sake" he is making a claim that stretches beyond the plain meaning that the text had in its original context. His interpretation arises out of his need to gain and give insight into his situation (his need of financial support). It is a "creative" or "depth" interpretation of the kind that we have spoken of before.

New Testament: Looking Back at the Old Testament

In the previous chapter we spoke about the "creative" way in which the Hebrew Bible was employed by the Jewish commentators of the Dead Sea community and by rabbinic Judaism. We observed that their method of approach was similar to that of early Christians who "preached Christ" out of the Old Testament. Now let us look more closely at some passages that occur in the Gospels and elsewhere. We will concentrate at first on some texts in the Gospels that employ the term "fulfill." A consideration of these passages will reveal that the Greek word translated "fulfill" has the meaning of "corresponds to," "is similar/analogous to," or even "reminds one of."[11]

11. This latter expression ("reminds one of") may be the sense behind Matt. 2:23 if Walter Kaiser is correct. The Gospel text reads: "He [Jesus] will be called a Nazorean." Kaiser thinks this is a play on the term for "branch" that is used in Isa. 11:1 and comments: "Matthew must have had a twinkle in his eyes as he set forth that pun, a literary device that prophets loved to employ." See his book, *The Messiah in the Old Testament* (Grand Rapids: Zondervan, 1995), p. 35.

Hosea 11:1 and Matthew 2:15

The original context of these two passages is well known to biblical scholars. Hosea 11:1, stemming from the eighth century B.C.E., recalls the divine intervention on behalf of the Hebrews in Egypt when God brought Israel (God's child) out of Egypt (cf. Exod. 4:22-23). Matthew, writing some seven hundred years later than Hosea, speaks of the time when Mary, Joseph, and the infant Jesus are returning from Egypt to Israel after the death of Herod. Matthew refers to the Hosea passage and declares: "This was to *fulfill* what had been spoken by the Lord through the prophet, 'Out of Egypt I have called my son'" (emphasis mine).

The use of the term "fulfill" does not intend to convey an exact fulfillment of a seven-hundred-year-old prediction. Almost every biblical scholar agrees that the text in Hosea has in mind the nation of Israel. This text in its context contains no reference to Jesus. But the Gospel writer finds it appropriate to call upon this passage as he tells the story of Jesus' return from Egypt to Israel. He is struck by the similarity existing between Israel and Jesus. These two special children (Israel and Jesus) have both made their exodus from Egypt!

But, of course, there are significant differences between the text in Matthew and that of Hosea. In the Matthew narrative it concerns a young child and not a nation, as in Hosea. Further, the people referred to in Hosea are escaping Egyptian oppression, but the context in Matthew is radically different. Here the family of Jesus was not fleeing persecution in Egypt; rather for Jesus, Mary, and Joseph, Egypt was a place to which they fled to escape danger in their own land. For Jesus, Egypt was a place of security! But these differences are not problems for Matthew because he sees only the similarities: both narratives, to his mind, speak about God's intervention to bring about deliverance. J. Gordon McConville comments:

> When Hosea wrote the line he had in mind God's calling of his "son" Israel out of slavery in Egypt. When Matthew lines it up with the return of the child Jesus from his Egyptian refuge on the death of Herod (Mt. 2:15), he is scarcely claiming that this is what Hosea had in mind. Rather, he is asserting that there is a true connection, at a *deep level*, between the two events.[12]

12. J. Gordon McConville, "Messianic Interpretation of the Old Testament in Modern Context," in *The Lord's Anointed: Interpretation of Old Testament Messi-*

It is little wonder that Matthew calls to mind the God of the exodus; it is a major theme in the Old Testament. The Isaian prophet of the exile, for example, aroused his dispirited people by reminding them of the character of their God. It was clear to him that Israel's captivity among the Babylonians was analogous to the slavery of the Hebrews in Egypt. Calling attention to what God did for the Hebrews enslaved in Egypt, the prophet proclaims a message of deliverance: the God of the exodus is alive and powerful; he will once again deliver Israel with a second exodus from a second Egypt. In similar manner, Matthew 2:13-15 declares that the God of the exodus is continuing his saving, preserving activity: he rescues Jesus (his child) from Herod, a new pharaoh, just as he once rescued Israel (his child) from the Egyptian pharaoh.[13] The rescue and protection of Jesus is a continuation and the reaffirmation of God's ability to protect those who look to him — a capability impressively revealed in the exodus.[14]

Hosea 11:1 comes "alive" in the Christian community's reflection on Jesus, but the new life infused in this text comes from *Christian* "depth" or "creative" understanding, *not* merely from transmitting the plain meaning of the text. Philip A. Cunningham states it well:

> Looking backwards into the Hebrew Scriptures through the lens of his post-resurrectional experience of Jesus, the evangelist perceives implications not apparent in the text itself. . . . by reading the Hebrew Scriptures in the light of the Raised Jesus, the evangelist has come to believe that the story of Jesus recapitulates the story of Israel.[15]

---

anic Texts, ed. Philip E. Satterthwaite, Richard S. Hess, and Gordon J. Wenham (Carlisle, Pa.: Paternoster; Grand Rapids: Baker, 1995), p. 13, emphasis mine.

13. It is frequently observed that Matthew's narrative concerning Jesus is a *re-presentation* of the history of Israel; that is, Jesus is presented as a collective/corporate person who in some sense repeats what happened to Israel (e.g., the flight to and exodus from Egypt as well as the temptations in the wilderness). See most recently, Jürgen Moltmann, "Jesus zwischen Juden und Christen," *Evangelische Theologie* (1995): 58.

14. See further the comments of Zenger, pp. 128-29, as well as those of Sean McEvenue, *Interpretation and the Bible* (Collegeville, Minn.: Glazier, 1994), pp. 174-76.

15. Philip A. Cunningham, "The Synoptic Gospels and Their Presentation of Judaism," in *Within Context: Essays on Jews and Judaism in the New Testament,* ed. Dan P. Efroymson et al. (Collegeville, Minn.: Liturgical Press, 1993), p. 53.

Writing after the experience of the resurrection, Matthew believes that the rescue of Jesus, God's "son," from Herod is a special continuation and reaffirmation of God's earlier preservation of his other "son," Israel. When we look at this kind of interpretation today, we recognize that such an approach has a *witness* character which identifies it as a "depth" or "believer" exegesis.

Psalm 41:9 and John 13:18

One more example of an analogical relationship between an Old and New Testament text may be seen in the citation of Psalm 41:9 in John 13:18. In the latter passage, Jesus is speaking of his betrayal and, in so doing, declares: "But it is to *fulfill* the scripture, 'The one who ate my bread has lifted his heel against me'" (emphasis mine). Psalm 41, however, has its own context; it is not a prediction or a recognizable promise of Jesus. Instead of focusing on Jesus and Judas, the psalmist is speaking about a painful, centuries-deep experience. A great number of people know this experience all too well: the hurt of being betrayed by one who appeared to be a true friend. This tragic happening is picked up by proverbial wisdom in Israel: "Profuse are the kisses of an enemy" (Prov. 27:6). It is also recognized in the wisdom literature of Egypt: "It was he who ate my food that raised up troops [against me] and he to whom I had given my hands that created terror thereby."[16]

Jesus' experience of what was taking place in his own inner circle brought to mind the hurt of the psalmist who was cut down by the pretense of friendship and loyalty. Mirrored in the familiar human story of betrayal, John sees the unthinkable: Jesus betrayed by one of his own disciples. Betrayal of a friend took place long before Jesus and continues to take place in our own day. But, that this betrayal happened to Jesus was especially tragic because he was seen to be one who stood in a special relationship to God. For the Christian believer it was the betrayal to end all betrayals. In this terrible event, we are not looking at promise, forecast, or prediction but at an all-too-frequent human oc-

---

16. "The Instruction of King Amen-em-het," lines 20-22. This reconstructed text is cited in *Ancient Near Eastern Texts* (Princeton: Princeton University Press, 1955), p. 418.

currence that repeated itself in the life of one in whom early Christians experienced the presence of God.

Jeremiah 31:15 and Matthew 2:16-18

Matthew's use of Jeremiah 31:15 is yet another illustration of the term "fulfill" having the meaning of "is similar to" or "stands in analogy with." The Gospel writer has in mind Herod's murder of Jewish children when he announces:

> Then was *fulfilled* what had been spoken through the prophet Jeremiah:
>
> > "A voice was heard in Ramah,
> >   wailing and loud lamentation,
> > Rachel weeping for her children;
> >   she refused to be consoled, because they are no more."
>
> (emphasis mine)

The text in Jeremiah refers to the hopeless situation of the Israelites who were suffering exile in the environs of Babylon. To understand the text, one needs to remember that Jacob and Rachel are regarded as parents of the nation Israel. Mother Rachel is depicted weeping over the suffering of her children in a foreign land.

Again, this passage is not intended as a prediction or promise of the murderous program of Herod; rather, his slaughter of the children reminded Matthew of a similar event recorded in Jeremiah.[17] Matthew envisions Rachel crying once again over the suffering of her children. But "children" this time does not mean adult Israelites and their families (that is, the exiles); the Matthew narrative has in mind actual children.

The event that brought bitter tears to the eyes of Rachel is an "alive" event. It did not come to an end with her. It actualized itself in the sad event that happened in the time of Matthew. In a time long ago

---

17. Douglas Moo observes that Matthew's reference to Jer. 31:15 is "appropriate and theologically profound," but he also says it needs to be stressed again that the 'fulfillment' of this Old Testament text does not imply that Matthew views it as a prophecy." See his chapter, "The Problem of Sensus Plenior," in *Hermeneutics, Authority, and Canon*, ed. D. A. Carson and J. D. Woodbridge (Grand Rapids: Zondervan, 1986), p. 206.

Rachel cried bitterly for her children (the Israelite exiles); she cried again for her children (the babies) in the time of Matthew. The murder of the young children was a part of the "event of Jesus," and therefore it had special significance.

However, the children of Rachel and Jacob have continued to suffer, and Rachel's tears have not ceased. Her body shook helplessly with terrified cries as Hitler, a new Herod, attempted to erase Jewish presence from Europe. A sermon on the Jeremiah text, therefore, should not deal simply with the tragic events of the past, whether that past is the suffering of the exiles or the murder of the Jewish children reported by Matthew; rather Christians should be reminded that the Jeremiah passage is analogous to events that have taken place (found "fulfillment") again and again among Jews — and among numerous minority societies in our world.[18]

Christian "Depth" Preaching Favors the Septuagint

In the above discussion we have emphasized that New Testament authors, looking back from their experience of Christ's ministry, death, and resurrection, have selected certain passages from the Old Testament which remind them of him. Sometimes this could be done by employing the Hebrew text of the Old Testament. But more often, texts "pointing to" Jesus were discovered in the Septuagint, the principal Greek text of the Old Testament.[19] E. Earle Ellis summarizes the scholarly consensus as follows:

> In their textual form the [New Testament] citations . . . frequently
> follow the Septuagint, both because this Greek version was used in
> Palestine and in the Diaspora and, at times, because the Septuagint

18. See further Walter Brueggemann's insightful comments on Jer. 31:15 and Matt. 2:18 in "Texts That Linger, Words That Explode," *Theology Today* 54 (1997): 183-86.

19. The Septuagint represents a translation of a Hebrew text which is somewhat different from the Hebrew text that is presently read (e.g., as published in the *Biblia Hebraica*). Apparently, the translation was undertaken by Jews in the middle of the third century B.C.E. It was used within the Jewish community for a time, but later on was adopted by the Christian community as its version of scripture. The church was heavily dependent upon the Septuagint until the time of Luther (sixteenth century).

rendering fit the writer's viewpoint. For the same reasons some citations, on occasion against the Septuagint, agree with the Hebrew text (Matt. 2:15) or with the targum (cf. Eph. 4:8). *Ad hoc* renderings usually serve an interpretive interest.[20]

For many centuries since the New Testament period, the Septuagint has been the Bible of the church. In our day, in fact, a number of scholars believe the church should prize this Greek Bible over the Hebrew text. H. Gese, for example, argues against accepting fully the Hebrew Bible canon, for, he says, in using the Hebrew Bible in its traditional form (i.e., the Masoretic text) "the continuity with the New Testament is broken off."[21] Gese's comment is important because, as is well known, a Christian interpretation of some Old Testament texts depended entirely on citations taken from the Septuagint. The following New Testament passages appeal to the Old Testament texts as those which "point" to Jesus. In each case the Christian witness is only possible because the citation is from the Septuagint.

Hebrews 10:5 and Psalm 40:6 (Heb. 40:7; Grk. 39:7)

A comparison of the citation in Hebrews 10:5 with the Greek and Hebrew versions of Psalm 40:6-8 illustrates the truth of the above sentence. The author of Hebrews declares that animal sacrifices are not acceptable offerings for sin and then cites the Greek text of Psalm 40:6:

> "Sacrifices and offerings you have not desired,
> but a *body you have prepared for me. . . .* " (emphasis mine)

Hebrews 10:10 picks up this reference to *body*, proclaiming: "And it is by God's will that we have been sanctified through the offering of the

---

20. E. Earle Ellis, *The Old Testament in Early Christianity* (Tübingen: Mohr, 1991), p. 71.

21. H. Gese, *Vom Sinai zum Zion* (Munich: Chr. Kaiser Verlag, 1974), p. 16, cited and translated by M. H. Goshen-Gottstein, "Tanakh Theology: The Religion of the Old Testament and the Place of Jewish Biblical Theology," in *Ancient Israelite Religion,* ed. P. D. Miller, Jr., et al. (Philadelphia: Fortress, 1987), p. 643 n. 64. See the important discussion concerning a revised appraisal of the Greek Bible (LXX) by Mogens Müller in *The First Bible of the Church: A Plea for the Septuagint* (Sheffield: Academic Press, 1996).

body of Jesus Christ once for all" (emphasis mine). The New Testament author cites Psalm 40:6 from the Septuagint Greek text and *not* from the Hebrew text because the latter would not enable him to make the connection between Jesus and this psalm. The Hebrew text of Psalm 40:6 reads: "You have given me an open ear [literally: Ears you have dug for me]." This reading gives no support to the author's line of thought. Only the Septuagint provides the possibility for a Christian "depth" interpretation which expresses the conviction that the sacrifice of Christ was in some way grounded in the ancient scripture.

Hebrews 2:7 and Psalm 8:5 (Heb. and Grk. 8:6)

A further illustration of the New Testament's dependence on the Septuagint for a Christian interpretation is found in Hebrews 2:7. The author calls Psalm 8:5 as a witness to the proclamation that God has incarnated himself *for a time* in the person of Jesus. The Hebrew text of the psalm yields little promise for a "depth" exegesis; it speaks of human beings (literally "him") whom God has created and then declares:

> Yet you have made him a *little lower* than God,
> and crowned him with glory and honor. (emphasis mine)

The Hebrew term translated "little lower" (lit. "to lack but a little") has within it a spatial dimension; it refers to human beings as standing a little under God. The Hebrew text, therefore, offers little potentiality of speaking about Jesus as one who came from and — after a length of time — returned to God. To the one believing in Christ, however, the Septuagint translation was an open door waiting for a christological interpretation to enter, and therefore its words are quoted:

> Yet you have made him *for a little while* lower than the angels;
> you have crowned him with glory and honor. . . . (emphasis mine)

The Greek term in the above text, translated "for a little while," has *both* a spatial ("a little lower") and a time sense ("a little while"), therefore it offers striking confirmation of the New Testament witness. Brevard Childs's remarks underscore the above comments: "The New Testament writer, working on the basis of the Greek Old Testament text, has been able to move his interpretation into an entirely different direction from that of the Hebrew Old Testament. The psalm becomes a Christological proof text for the Son of Man who for a short time was humiliated, but who was then exalted by God. . . ."[22]

Galatians 3:15-18 and Genesis 17:7-8

Galatians 3:15-18 provides yet another example of the New Testament's use of the Greek Bible (Septuagint) to provide contact with an Old Testament text. Paul is attempting to demonstrate that Christ, rather than non-Christian Jews, is the descendant of Abraham. To make his point, he refers to Genesis 17:7-8, but he does so according to the text of the Greek Bible rather than that of the Hebrew text. Paul's argument in Galatians 3:16 rests on an accident of language. The Greek word Paul relies on to carry his argument has a singular and a plural form, whereas the Hebrew term occurs always in the singular. Paul states his argument:

> Now the promises were made to Abraham and to his offspring; it does not say, "And to offsprings," as of many; but it says, "And to your offspring," that is, to one person, who is Christ.

Paul's argument holds literary water; the Greek Bible supports his declaration. However, had he used the Hebrew text, he could not have made his point, because the Hebrew word for "offspring" is, as the English word "sheep," always singular, even though it often has a plural meaning. When the Hebrew text was translated into Greek, the translators rendered the Hebrew word with a singular Greek term. But in making this decision, they represented wrongly the text of Genesis because the Hebrew term, though singular in form, was plural in meaning (i.e., the Genesis text refers to "descendants," not "descendant").[23]

22. See Brevard Childs's chapter, "Psalm 8 in the Context of the Christian Canon," in *Biblical Theology in Crisis* (Philadelphia: Westminster, 1970), pp. 151-63 (the citation is from p. 157). See Childs's further comments in which he argues for the validity and the necessity of a "theological" (christological) approach to the Old Testament by the Christian interpreter (pp. 157-58).

23. Concerning Gal. 3:15-18 and some other passages, see comments by Donald Juel, "New Testament Reading of the Old: Norm or Nuisance?" *Dialog* 31 (1992): 183-86. A further example of New Testament authors using the Septuagint text to give support to a Christian interpretation is provided by Robert

Matthew 1:23 and Isaiah 7:14

One of the most well-known passages of the Old Testament that is cited as being "fulfilled" in the New Testament is Isaiah 7:14. An angel announces to Joseph that Mary will bear a son whom "'you are to name . . . Jesus, for he will save his people from their sins'" (Matt. 1:21). The Gospel writer then declares (1:22-23):

> All this took place *to fulfill* what had been spoken by the Lord through the prophet:
>
> "Look, the *virgin* shall conceive and bear a son,
> and they shall name him Emmanuel,"
>
> which means, "God is with us." (emphasis mine)

The Gospel author cites the Old Testament from the Greek text rather than from the Hebrew because the latter text offers little possibility for Matthew's specific Christian witness; it reads simply "young woman" *('almah)*. Matthew's announcement of a "virgin" birth finds confirmation only in the Septuagint.

The Hebrew text of Isaiah 7:14 is not referring to some supernatural happening that is to take place, but to a very natural birth of a son by a young woman. The context in which Isaiah 7:14 occurs has to do with Ahaz, king of Israel, who seems to be yielding to pressure to join a rebellion against Egypt. Isaiah sees danger in such a decision and urges him to put his trust in God. The prophet gives him a *sign* that this is a right decision. The sign is that a young woman will give birth to a son and will call his name Emmanuel. The *sign* is not rooted in the manner of birth (i.e., in some unusual or unnatural birth), but in the name given to this child, namely, Emmanuel, which means "God is with us." Just as Isaiah's two sons had special names and therefore served as *signs* for the people, so this name given the child is a sign — a sign that God is with his people.

In the past the church has often regarded Isaiah 7:14 as a direct

---

Davidson, *The Vitality of Worship: Psalms 1–72,* International Theological Commentary (Grand Rapids: Wm. B. Eerdmans Publishing Co., 1998), p. 55. He refers to Paul's use of Ps. 14:2-3 in Rom. 3:10-11. He notes that Paul's citation follows the Greek text, "which takes us far beyond its original reference [i.e., in the Hebrew text]."

prophecy of Jesus. Today, Christian scholars representing conservative and mainline traditions view the text differently. J. Gordon McConville observes that "predictions which have been taken messianically in the New Testament do not necessarily fit the mould of the promised Davidic king in the Old. The famous Immanuel prophecy (Is. 7:14) is a case in point, since it is not at all clear that it referred to a royal child, and appears to have its fulfilment in the immediate context of Ahaz's reign."[24] Among a number of questions that McConville raises is the issue of whether Isaiah 7:14 takes on a messianic sense for the one who, as a follower of Christ, reflects on this text. Expressing a view similar to that of McConville is Alden Thompson. He suggests that Matthew "fills the original prophecy [of Isaiah 7:14] full of new meaning." Further, he comments that if we wish to "find out what Matthew meant we must read Matthew; to find out what Isaiah meant we must read Isaiah."[25]

Matthew, speaking out of his Christian experience, finds the Greek text of Isaiah 7:14 to be a fitting scriptural reference to support his understanding of Jesus as one born of a virgin. The Hebrew text, which speaks about a natural birth and a natural child who will bear a meaningful name, lends no clear support to Matthew's Christian interpretation. But, fortunately, both the Greek and Hebrew texts of Isaiah 7:14 preserve the "name" of this child: Emmanuel: God is with us. We do not know of anyone in the Old Testament — or in the New Testament — who has this name. In Matthew the child is named Jesus, not Emmanuel. Nowhere in the New Testament is Jesus addressed as Emmanuel. "Emmanuel" in Isaiah 7:14 *and* in Matthew 1:23 refers to the child's significance: he represents God's presence in this world. Without the use of the Greek version of the Bible, Matthew could have made this latter point, but he could not have developed the idea of a virgin birth.

Isaiah 9:6 (Heb. and Grk. 9:5) Not Cited in New Testament: Why?

A further illustration of the church's use of the Greek rather than the Hebrew text of the Old Testament may be seen in the *absence* of a remark-

---

24. McConville, p. 14; cf. p. x.
25. Alden Thompson, *Who's Afraid of the Old Testament God?* (Grand Rapids: Zondervan, 1989), p. 23.

able passage in the New Testament. For centuries Christians have believed that Isaiah 9:6 (Heb. v. 5) points most definitely to Jesus Christ:

> For a child has been born for us,
>   a son given to us;
> authority rests upon his shoulders;
>   and he is named
> Wonderful Counselor, Mighty God,
>   Everlasting Father, Prince of Peace.

This "messianic" text, however, is nowhere cited in the New Testament! What New Testament writer could or would overlook such a marvelous description of Jesus Christ?! The absence of this text may be due to a number of factors, but one of them no doubt concerns the fact that early Christians were using the Greek Bible instead of the Hebrew scripture. In the Septuagint the exceptional titles given the child in the Hebrew text are missing. In their place the Greek text gives only the following: "His name will be called messenger of great counsel." In Greek Isaiah 9:6 is still a beautiful passage, but it lacks the colorful titles of the Hebrew text, which have played such a prominent role in Christian music, liturgy, and theology. The Septuagint text therefore did not serve readily the christological interpretation that Matthew had in mind.

Summary

The authors of the New Testament held the Old Testament to be sacred scripture and looked to it for confirmation of the Christian proclamation. Early Christians were convinced that this scripture flashed light on the present and gave understanding of what was taking place in the event of Jesus. As the people of Qumran turned to the scripture to gain insight into what was taking place in their time, so the New Testament authors looked to the Old Testament to validate their understanding of Jesus and his ministry.

The New Testament community was not interested in a general understanding of the Old Testament. Rather, Christians searched the older scripture in order to find those passages which would corroborate their faith in Jesus. Their choice of passages was very selective. The greater part of the Old Testament was ignored; most of the citations came from Isaiah and the Psalms.

Clearly, the New Testament writers did not first consult the Old Testament and then form their opinion about Jesus. On the contrary, they moved from Jesus to the Old Testament scripture. Viewed in the light of Christ, certain texts took on new meaning which gave early Christians fuller insight into this figure in whom they experienced the presence of God.

The New Testament interpretation of the Old Testament represents a new reading of scripture[26] which, as previously noted, may be characterized as "insider" or "believer" exegesis. It understands the Old Testament against the background of faith in Jesus. When an "outsider" confronts the plain sense of an Old Testament text, the path from the Old Testament to Jesus is unclear. But to the insider, the ambiguities disappear; the text seems to lean or lead toward Jesus. The insider's depth probe of the ancient scripture provided the words and imagery that enabled early Christians to understand and articulate to others the significance and identity of Jesus.

Concluding Observations

As we conclude our discussion, we wish to underscore comments made at the end of the last chapter. There we commented that Christians have often denounced Jews for their failure to see prophecies, predictions, or promises of Jesus in the Old Testament. It was, in the eyes of the church, an act of rebellion against God and God's Word. However, these accusations can hardly represent the truth if in fact Christians have found Jesus in the Old Testament only after looking back from their experience with him.

Both rabbinic Judaism and Christianity relate to the earlier scripture by means of "look-back exegesis." The Old Testament renews itself — even if somewhat differently — in the interpretations of these two communities.[27]

26. See the comments of Nikolaus Walter, "Urchristliche Autoren als Leser der 'Schriften Israels'," *Berliner Theologische Zeitschrift* 14 (1997): 64, 76.

27. See further, Rolf Rendtorff, "Toward a Common Jewish-Christian Reading of the Hebrew Bible," in *Hebrew Bible or Old Testament*, ed. R. Brooks

Regarding Christian interpretation as "look-back exegesis," it is not as if the church is relating the Old Testament texts to one (i.e., Jesus) who is alien to the traditions of Israel. No, the witness of the New Testament as a whole testifies of Jesus the Jew, a child of Israel, who lived out of the rich traditions that he had received. These traditions, interpreted in his ministry, death, and resurrection, are handed on to those who follow him. No doubt it was the Jewishness of Jesus as well as that of his teaching that impelled Samuel Sandmel to observe: "Indeed, of the many varieties of Judaism which existed in the days of Jesus, two alone have abided into our time, rabbinic Judaism and Christianity."[28]

---

and J. J. Collins (Notre Dame: Notre Dame University Press, 1990), pp. 89-107. He comments that the Hebrew Bible achieved its present form before the rise of rabbinic Judaism and Christianity, "therefore neither a rabbinic nor a Christian interpretation of the Hebrew Bible can be historical." Neither rabbinic Judaism or Christianity interprets the Hebrew Bible in its *own* context. Both of these later traditions have developed their own peculiar approaches to this scripture (pp. 101-2). For similar views see Zenger, pp. 140-41; Klaus Koch, "Der doppelte Ausgang des Alten Testaments in Judentum und Christentum," in *Jahrbuch für Biblische Theologie: Altes Testament und christlicher Glaube*, 6, ed. B. Janowski and M. Welker (Neukirchen-Vluyn: Neukirchener Verlag, 1991), pp. 240-42; and James Charlesworth, "Exploring Opportunities for Rethinking Relations among Jews and Christians," in *Jews and Christians: Exploring the Past, Present, and Future*, ed. James Charlesworth (New York: Crossroad, 1990), pp. 41-42.

28. Samuel Sandmel, *We Jews and Jesus* (New York: Oxford University Press, 1965), p. 151. See also recently Bruce Chilton and Jacob Neusner, *Judaism in the New Testament: Practices and Beliefs* (London: Routledge, 1995), pp. xvii, 4-10, who declare: "People take for granted that Judaism contributes a principal formative force for the emergence of New Testament Christianity. We understand the New Testament solely in the setting of Judaism. We propose, by contrast, that we understand the New Testament still better when we regard it *as the statement of Judaism,* that is, from its writers' perspective, the New Testament at every point formed that very same Judaism that the Old Testament had adumbrated." For further comments see pp. 4-10. According to these authors, Christianity is one of a "number of Judaisms" (pp. xvi-xviii).

CHAPTER 4

Jesus and the Sinai Covenant

DIVERSE THINKING IN THE NEW TESTAMENT

Synopsis

For centuries the church has held that the Sinai covenant, with its focus on law, has been superseded by the New Testament proclamation of the grace of God present in Jesus Christ. It is usually assumed that this judgment is *the one* view in the New Testament. Admittedly there are a number of passages in the New Testament that convey a negative image of both the law and the Sinai covenant (e.g., John 1:17; Gal. 4:21-31; 2 Cor. 3:12-18). What is often overlooked, however, is that there are other texts in which this covenant is portrayed differently: its teachings continue to guide the early Christian community (e.g., Acts 21:17-26; Matt. 5:17-19; Luke 10:25-28). The following pages will concentrate attention on the tensions created by these two views and will give extended discussion to the remarkable chapters in Romans 9–11, in which Paul affirms the continuing validity of the Sinai covenant.

Sinai Superseded by the New Covenant

The words of John 1:17 have often been seen to summarize the New Testament's view of the Sinai covenant and its teaching: "The law indeed was given through Moses; grace and truth came through Jesus Christ." This judgment of John does not actually declare that the law is superseded by the grace and truth of Jesus, but it clearly conveys the writer's opinion that "grace and truth" is something quite different from "law," and much to be preferred. It is not a positive statement concerning law!

This negative understanding of the Sinai covenant finds strong advocacy in a number of other New Testament passages, especially in Galatians 4:21-31, 2 Corinthians 3:12-18, and Hebrews 8:13 (cf. 10:14-16). The Corinthians passage declares that Jews are unable to keep this covenant, and Hebrews 8:13 (cf. 10:14-18) asserts that the covenant at Sinai is aged and obsolete. In Galatians 4, the "old" covenant is not only old but apparently not even a fully valid part of the Israelite tradition. The covenant at Sinai is represented by Hagar, the mother of Ishmael and the Ishmaelites; the "Jerusalem above," on the other hand, corresponds to Sarah, the mother of Israel. Earlier Paul had declared that Christians through Christ, who is the seed of Abraham (Gal. 3:16), have Abraham as their ancestor. Now in Galatians 4:21-31 he asserts that Christians are the children of Sarah. In these passages Paul is claiming that the Christian movement is the "true" Israel.[1] Although various scholars provide helpful comments which lighten the negative stance of these passages,[2] the strong words of disavowal need

---

1. This dispute about the identity of the true people of God is not a new one. Already in the Hebrew Bible we find evidence of fierce debate on this topic, for example: Jer. 24:4-10; Ezek. 11:14-21; 33:23-29; Isa. 41:8-9; 51:1-2. See our discussion of Neh. 9:6–10:1 and the above texts in "Faithful Abraham and the *'ᵃmānâ* Covenant: Nehemiah 9,6–10,1," *Zeitschrift für die Alttestamentliche Wissenschaft* 104 (1992): 249-54. Apparently this controversy continued in postbiblical Judaism. For example, Bruce Chilton and Jacob Neusner, *Judaism in the New Testament: Practices and Beliefs* (New York: Routledge, 1995), p. 5, maintain that what early Christians "set forth in the New Testament must qualify as Judaism, and they insisted (as vigorously as any other Judaic system-builders) the only Judaism." The discussion of what community constitutes the true Judaism continues into the present day inside of traditional Jewish movements. A minority of orthodox rabbis (i.e., the Union of Orthodox Rabbis), for example, declared recently that Conservative and Reform Jews do not practice Judaism. Further, see the strong exclusionary language used of Jews embracing Reform Judaism by the former Chief Rabbi in Israel, Ovadia Yosef, as reported in the *Chicago Jewish Star*, December 5-18, 1997, p. 6. Such controversies, as is well known, have their counterpart within Christian circles.

2. See, for example, the following contributions: Erich Zenger, *Das Erste Testament: Die jüdische Bibel und die Christen* (Düsseldorf: Patmos, 1991), pp. 106-8 and 123-24; Rolf Rendtorff, *Canon and Theology* (Minneapolis: Fortress, 1993), pp. 201-3; Donald Hagner in *Hebrews*, A Good News Commentary (New

to be heard. These passages have contributed greatly to the strong negative view of Judaism in the Christian community.

The Continuing Validity of the Sinai Covenant

Frequently Christians have assumed that the New Testament presents a unified understanding of the relationship of the Christian community to the Sinai covenant and to the law (Torah). Further, it is thought that the texts cited above represent that one, unified view. Biblical scholars are increasingly aware, however, that diversity of thought is present in the New Testament[3] as well as in the Old Testament and Judaism. With others we believe that the above passages that speak negatively of the Sinai covenant and Jews represent the thinking of *some* — but not of all — leaders in the early Christian movement. These texts stand in tension with or in opposition to a number of other New Testament passages which present a more favorable view of the Sinai covenant and its emphasis on Torah (law). The following paragraphs point to some of these "positive" passages. To illustrate the tensions that existed in the early Christian movement, we are placing the positive passages alongside of the more negative texts.

York: Harper & Row, 1983), p. 104; Brevard Childs, *Biblical Theology of the Old and New Testament: Theological Reflection on the Christian Bible* (Minneapolis: Fortress, 1993), p. 439.

   3. The following references point to some of the diversity of views in the New Testament. See, for example, the conflict existing between: Paul and Peter (Gal. 2:11-14); Paul, Barnabas, and the Jerusalem leadership (Acts 15); Gal. 3:6 and James 2:21-24 (regarding faith and works); Rom. 13:1-7 and the book of Revelation (regarding the Roman state). Bruce Chilton and Jacob Neusner remark: "We can no longer speak of a single governing Judaism, any more than the diversity of earliest Christian writing [i.e., in the New Testament] sustains the view of a single Christianity . . ." (p. xvi). For a full discussion of diversity within the New Testament, see Chilton and Neusner, pp. 98-128 and 160-88. See further the thorough discussion of John Reumann in *Variety and Unity in New Testament Thought* (Oxford: Oxford University Press, 1991), who holds that what unites the great diversity found in the New Testament is the figure of Jesus and the experience of faith (p. 290).

Hebrews versus Luke's Portrayal of Paul

The author of Hebrews was convinced that Jesus' death and resurrection brought to an end the Sinai covenant with its cultic expression; this ancient covenant, he declares, is "obsolete" (8:13).[4] If the author of Acts is correctly representing the thinking of some parties within the very early church, then it is apparent that neither Paul nor the Jerusalem leadership could have supported the judgment of the author of Hebrews. The narrative in Acts 21:17-26 tells of Paul's visit to Jerusalem, where he was met by leaders of the Jerusalem Christian community. They rejoiced in Paul's successes but were also worried about rumors circulating that Paul was undercutting the law. Such rumors were upsetting Jewish converts to Christianity who were "zealous for the law." These leaders said: "'They [the Jewish converts] have been told about you that you teach all the Jews living among the Gentiles to forsake Moses, and that you tell them not to circumcise their children or observe the customs'" (v. 21). The elders of Jerusalem ask Paul to undergo a "rite of purification" together with four others and to pay the costs involved. Paul does what they ask him to do, and in this way demonstrates that he is *not* teaching "Jews living among the Gentiles to forsake Moses." Verse 26 describes what was done: "Then Paul took the men, and the next day, *having purified himself,* he entered the temple with them, making public the completion of the days of purification when *the sacrifice would be made for each of them*" (emphasis mine). One would hardly expect the author of Hebrews to act as Paul did. His view of the law (especially its cultic aspect regarding purification and sacrifice) would have prohibited him from agreeing to the requests of the Jerusalem elders.

---

4. William Lane, *Hebrews 1–8,* Word Biblical Commentary, vol. 47A (Dallas: Word, 1991), pp. cxlvi-cl, believes that the author of Hebrews "appears to have received his theological and spiritual formation within the hellenistic wing of the Church" (p. cxlvii). The author's negative view of the "old" covenant (especially its cultic manifestation) may be due to the influence of this tradition (p. cxlix). The viewpoint of Hebrews reveals some continuity with that of Stephen, who also appears to reflect the influence of the Hellenistic tradition (p. cxlix). See also Chilton and Neusner, pp. 181-88, who refer to the above commentary by Lane with approval and discuss the book of Hebrews under the title "Hebrews' New Religion."

Hebrews versus the Presentation of Jesus in Matthew and Luke

Lending further doubt to the belief that Hebrews represents the standard view of the New Testament concerning the old covenant is a comparison of this book with Matthew's view of Jesus (Matt. 5:17-19). The words of Jesus regarding the law do not lead one to believe that the so-called "old" covenant given at Sinai was obsolete (Heb. 8:13):

> "Do not think that I have come to abolish the law or the prophets; *I have come not to abolish but to fulfill.* For truly I tell you, until heaven and earth pass away, not one letter, not one stroke of a letter, will pass from the law until all is accomplished. Therefore, *whoever breaks one of the least of these commandments,* and teaches others to do the same, will be called least in the kingdom of heaven; *but whoever does them and teaches them will be called great in the kingdom of heaven."* (emphasis mine)

In the Gospels we find numerous examples of Jesus in conflict with Jewish leaders about the interpretation of the law, but nowhere is it suggested that the law given at Sinai lacks validity. Further, Jesus never says people should believe in him as opposed to obeying the law. In fact, in Matthew 23, where Jesus attacks fiercely the Pharisees, the famed interpreters of the law, he does *not* say to his disciples: "Believe me — not the Pharisees." Rather, he declares: "'The scribes and the Pharisees sit on Moses' seat; *therefore, do whatever they teach you and follow it . . .'"* (vv. 2-3, emphasis mine). To be sure, Jesus cautions them not to do what the Pharisees do; that is a part of his conflict with them. However, apparently he has no basic conflict with the Pharisees about the validity of the law of Moses or even with their interpretation!

Yet again we should give attention to another passage that was long overlooked or undervalued by many interpreters, namely, Luke 10:25-28:

> Just then a lawyer stood up to test Jesus. "Teacher," he said, "what must I do to inherit eternal life?" He said to him, "What is written in the law? What do you read there?" He answered, "You shall love the Lord your God with all your heart, and with all your soul, and with all your strength, and with all your mind; and your neighbor as your-

60

self." And he said to him, *"You have given the right answer; do this, and you will live."* (emphasis mine)

The exhortation which concludes this last statement of Jesus is not thrown at the lawyer to bring him to despair; Jesus is not attempting to make him aware that he could not do all the law and therefore could not live.[5] Further, it was not an attempt to indicate to the lawyer that because he could not do the law, he needed to believe on Jesus. Not one word about this! Rather, the concluding exhortation ("do this, and you will live") is taken from Leviticus 18:5: "You shall keep my statutes and my ordinances; by doing so one shall live; I am the LORD." This Old Testament text is not a threat but a promise! Here, as elsewhere in the Old Testament, following the path of the law (Torah) meant finding life. It is inconceivable that God would give Israel a law that it could not obey! The God of Israel is not such a God, as Deuteronomy 30:11-14 testifies: "Surely, this commandment that I am commanding you today is not too hard for you, nor is it too far away. . . . No, the word is very near to you; it is in your mouth and in your heart for you to observe." The law was given, as we well know today, not to press people down; it was gifted to Israel so that people could live and find fulfillment.

The straightforward affirmation of the law in the above passage (Luke 10:25-28) is often lost to the reader because interpreters too often focus on the seeming bad attitude of the lawyer (that is, "a lawyer stood up to *test* Jesus"). Or this text is passed by quickly because it does not seem to fit with some other passages in the New Testament (e.g., Paul in Galatians). It is striking that nowhere in the teaching of Jesus do we hear him talking about the covenant and the law as a teaching to be rejected because it is obsolete. It is increasingly apparent to both Christian and Jewish scholars that Jesus was one whose life and teachings

---

5. In certain traditions within the church, it has been long taught that because no one could obey the law the way that God expected, all people were placed under condemnation. From this condemnation, so it was held, people could only be saved by believing in Jesus, who in himself fulfilled the law for humankind. This view rested on the false assumption that God held the people (i.e., Israelites) to a *perfect* fulfillment of the law and that failure provided no possibility for forgiveness. But such is not the teaching of the Old Testament, as may be seen by the following passages which speak of divine forgiveness: Exod. 34:6-7; Pss. 32:5; 51:1-2; 103:15; 130:3-4. A God who gave a divine teaching that no one could obey or who would not forgive when sincerely asked is not the God that Israel knew and loved.

were shaped by Torah.[6] Rendtorff observes that although conflict existed between Jesus and the Pharisees, this conflict was an inner-Jewish conflict and had to do with the *interpretation* of Torah, not with its validity. In addition, he calls attention to the remarkable fact that in the Gospel narratives which report the trial of Jesus, there is no mention of his rejection of Torah — no accusation that his interpretation was false.[7]

Paul in Galatians Compared to Jesus in Luke-Acts

For many readers of the New Testament, Paul's epistle to the Galatians presents the authentic view of law in the New Testament — a view that by and large seems negative (3:1-5, 10-14, 15-18). The dramatic allegory of Hagar and Sarah in 4:21-31 is a part of this negative depiction. It likens Mount Sinai to Hagar (mother of Ishmael and the Ishmaelites) and "Jerusalem above . . . our mother" to Sarah, the mother of the Israelites. In this comparison the covenant with Moses is set very definitely at a second level; it does not appear to represent true Israelite faith. It may be that Paul's ardent desire to persuade Gentile converts to stand firm against a more Jewish interpretation of faith led him to an illustration that overreached the truth; he said more than he intended to say. In any case, this allegory does not fit the figure of Paul in Acts 21:17-26 (discussed above), nor does it bond well with the words of Paul in Romans 7:12, 14 (the law is holy, just, good, and spiritual).

Further, the allegory in Galatians, in which Mount Sinai is associated with Hagar, who bears "children for slavery," stands in conflict with Luke's narrative concerning the experience of Jesus on the Mount

6. See Brad H. Young, *Jesus the Jewish Theologian* (Peabody, Mass.: Hendrickson, 1995). In J. Charlesworth, ed., *Jesus' Jewishness: Exploring the Place of Jesus within Early Judaism* (New York: Crossroad, 1991), consult the articles of James Charlesworth, John P. Meier, David Harrington, and David Flusser. For an up-to-date summary of present-day scholarship concerning the relationship of Jesus to Judaism, see the fine article contributed by James Charlesworth ("Jesus Research Expands with Chaotic Creativity") in *Images of Jesus Today,* ed. J. Charlesworth and W. P. Weaver (Valley Forge, Pa.: Trinity Press International, 1994), pp. 1-41 (with extensive notes).

7. Rolf Rendtorff, "Die Bedeutung der Tora für die Christen," in *Begegnungen mit dem Judentum,* ed. B. Rübenach (Stuttgart: Kreuz Verlag, 1981), pp. 216-17.

of Transfiguration (Luke 9:28-36). This event, occurring on top of a mountain, is meant to recall the revelation on Mount Sinai. Here Jesus was, as was Moses earlier, enveloped by divine glory (v. 29; cf. Exod. 34:29). And while standing on this mountain with his disciples, Jesus sees and speaks with Moses and Elijah. Both are men of Torah and firmly linked to the Sinai covenant (Exod. 19 and 1 Kings 19:8).

Why Do "Negative" and "Positive" Views of the Sinai Covenant Exist?

How is one to understand the existence of positive and negative views regarding the Sinai teaching (law) in the New Testament? Rolf Rendtorff addresses this issue.[8] He notes, as do many others, that the very early Jesus movement was a movement *within* Judaism. Jesus lived as a Jew and obeyed Torah as he understood it. True, other Jewish leaders opposed at times his interpretation of the law, but as we have already noted, no one ever accused him of rejecting its validity. One can be certain that if Jesus had proclaimed that the law was obsolete or that the covenant at Sinai was invalid, his opponents would have made the most of it.

This regard for Torah which Jesus had, observes Rendtorff, was less and less remembered as the followers of Jesus became more sharply separated from other Jews because of their conviction that he was the Messiah. Further, the memory of the Jesus movement as one that took place inside of Judaism faded rather quickly as, increasingly, the followers of Jesus were found among the Gentiles. These Gentile converts had no experience or recall of the commonality that existed between Judaism and the Jesus movement. It is this increasing Gentile character of the church that provides an understanding of the rise of Marcion later on, who called for a rejection of all that was Jewish in Christianity.

Rendtorff argues further that in the context of a movement increasingly dominated by Gentiles, the discussion of Torah undertook a change. It became a discussion *inside of the Christian movement.* The basic question, as it is seen in Galatians, is whether Gentiles must become

---

8. For comments in the following four paragraphs, see Rendtorff, "Die Bedeutung der Tora," pp. 216-21.

Jews and obey the law in order to enter the Christian movement. This controversy did not address, primarily, the significance of Torah for Christian lifestyle, rather it focused on the question of whether or not obedience to the Torah was necessary for the salvation of the Gentiles. As the controversy developed within the Christian movement, it took on an anti-Jewish cast. Christians began to view the teaching of Jesus and Paul as an attack on Jews and the Mosaic covenant. This happened despite the fact that *Jesus' conflict* with the Pharisees was basically an *inter-Jewish* disagreement regarding the interpretation of Torah,[9] whereas *Paul's teaching* had to do with an *inter-Christian* controversy in which Paul declared that, for Gentiles, the Torah was not necessary for salvation.

Throughout the history of the church, up to the present time, Christians have taken a negative stance to the Sinai law (Torah) because they have not paid full attention to the contexts in which comments about Torah are made. With regard to the place of Torah in Christianity, Rendtorff declares that unquestionably, for Christians, the Torah is not necessary for salvation; Christians have entered into salvation through Jesus Christ. Although this is true, it does not mean that Christians are completely free from law. Both Jesus and Paul assume the legitimacy of Torah as "instruction" for responsible living.

9. The conflict between the early Jesus movement and traditional Judaism could at times be very intense, as the Gospels reveal, but one should not immediately conclude that Jesus' conflict with traditional Judaism placed him outside of the Jewish community. Alan Segal's words, which are echoed by many Jewish and Christian scholars, states the situation well: "Conflict was characteristic of Jewish Christian relations from the beginning. Yet the New Testament's many uncomplimentary references to Jews have been misinterpreted by both Jews and Christians. *The argument between Judaism and Christianity was at the beginning largely a family affair.* After Christianity separated from Judaism, the polemical passages in the New Testament were read in an unhistorical way, as testimony of hatred between two separate religions, when they should have been read as strife between two sects of the same religion." See Alan Segal, *Rebecca's Children: Judaism and Christianity in the Roman World* (Cambridge: Harvard University Press, 1986), p. 142, emphasis mine.

Paul in Galatians and Romans 9–11: Differing Emphases

At this point it is necessary to comment briefly about Paul's perplexing words in Romans 9–11, which have come into special prominence since the time of the Shoah (Holocaust). In the view of Krister Stendahl, these passages are the "climax" of the book of Romans.[10] Although in Romans 9–11 we discover a different stance toward Jews and the Sinai covenant, some passages appear to confirm the thinking of Galatians. For example, in Romans 9:30-32 Paul seems to be saying that Gentiles who stood outside the law have in fact achieved righteousness while Jews who strove for righteousness through the law did not find it because they failed to fulfill the law. Further, in Romans 11:15 Paul speaks about the rejection of his own people. Such passages give the impression of being at one with the Galatians outlook (e.g., 2:15-17; 3:10-12, 15-18) and therefore supportive of the traditional Christian view of Jews as a people rejected by God.

Romans 9–11: Jews Have Stumbled but Have Not Fallen

However, if Romans 9–11 stands in some continuity with the thinking of Galatians, so too does it offer elements of discontinuity. Brevard Childs declares: "In spite of the clarity of Paul's thought respecting the discontinuity between the old and the new, the full complexity of his theology only emerges when one considers another approach to the subject of the people of God which he develops in Romans 9–11."[11]

These three chapters in Romans, in which Paul is attempting to deal with the existence of two peoples (his "own people" and Gentile believers), give us insight into the pain endured by the apostle. He is convinced that he has experienced something "new" in Jesus Christ. It is a divine "newness" that in Paul's view confirmed and carried forward the

10. Krister Stendahl, *Paul among Jews and Gentiles* (Philadelphia: Fortress, 1976), p. 4.

11. Childs, p. 435. See also Peter Fiedler, who believes that Romans 9–11 provides a correcting counterbalance to other passages in Paul's letters that appear to take a negative view of the Sinai covenant: "Stand und Perspektiven des christlich-judischen Dialogs," *Bibel und Liturgie* 65 (1992): 146-47.

Old Testament witness regarding the will of God for his people. He hoped that all Jews would embrace this person. But only a remnant "believed" in Jesus as God's special messenger of newness; most Jews did not share Paul's enthusiasm for him. They "rejected" him. But why? Did these Jews refuse to follow Jesus because they were blinded by their wickedness? If so, then perhaps it is only right that God rejected them. For centuries the church has acted as if the Jews rejected Jesus out of their own wickedness. *But Paul does not attribute Jewish rejection of Jesus to their evil character.* They are not portrayed as major sinners. Speaking of the Jews in Romans 11:11-12, Paul asks and then answers his own question: *"Have they stumbled so as to fall? By no means!* But through their stumbling [or: transgression] salvation has come to the Gentiles, so as to make Israel jealous. Now if their stumbling means riches for the world, and if their defeat means riches for Gentiles, how much more will their full inclusion mean!" (emphasis mine). Further, in verses 28-29, the apostle declares (cf. 9:4): "As regards the gospel they are enemies of God for your sake; but as regards election they are beloved, for the sake of their ancestors; for the gifts and calling of God are irrevocable." In 1 Thessalonians 2:14-16, one of Paul's earliest writings, Paul speaks of wrath coming upon Jews as payment for the killing of Jesus and opposition to the gospel. The texts cited above strike a very different note.[12] Jews may have stumbled, but they have not fallen!

Jews Have Not Fallen: God Has "Hardened" Them

So Jews have stumbled but not fallen. They are not rejected by God because of their wickedness. Paul does, of course, mention Israel's sinfulness (11:26-32); it is a part of Israel's stumbling. But they have "not fallen." Why then have only a remnant followed Jesus? Why does the majority remain in "unbelief"? Is there a reason? The one reason proclaimed by the Christian church for ages (i.e., Jewish wickedness) is the one that Paul rejected.

Paul stands at odds with this traditional view of the church and offers another explanation. His answer is rooted in Old Testament pas-

12. See the comments of Terrance Callan, "Paul, the Law, and the Jewish People," in *Within Context: Essays on Jews and Judaism in the New Testament,* ed. D. P. Efroymson et al. (Collegeville, Minn.: Liturgical Press, 1993), pp. 23-37.

sages that speak of God's sovereignty in electing some and hardening others.[13] Paul believes that God in his divine sovereignty has hardened the heart of Jews so that *they cannot believe*. He declares as much in Romans 11:7-8 (see also 9:13ff. and 11:5ff.): "What then? Israel failed to obtain what it was seeking. The *elect* obtained it, but *the rest were hardened*, as it is written, 'God gave them a sluggish spirit, eyes that would not see and ears that would not hear, down to this very day'" (emphasis mine). The above view of Paul is interpreted by Otfried Hofius in the following citation:

> If therefore the vast majority of Israel fails to acknowledge the salvation of God and thus does not believe in Christ, the reason can only lie in the fact that God has not let the gospel become the saving and faith producing [power] for that majority. . . . God himself . . . has "hardened" Israel, with the result that it cannot accept salvation now realized in Christ. . . . This divinely ordained hardening is by no means God's answer to the unbelief of Israel. On the contrary, Israel's unbelief is the mode and form of exclusion from salvation.[14]

In basic agreement with the view of Hofius is Jürgen Moltmann, who declares: "The 'No' of Israel is not identical to the 'No' of unbelievers who exist everywhere. It is a special 'No' and as such, must be respected." He holds that Israel's overwhelming "No" is seen by Paul in Romans 9–11 as the will of God. Israel is not "hardened" or left out because it said "no" to belief in Jesus. The truth is the reverse: Israel as a whole could not believe because God had "hardened" Israel.[15]

Further, says Moltmann, this "hardening" should not be thought of as if God had rejected his people or as if it were a judgment on the moral character of Israel. It is not a "final judgment of God," but is an

13. See, e.g., his reference to the electing of Jacob over Esau and the hardening of Pharaoh in Rom. 9:13-17. Verse 18 concludes: "So then he has mercy on whomever he chooses, and he hardens the heart of whomever he chooses."

14. Otfried Hofius, "'All Israel Will Be Saved': Divine Salvation and Israel's Deliverance in Romans 9–11," *Princeton Seminary Bulletin*, Supplementary Issue 1 (1990): 27; see also pp. 29 and 32. So also Childs, p. 435: "Israel's unbelief is part of God's mysterious purpose which works toward the salvation of the Gentiles."

15. Jürgen Moltmann, "Jesus zwischen Juden und Christen," *Evangelische Theologie* (1995): 56-57. Such also is the opinion of Vittorio Fusco, "Luke-Acts and the Future of Israel," *Novum Testamentum* 38 (1996): 6-8.

act which has a definite goal in mind, that is, the inclusion of the Gentiles. Israel's blindness caused by the divine hardening will last until the time of the coming in of the Gentiles.[16]

God Will Unharden ("Save") Jews

According to Paul, God has "hardened" the many in Israel, but he has not rejected Israel (11:1); he has called forth a remnant of Israel, that is, those Jews who have become Christians. But, in Paul's thought, this establishment of a remnant by God is not the end of God's outreach to Israel. True, the rest of Israel remains in unbelief because God has "hardened" them, but this is only a temporary hardening. It will come to an end (in a time known only to God) when "the full number of the Gentiles has come in" (11:25). At that time "all Israel will be saved."

The God of Israel, according to the Hebrew tradition, is one who acts according to his own mysterious counsel. He is the sovereign Lord who is not to be questioned on the basis of human logic (Isa. 45:9-11). He has made his sovereign decision that only a remnant will believe in Jesus and has hardened the rest of Israel in unbelief. But the time is coming when God will exercise his sovereignty once again with the result that "all Israel" will be saved. God's concern for Israel, then, is not replaced by his embrace of Gentiles; he is ever the God of Israel, to whom he has given "the adoption, the glory, the covenants, the giving of the law, the worship, and the promises" (9:4) and who, "as regards election . . . are the beloved . . . for the gifts and the calling of God are irrevocable" (11:28-29).[17]

This emphasis is a surprise for contemporary Christians who have grown up thinking that Jews have been rejected by God because of their sinfulness. Paul is speaking of something (i.e., sovereign election and hardening) which, for us today, eludes understanding. We are uneasy with this approach and find ourselves hesitant to accept it. It is hard for us to be open to such an explanation because we have democratized God; we believe that God must give a reason (which we will understand) for doing what he wishes to do. The ancients, how-

---

16. Moltmann, pp. 56-57. Again, see the comments of Fusco, pp. 6-8.
17. For the above discussion see Hofius, pp. 29-39.

ever, were not of such a mind. They accepted God's Godness and bowed before his mysterious sovereignty.[18] He hardens the heart of an Egyptian pharaoh, chooses Jacob over Esau, and selects the Persian, Cyrus, as his "messiah" to restore the exiles to the land (Isa. 45:9-11; cf. v. 1). These actions are God's affair. God does what he chooses to do. Paul believes that God is acting in such a manner in his day. In this explanation of a temporary hardening of Israel (producing unbelief), Paul is attempting to hold together the enthusiastic response of the Gentiles to the gospel while maintaining God's commitment to Israel. Israel is still in the caring hand of God; all of Israel will be saved when God wills it.[19]

This emphasis of Paul that all Israel will be saved reminds us once again of the diversity of thinking in the New Testament. Paul's confidence in Romans 9–11 differs considerably from the point of view represented in Matthew 8:11-12 and 21:43. The former passage declares that the Jews ("heirs of the kingdom") "'will be thrown into the outer darkness, where there will be weeping and gnashing of teeth.'" Matthew 21:43 continues this theme, declaring, "'the kingdom of God will be taken away from you [Jews] and given to a people that produces the fruits of the kingdom.'"[20] Such views are not represented in Romans 9–11.

What Does "Be Saved" Mean?

But what does it mean that Israel will be "saved"? The word is so common in Christian theology that we do not even ask the question. But Krister Stendahl's following observation makes us aware that Christians may have been too certain of understanding what Paul meant when he used the word "save." He points out that Paul *does not say* that with the coming of the end

---

18. The books of Job and Ecclesiastes together with the psalms of lament provide the exceptions to this rule.

19. The emphasis on God's sovereign and solitary decision to choose some and not others is upheld by the Old Testament passages listed above. An attempt to interpret Jer. 31:31-34 in a similar manner (ie., God acting by himself to write the law on the heart) does not find support in related passages. See our discussion in the next chapter.

20. Cf. Luke 13:23-29. See the discussion of David Flusser, *Judaism and the Origins of Christianity* (Jerusalem: Magnes Press, 1988), pp. xxiii-xxiv.

Israel will accept Jesus as the Messiah. He says only that the time will come when "all Israel will be saved" (11:26). [However, as Stendahl notes elsewhere, Paul does not here define what "saved" means.] It is stunning to note that Paul writes this whole section of Romans (10:18–11:36) without using the name of Jesus Christ. This includes the final doxology (11:33-36), the only such doxology in his writings without any christological element.[21]

Paul's failure (1) to state specifically that "saved" means believing in Jesus and (2) to use the name of Jesus in this long, crucial section of the epistle is surprising. It should alert us to Paul's own divided state of mind. He is attempting to hold together paradoxical elements: God has done something new in Jesus Christ, *but* in so doing he has not rejected Israel as his people. True, *some* of the Jewish branches in the olive tree (Rom. 11:17-20) were broken off and a Gentile "wild root" was grafted in. However, it is noteworthy that Paul does not say that all of the branches in the olive tree were broken off, nor does he say that the olive tree itself (God's covenant with the Jews) was destroyed. Brevard Childs comments: "Against those Gentile Christians who have no further need of Israel, Paul makes it fully clear that there is only one people of God, that is Israel, into which olive tree a 'wild shoot' (the Gentiles) has been engrafted."[22]

Romans 9–11: Paradoxical Thinking

In Romans 9–11, Paul gives expression to the paradoxical situation in which he finds himself. He attempts to find the right words and images which truly reflect his own and his community's experience of God in Christ *and* his conviction concerning Israel's continued election by God. This dual witness is, as Childs notes, not "harmonized" by Paul; he lets both affirmations stand.[23]

---

21. Stendahl, p. 4.

22. Childs, p. 436. Within the New Testament itself, Childs sees a moving away from this Pauline view that there is only one people of God, namely, Israel. He asserts (p. 437): "Here [i.e., in the Pastoral Epistles] it is quite clear that the church has now assumed the role of the new people of God. One misses the complex dialectic of Paul in seeking to relate Jew and Gentile" (e.g., Titus 2:14).

23. Childs, p. 436. So also Isaac Rottenberg, "Thank You, but No Rabbi

The church has had difficulty letting these two truths exist together; it has only heard Paul's words that speak of rejection. Similarly,
by the way, for centuries the Christian community only heard Jesus
speaking against Jews and failed to perceive how fully Jewish he himself
was and how fully he affirmed the Jewish tradition. Paul's view of the
relationship between Jews and Christians will be misunderstood if attention is not given to the above-cited passages in Romans 9–11. It is by
ignoring these positive texts that the church has been able to speak of
the Jews as rejected by God while at the same time affirming that Christians are the new people (even the new Israel) of God.

Paul's Qualifying Statements: Few but Important

Admittedly, only a few verses in Romans 9–11 affirm that (1) the Jews
have not fallen and (2) the divine promises made to them still hold.
Still, we need to listen to them because elsewhere two or three verses
have been very important for understanding the diversity in the Bible.
Following are two examples.

For centuries the author of Isaiah 40–55 was looked upon as one
who consistently envisioned the inclusion of Gentiles as equals into Israel's religious life. To achieve this generous view of the prophet, scholars passed by such passages as Isaiah 45:14 and 49:23 which speak of
Gentiles as coming over to Israel *in chains, bowing down* and *licking the
dust of Israelite feet.* These passages were ignored by many scholars (or
seen as additions) because they contradicted the generally accepted
view mentioned above. Only two texts proclaim boldly the prophet's
nationalistic ardor, but if they are overlooked the interpreter is led
astray.

Another text, from the New Testament, which appears to present a
"nationalistic" coloring is Acts 3:19-21. It hints of diversity of thought in
the early Christian community regarding the future. This passage de-

---

Neusner," *Journal of Ecumenical Studies* 29 (1992): 272, and Ellis Rivkin, "Paul's
Jewish Odyssey," *Judaism* 39 (1989): 225-34. Rivkin points out: "Israel's rejection of Christ did not . . . carry with it God's rejection of Israel, anymore than Israel's rejection of the prophecies of Amos, Isaiah and Jeremiah carried with it
God's rejection of his people whom he foreknew." If, says Rivkin, the prophets
could castigate the Israelites and yet speak words that affirm them as the children
of God, why could not Paul have done the same (pp. 230-31)?

clares that Jesus, the Messiah, must "'remain in heaven until the time of universal restoration [or: restoration of all things] that God announced long ago through his holy prophets.'" Commenting on this text, Arthur W. Wainwright suggests that it makes the "most sense if it is assumed that Luke continued to be influenced by Jewish expectations about the restoration of Israel" (cf. Acts 1:6-11; Luke 2:38 and 24:21).[24]

With regard to the few texts in Romans which speak positively about the Jews and the Sinai covenant (e.g., 9:4-5; 11:11, 17-24, 28-29), it is astounding that they appear at all in Paul's writings. It is astonishing for two reasons: (1) Paul is convinced that Jesus, sent by God, has opened a new way of life for him. Further, (2) he knows the accusations that are being made against the Jews; that is, that they have rejected Jesus and killed him (1 Thess. 2:14-16). In view of both of these reasons, why is he affirming that the Jews have not fallen and that their election is irrevocable? Why does he not say that God has uprooted the olive tree and planted a new one? The uprooted olive tree would provide a good parallel to a covenant that had been "set aside" (2 Cor. 3:11), spoke of "slavery" (Gal. 4:24), and was "obsolete" (Heb. 8:13). Paul could not use such imagery in Romans 9–11; it misrepresented his dual experience of being in Christ and in Israel.

Qualifications: Never as Numerous as Affirmations

In our above discussion we have observed that Paul's views in Romans 9–11 qualify statements made elsewhere in his writings. Qualifications play an important role in addressing complex issues. They occur, for example, when an author or speaker feels that an issue has been made too simple — or believes that too many overstatements have been made. Qualifications, by their very nature, do not occur as often as the affirmations that one makes. Nevertheless, when we listen to speeches of

24. Arthur W. Wainwright, "Luke and the Restoration of the Kingdom to Israel," *Expository Times* 89 (1977): 78. For a similar view see Larry R. Helyer, "Luke and the Restoration of Israel," *Journal of the Evangelical Theological Society* 36 (1993): 324-29. Compare also Robert Tannehill's comments in "Israel in Luke-Acts: A Tragic Story," *Journal of Biblical Literature* 104 (1985): 84. Fusco, p. 3, observes that "Luke-Acts refers repeatedly . . . to the 'hope of Israel'" and observes that although "this hope has as its primary object the resurrection of the dead, it retains an aspect of nationalism."

any kind, our ears are alert to the qualifications. Further, the person who is speaking makes these qualifiers knowing, or at least hoping, that they will be heard. Qualifying statements are important because their use enables a speaker to make forthright affirmations while showing awareness of an issue's complexity. Paul may very well have a right to complain that his qualifying comments have been ignored. Such statements by Paul are an attempt to take into account the existence of paradoxical truths.

Finding Appropriate Language for the New Experience

Some years ago there appeared in the old *Chicago Daily News* an article by a sociologist who observed that changes were taking place in society that went beyond our capacity to describe exactly. He was simply affirming that experience was, as usual, preceding our vocabulary.[25] This was the situation with Paul. He believes in Jesus and knows from personal experience and from the witness of the Christian community that something new has happened. But he cannot explain fully how this has come to be or what it means fully for Jews. Even though this newness fills the apostle with extravagant praise, he cannot believe that Jews have fallen completely or that God has rejected them. Paul in these chapters, unlike some Christian leaders in the post–New Testament period, does not declare that the new Christian movement constitutes the "people of God" or the "new Israel."[26] Further, he believes that this newness in Christ is rooted in the soil of Israel's faith. In his view, the Christian movement represents grafted-in branches of the olive tree, Israel. The image is expressive of his thinking and experience, but, apparently, he is

25. David Tracy, *On Naming the Present: Reflections on God, Hermeneutics, and Church* (Maryknoll, N.Y.: Orbis, 1994), p. 3, remarks concerning the ambiguity of our age. He declares: "We live in an age that cannot name itself."

26. Regarding such affirmations by the early church founders, see the comments of Jaroslav Pelikan, *The Christian Tradition: A History of the Development of Doctrine*, vol. 1 (Chicago: University of Chicago Press, 1971), pp. 21 and 26. On Jewish reaction to these assertions, note the interesting discussion of Marc Hirshman in "The Core of Contention: 'They Are Not Israel . . . We Are Israel,'" in *A Rivalry of Genius: Jewish and Christian Biblical Interpretation in Late Antiquity* (Albany: State University of New York, 1996), pp. 13-22.

unable to find a straight-line, unqualified explanation of what has taken place in Christ. Paul is reluctant to concretize this new experience in Christ with dogmatic terminology that would exclude Jews who remained faithful to the divine teaching given at Sinai. The newness that arrived in Christ did not mean that what had gone before was invalid.

Speaking out of the context of the portrayal of early Christianity in the book of Acts, Jaroslav Pelikan notes that "the earliest Christians were Jews, and in their new faith they found a continuity with the old. . . . Clearly, they recognized that something new had come — not something, brand-new, but something, newly restored and fulfilled."[27] The borders that separated Judaism from the Christian movement were not all that clear despite the Christian conviction that something new had arrived in Jesus. This ambiguity gave rise to differing views of the relationship existing between the two communities — views that espoused both continuity and discontinuity.

27. Pelikan, p. 13.

CHAPTER 5

Israel and the "New Covenant" in Jeremiah 31:31-34

FAITHFULNESS TO SINAI TEACHING *IS* THE NEW COVENANT

Synopsis

In highly colored language that combines hyperbole with irony, Jeremiah 31:31-34 indicates the need for radical change. Elsewhere the prophet has called upon Israelites to repent, be washed and circumcised. Added to these demands for change is Jeremiah's announcement of a new covenant in which the law (Torah) will be written on the heart.

On the surface, this prophetic text appears to speak of God's decision to establish a new and different kind of covenant with Israel. When, however, this prophecy of a new covenant is compared with other passages from Jeremiah, Ezekiel, and Deuteronomy, one sees it in a different perspective. It becomes evident that, while the prophet is speaking dramatically of God's role in bringing about change, he is not denying the ability of human beings to respond sincerely to God's initiative.

The "new covenant" is not completely new or different; it is the Sinai covenant presented ironically under another designation. Jeremiah 31:31-34 was directed to Israel, and the plain meaning of the text found fulfillment in that community. We reserve to the next chapter a discussion of the relationship of this prophecy to Jesus.

Jeremiah 31:31-34: A Prophetic Word to Israel and Judah

Jeremiah's announcement of a new covenant in 31:31-34 has its context in a series of prophecies recorded in chapters 30–31. These latter chapters address the experience of Israelites who are suffering captivity in a foreign land; they offer challenge and hope to the exiles in Babylon. The prophet's message draws upon God's earlier saving act in the time of Moses. At that time God brought the Hebrews out of Egypt and covenanted with them at Sinai. Now, in a similar situation, God will bring the exiles out of Babylon (31:7-14) and make a "new covenant" with "the house of Israel and the house of Judah."

Nowhere in 31:31-34 or in its broader context is there any indication that this announcement of a new covenant is to have its fulfillment hundreds of years later. The oracle is not a vision into the far-flung future. The plain sense of the passage points to a covenant with Israel and Judah, that is, with the people who lived in the general time period in which Jeremiah exercised his prophetic calling. And this covenant that God is making with Israel and Judah will never cease to be valid: it will last as long as the sun, moon, and stars endure (31:35-36). A similar promise of eternal validity is made regarding God's covenant with the Levitical priests who are the ethical-cultic ministers of the Sinai covenant (33:18-22).

Throughout the book of Jeremiah, the prophet calls for a return to God which means a turning back to the Sinai covenant (e.g., 7:1-15). There is no indication that he is looking forward to a new, different kind of covenant. Any interpretation of this *one* passage in 31:31-34, which speaks of a "new covenant," must keep this general context in view. If Jeremiah had in mind a *new* and significantly *different* covenant, he has given little attention to it. If such a covenant were a major theme for him, one would expect that it would appear unambiguously throughout his writings. But as a matter of fact, this kind of definiteness is lacking. This leads us then to inquire further concerning the use of "new" in the expression "new covenant."

The "New" or "Renewed" Covenant

Christians have traditionally assumed that "new" in "new covenant" means something "unique" or "qualitatively different." It has been thought that it indicates a relationship to God that was unknown to people who lived before the time of Jesus. True, the Hebrew term translated "new" does at times indicate something akin to "completely new" or "different." This meaning may be seen, for example, in such phrases as a "new" king, house, garment, or rope (e.g., Exod. 1:8; Deut. 22:8; 1 Kings 11:29; Judg. 15:13). The Hebrew term, however, does not always reflect this meaning. It can, for example, be employed to refer to the "new moon" (1 Sam. 20:5, 18, 24, 27). "New" in this context does not mean something absolutely new because the "new moon" is not a uniquely new moon. It is in fact the very same moon that it was when it last appeared as a new moon. "New" in this expression speaks of "renewal" and of continuation; the "new" moon is a moon that becomes "new" again.

Yet another example of this same meaning for the Hebrew word "new" is found in Lamentations 3:22-23:

> The steadfast love of the LORD never ceases,
>   his mercies never come to an end;
> they are *new* every morning;
>   great is your faithfulness. (emphasis mine)

Once again it may be seen that "new" is not set over against something "old"; it does not point to something that is absolutely new or unique. The "new" in this text speaks of the renewal and continuation of the past. The love of God never ceases; it *renews* itself every morning.[1]

A further example of "new" having the sense of "renew" may be illustrated from a New Testament text (John 13:34). Jesus, addressing his disciples, declares: "'I give you a *new* commandment, that you love one another'" (emphasis mine). Clearly the "new" commandment here is not a unique commandment unknown before the time of Jesus (see, e.g., Lev. 19:18, 34). It is basically a renewed commandment, one of which the disciples needed to be reminded.

If the Hebrew term translated "new" has both the sense of "new" (as in "brand-new") and of "renew," then its meaning in any text can only be discovered by examining the context in which the term appears. This will be our task as we look further at Jeremiah 31:31-34. A preliminary comment deserves attention: in the Jeremiah

---

1. The employment of "new" in the following psalms has also the meaning of renewal and strengthening of one's praise: Pss. 40:3; 96:1; 144:9.

text "new covenant" is not set over against the "old" covenant. The expression "old covenant" does not occur in Jeremiah, nor anywhere else in the Old Testament.[2] Its *onetime occurrence* in the whole Bible is in 2 Corinthians 3:14. It may be that its rare appearance in the New Testament indicates that the tensions existing between Judaism and the Jesus movement had not yet fully hardened into "new" versus "old" covenant.[3]

Images of Change: Newness, Washing, Circumcision, Return

A reading of the book of Jeremiah leaves no doubt that the prophet is addressing Israelites at a critical period in their national life. He believes that a living, responsible relationship to God stands in question. Only radical change will save the nation from ruin. Attempting to pierce the self-satisfied spirit of his day, Jeremiah uses strong words which reflect both anger and disappointment. From the following

2. Thomas Römer's study of Jer. 11:1-11 and 31:31 may throw some light on this question. See his article, "Les 'anciens' pères (Jér 11,10) et la 'nouvelle' alliance (Jér 31,31)," *Biblische Notizen* 59 (1991): 23-27. Römer calls attention to the unusually close verbal ties that exist between these two texts and points to the occurrence of the term "old" in Jer. 11:10. However, "old" in this text is not related to an "old" covenant, but rather to the "ancestors of old." In chapter 11 Jeremiah accuses the people of returning to the "iniquities of their *ancestors of old.*" When, in Jer. 31:31, the prophet speaks of a "new covenant," he is *not* setting an old covenant over against a brand-new covenant. Rather, in the midst of brokenness, thinks Römer, Jeremiah is speaking of a *renewed* covenant relationship. See also Peter Fiedler, "Stand und Perspektiven des christlich-jüdischen Dialogs," *Bibel und Liturgie* 65 (1992): 146. Walter Brueggemann, in "Texts That Linger, Words That Explode," *Theology Today* 54 (1997), holds that continuity and discontinuity with the past is present in Jer. 31:31-34 and declares: "It is possible . . . to take the word 'new' as indicative of renewal, a reestablishment and revivification of the old" (p. 190).

3. Norbert Lohfink, *The Covenant Never Revoked: Biblical Reflections on Christian-Jewish Dialogue*, trans. J. J. Scullion (New York: Paulist, 1991), p. 18, calls attention to the fact that the community at Qumran (Dead Sea Scroll community) thought of themselves as the people of the "new covenant" (see, e.g., the Damascus Document 6:19; 8:21; 20:12), but they never interpreted this to mean that this was a brand-new covenant, different from that at Sinai, which separated their community from Judaism.

passages one can see that he employs varied imagery to dramatize his call for "newness."

It is a "newness" that must take place in the *heart.* Here at the center point where decisions are made, radical change is needed. Jeremiah addresses this need in 31:31-34 where he speaks of a "new covenant" in which God writes the law (the divine teaching) on the heart. But this is not the only place where he speaks of heart-depth change. Elsewhere, using other imagery, the prophet strikes home the same message, as the following citations reveal:

The *heart* is dirty with a religion-approved wickedness; it needs a thorough *washing* (4:14).

The *heart* is so thickly covered with a fleshly substance that it no longer is sensitive to right and wrong; the excess flesh must be cut off; *the heart must be circumcised* before it will be able to see, hear, and do the good (4:4).

The *heart* is in revolt; it has turned to its own way (18:11-12). *It needs to turn around* (3:12, 14, 22; 18:11). Only a complete repentance (turnaround) will prevent ruin.

The prophet is addressing people who are "skilled in doing evil" (4:22); he calls the Judeans to forsake their evil ways and follow the way of God. It is a summons to "newness." The terminology and imagery is other than that found in 31:31-34, but the message is the same: the Judeans must repent, be washed, and have their hearts circumcised if they are to be in a right relationship to God. When the prophet speaks of a "new covenant" and a law written upon the heart (31:31, 33), he is making use of one more image in his attempt to drive home the necessity of change.

A New (Renewed) Covenant: Faithfully Obedient to Sinai

The change that a "new covenant" calls for is the one ever on Jeremiah's mind: a genuine return to the Torah of the God of Sinai. The prophet laments continually the community's unfaithfulness to the divine teaching given at this mountain, for example:

Hear, O earth; I am going to bring disaster on this people,
  the fruit of their schemes,

because they have not given heed to my words;
and as for my teaching [law], they have rejected it.

(6:19; cf. 5:4-5; 9:13; 16:4; and 26:4)

What Jeremiah has in mind is to bring home to those who are "accustomed to do evil" (13:23) and "skilled" in doing it (4:22) the necessity of adhering to the Sinai covenant if they desire to avoid ruin. The following text carries the themes of the Sinai tradition:

> For if you truly amend your ways and your doings, if you truly act justly one with another, if you do not oppress the alien, the orphan, and the widow, or shed innocent blood in this place, and if you do not go after other gods to your own hurt, then I will dwell with you in this place, in the land that I gave of old to your ancestors forever and ever. (7:5-7)

Jeremiah would like the Judean leadership and all of Judean society to emulate the faithful life of King Josiah, who respected the teaching of Sinai and did "justice and righteousness" and "judged the cause of the poor and needy." To act in such a manner, the oracle continues, is to "know" God (22:15-16). *Josiah, in his faithfulness to the Sinai teaching, is a new covenant person!* There is no evidence that Jeremiah has given up on the Sinai covenant — no indication that he is looking to another kind of covenant. He believes that if the Judeans would return to covenant faithfulness (as exemplified by Josiah), then life would be what God intended it to be.

Despite Sins of People, God Holds to the Sinai Covenant

The Sinai covenant has not outlived its usefulness, nor has God rejected his people and broken the covenant with them. True, *they* have broken the covenant (31:32; 11:10), but Jeremiah is convinced that God, for his part, still holds to his responsibility within the covenant. He therefore prays:

> We acknowledge our wickedness, O LORD,
> the iniquity of our ancestors,
> for we have sinned against you.

Do not spurn us, for your name's sake;
  do not dishonor your glorious throne;
  remember and do not break your covenant with us.
(14:20-21, emphasis mine)[4]

Regarding the above passage, J. A. Thompson says: "There is a strange inconsistency in this plea, since it lays stress on Yahweh's obligations and overlooks the strong obligations of Israel to Yahweh."[5] The point that Thompson makes is generally true, even though here there is a confession of sin. But this citation from Jeremiah and the other texts listed in the preceding footnote underscore the unwavering commitment of God to the covenant made at Sinai. As Hosea noted (11:9), God is God and not a human being; the divine one, the holy one of Israel, will not bring full ruin upon the people to whom he promised his love.

The prophets reproached the Israelites severely for their sinfulness, yet they held the conviction that God had not rejected them; along with oracles of threat and judgment there exist promises of forgiveness and restoration (e.g., Isa. 43:1-7; Jer. 30:18; 31:2-6). The announcement of the new (or renewed) covenant (31:31) should not be seen as an indication that God has given up on the covenant made at Sinai. Such is not the case. It was Israel that broke the covenant relationship,[6] and it is Israel that must once again make a new covenant commitment.

The New Covenant: Renewal or a New Work of God?

However, the above sentence, which implies that the Judeans must take action to recovenant with God, appears to fly in the face of the very clear declaration of the text that it is God who takes action and not hu-

---

4. See also Ps. 106:43-45 and Neh. 9:32-33. For a further discussion of this theme see Fredrick Holmgren, "Remember Me, Remember Them: The Prayers of Nehemiah," in *Scripture and Prayer*, ed. C. Osiek and D. Senior (Wilmington: Glazier, 1988), pp. 33-45.

5. J. A. Thompson, *The Book of Jeremiah*, New International Commentary on the Old Testament (Grand Rapids: Wm. B. Eerdmans Publishing Co., 1980), p. 386.

6. See Erich Zenger, *Das Erste Testament: Die jüdische Bibel und die Christen* (Düsseldorf: Patmos, 1991), pp. 115-16.

mankind: "*I will* put my law within them, and *I will* write it on their hearts" (31:33, emphasis mine).

Many scholars believe that this declaration points to a time in the future when God, *all by himself,* will take decisive action to write his teachings on the heart. In support of this interpretation, it is noted that Israel has repeatedly broken its covenant with God. If now God makes once again a covenant with Israel just like the covenant made at Sinai, one can only expect that Israel will break this one also. What to do? The only guarantee that Israel will be obedient to the divine teaching (law), it is said, is for God to take sovereign action and to write this teaching upon the heart. Once God has created within the heart a "natural inclination" to obey the divine teaching, then it will no longer be necessary to teach people what is right (31:34), because everyone will do naturally what is right and good. In taking this sovereign action, so it is affirmed, God has guaranteed that Israel in the future will never say "No."[7] This view is articulated by Moshe Greenberg in his comments on 31:31-34: "This is a counsel of despair. There is no hope that humans in their present nature can observe the Torah. Salvation will come only when God intervenes and makes observing the Torah natural, so that it will no longer be necessary to learn it."[8]

We do not agree with Greenberg that Jeremiah 31:31-34 is a "counsel of despair" about the ability of the Israelites to obey God. Rather, we hold that this passage stands in harmony with the usual assumption of the lawgivers and the prophets that the Israelites were capable of turning around and obeying the divine teaching. Neither the lawgivers nor the prophets expected perfection; they called on the Israelites to be righteous, that is, to be responsible persons in their relationship to God and people. And they believed the Israelites were capable of this kind of righteous behavior. Josiah, as indicated earlier, pleased God with his acts of justice and kindness (Jer. 22:15-16). *It would be wrong to assume that Josiah was the only person in Israel capable of pleasing God.* Although it is true that people

7. So, e.g., Hans-Jürgen Hermisson, "Jeremiah 31,31-34," *Göttinger Predigtmeditationen* 83, no. 5 (1994): 239. See the chapter of Ronald Hals, who shares generally the view of Hermisson: "Some Aspects of the Exegesis of Jeremiah 31:31-34," in *When Jews and Christians Meet,* ed. J. J. Petuchowski (Albany: State University of New York Press, 1988), p. 92.

8. Moshe Greenberg, *Studies in the Bible and Jewish Thought* (Philadelphia: Jewish Publication Society, 1995), p. 19. A similar view from the Jewish tradition is represented by Richard Sarason, "The Interpretation of Jeremiah 31:31-34 in Judaism," in *When Jews and Christians Meet,* p. 110.

often say "No" to God, the Old Testament itself would not be in existence today if many people had not said "Yes" to God and the divine teaching (Torah)!

In the next few paragraphs we wish to discuss further the opinion suggested by Greenberg and others; namely, that Jeremiah 31:31-34 looks to a time when God will act by himself to create a "new" heart. We will do this by looking at some significant texts in the Old Testament that point in another direction.

God Doesn't Do It All by Himself

Biblical commentators, in general, have too often literalized the "God alone" language of the Bible; they have pressed religious speech too hard. The language of piety, ancient and modern, often reflects a fervor for God which attributes to God alone that which involves human participation.

Familiarity with the pietistic wing of the church may give some insight into the use of "God alone" language. For example, when young people give "witness" of what Jesus Christ has done for them, they often describe their experiences as if only God were involved. It is only in further conversation that one discovers that there is more to the story. An incident some years ago highlights this use of religious language. A church administrator visited our campus to speak to some young people who would soon be entering theological studies. He introduced the session by sharing his pilgrimage of faith. He spoke dramatically of God's part in his conversion, using such phrases as "God said" — "God touched me" — "God led me." After several minutes, he stopped and said: "That's not the way it really was!" He then proceeded to talk about people and events that were influential in his decision to follow Jesus Christ. It was then that the students heard "the rest of the story." This information proved interesting, but his listeners had already assumed, of course, that much more was involved in his decision to become a Christian than he had at first indicated.

In the following paragraphs we attempt to show that the Bible (1) at times speaks of change as if it were brought about by God alone and (2) at other times attributes these *same* changes to the actions of people. Such opposite emphases should not be seen as contradictions; the one emphasis does not rule out the other. The following illustrations from the Old Testament help us understand the use of the God-alone language in Jeremiah 31:31-34.

Concerning the Land

When we read the books of Joshua and Judges, we learn that *Israelites* were involved in the *taking* of the land of Canaan. Violence was present, blood was shed and people died (Josh. 8; 11; 12; Judg. 1). God took the land, but not without spears and swords wielded by human beings in hand-to-hand combat. God "needed" the army of Joshua to defeat the kings of Canaan. However, later on when this event was remembered, the participation of people is not mentioned; instead praise is directed to God, who *gave* the land to Israel (e.g., Ps. 105:44; Amos 2:9-10; Acts 7:45). For people of piety it was "natural" to emphasize the divine action involved in the taking of the land. If one is to appreciate *all that was involved,* however, one needs to listen to the texts of Joshua and Judges.

Concerning Circumcision

The following texts come closer to the issue regarding Jeremiah 31:31-34 because they have to do with heart religion. Deuteronomy 30:6 informs us that it is *God* who circumcises the heart: "Moreover, the LORD your *God will circumcise your heart* and the heart of your descendants, so that you will love the LORD your God with all your heart and with all your soul, in order that you may live" (emphasis mine). Those scholars who emphasize that God alone creates the new heart in Jeremiah 31:33 underscore the above text, but they often fail to give attention to the following two passages (Deut. 10:16 and Jer. 4:4)[9] where *people are urged to circumcise their own hearts:*

> *Circumcise, then, the foreskin of your heart,* and do not be stubborn any longer. (emphasis mine)

> *Circumcise yourselves to the LORD,*
>   remove the foreskin of your hearts,

9. So, e.g., Sarason, p. 110.

84

> O people of Judah and inhabitants of Jerusalem,
> or else my wrath will go forth like fire. . . . (emphasis mine)

As we noted, all three passages above have to do with "heart religion"; the first passage attributes the circumcision of the heart to God, but the following two texts call upon Israelites to circumcise their own hearts. In these passages one side (God) or the other (people) is emphasized. However, the emphasis on God should not be seen as denying the actions of people. Similarly, the underscoring of the actions of people should not be interpreted as if God had nothing to do with it.

Concerning a New Heart and Spirit

Once more we call attention to some texts that speak directly to the idea of a new heart. The passages cited below from Ezekiel speak as if a new heart and new spirit resulted only from the action of God:

> *I will give* them one [or: a new] heart, and *put* a new spirit within them. (Ezek. 11:19, emphasis mine)

> *A new heart I will give you,* and a new spirit I will put within you; and I will remove from your body the heart of stone and give you a heart of flesh. (Ezek. 36:26, emphasis mine)

However, countering the above language which strongly underlines divine action is another text from the same prophetic book. This text (Ezek. 18:30-31) presents another viewpoint, one that is often overlooked by scholars.[10] It points to the necessity of people taking action in the making of a new heart.

> Therefore I will judge you, O house of Israel. . . . Repent and turn from all your transgressions. . . . Cast away from you all the transgressions that you have committed against me, and *get yourselves* (Heb. *make for yourselves*) a new heart and a new spirit! (emphasis mine)

In summary: The above text from Ezekiel 18:31 (Israelites are urged to make for themselves a new heart) and those texts in Jeremiah 4:4

10. So Sarason, p. 110.

and Deuteronomy 10:16 (Israelites are to circumcise their own hearts) underscore the necessity of human decision and action; they do not, however, exclude divine activity.[11] Similarly, the "God alone" emphasis present in Deuteronomy 30:6, Ezekiel 11:19 and 36:26, as well as in Jeremiah 31:33 does not preclude the involvement of human action.

"O My God; Your Law Is within My Heart" (Ps. 40:8)

"Heart religion" has always been at the center of Israelite faith. In Jeremiah 31 the prophet is once more emphasizing the necessity of this kind of faith. In dramatic fashion and with hyperbolic speech (*"I will write . . . I will* put . . ."),[12] the prophetic oracle indicates that truehearted religion is what God expects; it is the only way to live before God. To have the law (the divine teaching) in one's heart, however, is not a new thought. It was the experience of those who committed themselves to the God of Sinai. Again we need to be reminded of Josiah. Was it not the teaching of Sinai, written deep on the heart of King Josiah, which caused God to rejoice in him? If the law had been written only on tablets of stone, then one finds it difficult to explain a person like Josiah (Jer. 22:15-16).

Further, one can hardly understand the expressions of faith and hope found in the book of Psalms if stone tablets were the final repository for the law. There were, of course, casuistic, legalistic persons in Israel who acted as if the law was something written on tablets and who found ways to circumvent it. But those people who had truly "met" the God of Sinai knew that the law's home was in the heart. Its presence there created life and lasting satisfaction:

---

11. The covenant reported in Neh. 9:38 (Heb. 10:1) underlines the activity of the Jewish leaders, but it should not be interpreted to be merely human activity as some understand it. Undoubtedly this passage assumes the presence and activity of God. See further Fredrick Holmgren, "Faithful Abraham and the '*ᵃmānâ* Covenant: Nehemiah 9,6–10,1," *Zeitschrift für die Alttestamentliche Wissenschaft* 104 (1992): 249-54.

12. Similar highly colored, exaggerated speech of a negative kind may be found in Jer. 17:1: "The sin of Judah is written with an iron pen; with a diamond point it is engraved on the tablet of their hearts, and on the horns of their altars."

"I delight to do your will, O my God;
    your *law* is within my heart."

(Ps. 40:8, emphasis mine)

The divine word recorded in Deuteronomy 30:11-14 declares that the commandment given Israel is "not too hard for you, nor is it too far away." In verse 14, the speech continues and affirms: "No, the *word* [i.e., the *commandment*] is very near to you; it is in your mouth and *in your heart* for you to observe" (emphasis mine). Further, as most Christians well know, Psalm 51 gives a beautiful expression of heart religion, but sometimes it is almost overlooked that this expression of piety roots in the Old Testament.[13] In this psalm that speaks about the heart and spirit, we are introduced to new terms and imagery: "truth" within (v. 6); "clean heart" and "new and right spirit" (v. 10); "a broken spirit; a broken and contrite heart" (v. 17). This variety of terms and images reminds us that the Bible speaks about "newness" in diverse ways.[14] With this in mind, we realize that Psalm 51 is not an isolated example of heart religion. Other psalms, using a variety of terms and images, witness of this same inner piety (e.g., Pss. 42–43; 103; 119; 130; 139). In such psalms the divine teaching is not written on tablets, it lives within the heart.

The Law: No Enemy to Heart Religion

The new covenant described by Jeremiah 31:31-34 is a covenant in which the law stands at the center.[15] It is the love of God's law that

13. Lohfink holds that Jer. 31:31-34 "was only fulfilled in its definitive, eschatological fullness in Jesus of Nazareth" (p. 57). However, he observes that Israelite/Jewish faith is not merely "material and external." As an example of inner faith, he points to Psalm 51 and declares: "Ps. 51:12 shows that even before the post-exilic rebuilding of the walls of Jerusalem God disposed to confer on Israel the very essence of the promised 'new covenant', a heart stamped with the torah" (p. 55).

14. See also Ezek. 16:53-63, which speaks of God's dismay at the people's sins yet promising forgiveness (v. 63), the restoring of the fortunes of Israel (v. 53), and the establishing of "an everlasting covenant" (v. 60).

15. See the fine comments of Michael Wyschogrod concerning the law (Torah) in "The Impact of Dialogue with Christianity on My Self-Understanding as a Jew," in *Die Hebräische Bibel und ihre zweifache Nachgeschichte*, ed. E. Blum et al. (Neukirchen: Neukirchener Verlag, 1990), pp. 725-36. Without the law and its observance, declares Wyschogrod, there is no Judaism. But he rightly underscores the

87

nourished the piety of the Israelites — a piety beautifully expressed in the book of Psalms, which still today has a prominent place in Christian worship. In the past, Christians have spoken of the "Old Testament" law in terms of a heavy burden that weighed down the Israelites and Jews. But it is evident that the law is no burden for the psalmists, Jeremiah, or the prophets generally. Rather, for them, this divine teaching is life-giving; it is a blessing bestowed by a "covenant of love."[16] For this reason, when Jeremiah speaks about genuine faith, he must also speak of the law. It is no doubt for the same reason that Jesus gives such strong support to the law; his mission is not to "abolish" but to "fulfill" it. The law will stay in force as long as heaven and earth exist; until they come to an end, "'not one letter, not one stroke of a letter, will pass from the law until all is accomplished'" (Matt. 5:17-20). True, as we noted above, Jesus may have been at odds with some Jewish interpreters of the law, but he did not advocate its rejection.

Jeremiah's "New Covenant": Unique?

Although many interpreters attempt to find something "uniquely new" in Jeremiah 31:31-34, it is generally admitted that the description of the new covenant is suitable as a description of the so-called "old" Sinai covenant. In both covenants the law stands at the center. Also, both covenants are covenants made with Israelites. A third aspect which characterizes both covenants is the promise of forgiveness of sins. Some interpreters hold that this latter aspect (forgiveness) is the "uniquely new" aspect of the new covenant. But a look at numerous Old Testament texts confirms that it is but another theme that both covenants share.[17] In the narrative about the second giving of the law at Sinai (Exod. 34), it is proclaimed:

> "The LORD, the LORD,
> a God merciful and gracious,
> slow to anger,

---

truth that Jews do not believe that they are "saved" by the law; rather it is the "mercy of God" that justifies (pp. 729-31).

16. The Sinai covenant is so described in the hymn "Song of Zechariah," *The Covenant Hymnal: A Worship Book* (Chicago: Covenant Press, 1996), p. 142.

17. See Rolf Rendtorff, "What Is New in the New Covenant," in *Canon and Theology* (Philadelphia: Fortress, 1993), p. 198.

and abounding in steadfast love and faithfulness,
keeping steadfast love for the thousandth generation,
forgiving iniquity and transgression and sin."

(34:6-7, emphasis mine)

It is to this God who richly forgives sin that Moses prays on behalf of a people who have acted wickedly: "'If now I have found favor in your sight, O Lord, I pray, let the Lord go with us. Although this is a stiff-necked people, *pardon our iniquity and our sin, and take us for your inheritance*'" (34:9, emphasis mine). To these texts we may add other passages from the Psalms (e.g., Pss. 51; 103; and 130). Further, and somewhat surprisingly to those who think postexilic Judaism is but a formal and dead religion, one discovers that Jews gave full confession of their sin because they were confident that their God was the one who was rich in forgiveness. Ezra confesses on behalf of the Jewish community: "'O my God, I am too ashamed and embarrassed to lift my face to you, my God, for our iniquities have risen higher than our heads, and our guilt has mounted up to the heavens'" (Ezra 9:6). One does not make such a confession unless there is both the experience and assurance of God's mercy and forgiveness. Nehemiah also confesses to God the wickedness of his people (Neh. 9:26-30) and shares Ezra's confidence in the mercy and love of God (9:31-32). The God of the so-called "old" covenant is not different from the God who makes the "new" covenant. Moses and the prophets would not be able to detect a different God or a different relationship in the "new covenant." Further, divine mercy and forgiveness is a prominent theme today in Jewish synagogues and temples. Two prayers illustrate this well:[18]

> Forgive us, our Creator, when we have sinned; pardon us, our King, when we transgress; for you are a forgiving God.

> Our Father, our King, be gracious to us and answer us, for there is little [lit. no] merit in us. Treat us generously and with kindness, and be our help [or: save us].

---

18. See *Gates of Prayer: The New Union Prayerbook* (New York: CCAR, 1975), pp. 39 and 393.

89

The New Covenant Promise: Irony

Most biblical scholars today agree that the "new covenant" shares major themes with the Sinai covenant, including the theme of forgiveness. But there remain still some expressions in Jeremiah 31:31-34 which, it is thought, point to something uniquely different in the new covenant. The prophetic oracle declares, for example, that this new covenant "will *not be like* the covenant that I made with their ancestors when I took them by the hand to bring them out of the land of Egypt — a covenant that they broke, though I was their husband, says the LORD" (31:32, emphasis mine).

Such a sentence following the announcement of a "new covenant" appears to point to something radically new and different. However, as we have mentioned earlier, we believe that this approach is one that presses religious language into literalism.[19] Here, as elsewhere in the Bible, one must ask not only what is written but how it is to be interpreted. We hold that the expression "not like" in the above citation should be considered as irony in which exaggerated speech and satire are included. For this approach to the text, we are indebted to Wilber Wallis, whose insight clarifies the significance of the oracle.[20]

Irony, as Edwin Good observes, roots in conflict — "a conflict marked by the perception of the distance between pretense and reality."[21] Although it displays itself in many patterns, basically irony is a type of speech in which a person says one thing but intends another. *An ironical statement means the opposite of what is said.* For example, one might say to an opponent: "You are right; the evidence that you have assembled in support of your view is overwhelming." If spoken with

---

19. Lohfink, pp. 45-48, emphasizes the rhetorical character of the language in Jer. 31:31-34 and holds that the intention is not to set the new covenant over against the Sinai covenant.

20. Wilber Wallis, "Irony in Jeremiah's Prophecy of a New Covenant," *Bulletin of the Evangelical Theological Society* 12 (1969): 107-10. See Fredrick Holmgren, "A New Covenant? For Whom?" *Ecumenist* (1984): 38-41.

21. Edwin M. Good, *Irony in the Old Testament* (Philadelphia: Westminster, 1965), p. 14. Good notes that sarcasm "is often equated with irony, in that it usually means the opposite of what it says" (p. 26). But, he continues, whereas sarcasm has the intent of wounding or destroying, "the basis of irony in a vision of truth means that irony aims at amendment of the incongruous rather than its annihilation" (p. 27).

irony, these words mean: "You are wrong; the evidence you have produced would not fill a thimble."

When irony is used in conversation and debate, the tone of voice used by the speaker often gives clear indication of its meaning. Irony, however, is often subtle; its character may be missed. For example, some time ago an article about the "Jesus People" appeared in a denominational paper. On the surface it seemed very critical of this community. Some readers perceived it as an attack and wrote the paper protesting what they considered to be unfair treatment of this Christian community. The editor was forced to append a note at the end of their protest which explained that the article was an ironical, satirical portrayal of that community. In actual fact, the article favored the Jesus People!

What does an ironical approach mean for our understanding of this famous oracle? Our suggestion follows. Jeremiah is addressing people who think they are in covenant with God, but, in fact, are not. The prophet speaks to them of a "new" covenant, but, as most scholars admit, this "new" covenant has the same character as the Mosaic covenant. Jeremiah's listeners, however, have a warped view of the covenant relationship with God; they have cast aside the divine teaching and yet expect God to be with them (Jer. 7). They have little awareness that they have broken the covenant bond. Without any bending of conscience they can say to a tree, "'You are my father,' / and to a stone, 'You gave me birth'" (2:27), and yet address God as "'my Father, you are the friend of my youth'" (3:4). With the use of such attack, hyperbolic language,[22] Jeremiah attempts to crack open minds and hearts that have been sealed shut. The true character of the covenant at Sinai has never gotten through their blindness, deaf-

---

22. A frequent element in prophetic oracles is exaggerated speech. See, e.g., Jer. 5:1:

> Run to and fro through the streets of Jerusalem,
>   look around and take note!
> Search its squares and see
>   if you can find *one person*
> who acts justly
>   and seeks truth. (emphasis mine)

With this statement we are not to believe that Israel was *actually* so corrupt that it lacked one person of upright character.

ness, rebellion, and deceit (5:21, 23; 9:5). They have never experienced the transforming Torah given by God at the sacred mountain. If these people, who are "accustomed to do evil," could recognize the covenant for what it truly was, it would be a new teaching *for them.* For this reason, Jeremiah speaks to them of a "new covenant . . . not like the covenant . . . made with their fathers."[23] Jeremiah declares, says Wallis, that "the basic matters of . . . religion were foreign to him [i.e., Israel], that his experience of these realities would be as revolutionary as a new covenant."[24] The prophet is using irony; he is saying one thing but intending another: *The ancient, Mosaic covenant is depicted under the guise of a "new" covenant.*[25]

Jeremiah adopts the ironic approach because he is addressing people who have hardly a glimmer of what the covenant is about. They have so little understanding of the basic character of the covenant that it is not sufficient to urge them to change a little here and a little there. They lack wholeness at the center; they need a new heart. In no other way can they know God.

Knowing the Lord without Being Taught

Those in the "new covenant" — in reality another name for the Sinai covenant — are the people who are whole at the center. They have repented from the heart; the heart has been washed and circumcised; the Torah (law) has been inscribed on the heart (Ps. 40:8). Such people "know God"; they need not be "taught" (Jer. 31:34). They have internalized the divine teaching from Sinai, and from the heart they know what God requires: "to do justice, and to love kindness, / and to walk humbly with your God" (Mic. 6:8).

Although Micah in the above text is proclaiming a message that is very similar to that of Jeremiah, he does not use the word "know" in his address. This term, however, is employed by Jeremiah; in the following passage he reveals his kinship with Micah and defines what is meant when he speaks of "knowing God." During a critical period of his pro-

23. See Römer, p. 27, who links the "new covenant" in Jer. 31:31-34 with the mention of the "iniquities of their ancestors [i.e., fathers] of old" in Jer. 11:10.
24. Wallis, p. 108.
25. See Zenger, pp. 108ff., who holds that the "new covenant" is essentially what we today call the "old" covenant.

phetic activity, Jeremiah launches a fierce attack on King Jehoiakim because this ruler's love of luxury and kingly glory meant oppression for
others; "injustice" and "unrighteousness" summed up his rule. In the
midst of these accusations, Jeremiah holds up Josiah (Jehoiakim's father) as an example of one who had true knowledge of God:

> Are you a king
>   because you compete in cedar?
> Did not your father eat and drink
>   and do justice and righteousness?
>   Then it was well with him.
> He judged the cause of the poor and needy;
>   then it was well.
> *Is not this to know me?*
>   says the LORD.   (22:15-16, emphasis mine)

In such words Jeremiah is affirming his bond with Micah: "*to
know the LORD*" means: practice justice and kindness. We underscore
what was mentioned above: those who have truly entered into a covenant relationship with God have no need to be taught by others concerning what it means to "know" him. God desires righteousness and
kindness. It is not a complicated affair; one does not need to be a lawyer
to figure that out. Such acts flow naturally from a heart devoted to God.
People who must be instructed in the basics of righteousness and kindness are those who stand outside of a *genuine* covenant relationship
(what Jeremiah is calling a "new" covenant). People who must *learn* the
basics of humaneness are people who have no idea of the character of
the God who has called them into covenant; his will has never taken
hold of them in the heart.

The issue that faced Jeremiah is similar to the one that arose in the
time of Amos (and, no doubt, in every period of history) — namely,
people who embrace religion but not God. Amos speaks of what is *es-
sential* in Israelite faith:

> Seek *me* and live;
>   but do not seek *Bethel*.   (5:4-5, emphasis mine)

Confronting the same kind of audience, Jeremiah uses a variety of
words, phrases, and images to call them to change — to let go of religion and embrace God. He declares that they

— must *repent,*
— *be washed,*
— *be circumcised,* and
— *enter (what will be for them) the new covenant* in which *the law will be written on the heart.*

The Judeans must enter anew — with sincerity — the covenant made with God at Sinai. When they do so, they will be in a new covenant in which they have no need of instruction on how to do the good; it will flow from the heart that knows God.

Summary

The plain sense of Jeremiah's announcement of a new covenant (31:31-34) concerns Israel and Judah. The prophet's message throughout is a call to return to and obey the Sinai covenant. Nowhere outside of the above text does Jeremiah speak with clarity and definiteness about another, different "new covenant." The major aspects of this new covenant are in fact characteristics of the covenant given at Sinai: both have to do with Israel, Torah, knowing the LORD, and forgiveness. It appears that the Sinai covenant is being presented to the Israelites as a new covenant. In this case, the discussion is not about a brand-new covenant that will be instituted at some time in the far future, but it concerns the "re*new*al" of commitment to the ancient covenant made through Moses at the sacred mountain. Jeremiah is calling for a deep-down change. Sometimes he speaks of this change in terms of repentance, of being washed and circumcised; in Jeremiah 31:31-34 he speaks of it in terms of a new or renewed covenant.

There are aspects in the description of the "new covenant" that lead some interpreters to believe that God will do what he never before has done: he will, by a sovereign act, implant his teaching in the heart of human beings so that they will do naturally what is right. However, when one compares this passage with other texts in Jeremiah and elsewhere, it becomes evident that this "God alone" language is not to be literalized. Here, as elsewhere in the Old Testament, the free willed response of people is respected and needed.

A further issue has to do with the prophet's declaration that this "new covenant" is "not like the covenant" that God made with Israel's

94

ancestors. This statement appears to suggest that the new covenant is a new and different kind of covenant. We believe, however, that these words should not be interpreted in a literalistic fashion but in terms of satirical irony. According to irony, one says one thing but means another. Jeremiah is speaking about the Sinai covenant, but he introduces it as a "new covenant" because the people he is addressing are so out of touch with the divine teaching (law) that *for them* this covenant would be a "new covenant."

We conclude, then, that despite the language used which appears to speak of a completely new covenant, this text contains one more call of Jeremiah to renew commitment to the Sinai covenant.

So far we have been speaking of the plain meaning of Jeremiah 31:31-34. Later communities, however, were drawn to this colorful prophecy, including that of Qumran as well as the early Christian movement. In chapter 3 we observed that New Testament authors used "depth" interpretation of Old Testament texts in order to provide a scriptural witness to Jesus (e.g., Hos. 11:1). Appropriated in a similar manner was the announcement of a "new covenant" in Jeremiah 31:31-34. In the next chapter we will discuss the relationship of this Jeremiah prophecy to Jesus.

CHAPTER 6

Jesus and the "New Covenant" in Jeremiah 31:31-34

ORIGINAL MEANING AND DEPTH INTERPRETATION IN TENSION

Synopsis

Jeremiah's announcement of a new covenant finds full meaning in Jesus. This is the conclusion of the New Testament authors as they probed the "depth" of this text in the light of their experience with him. Early Christians turned frequently to the Old Testament scripture in an attempt to understand more fully the significance of their meeting with Jesus (see our discussion in chaps. 2, 3, and 9). Jeremiah 31:31-34 is one more text that drew Christian attention and provided further insight into Jesus' identity: he is God's new covenant for humankind. What this conviction means for understanding the Old Testament and the relationship of Christians to Jews will focus our discussion on the pages that follow.

Hearing the Voices of Both Old and New Testaments

Our discussion of Jesus as the fulfillment of this ancient text will take the form of a dialogue with Norbert Lohfink, whose many writings on the Old Testament have earned him great respect in his home country of Germany as well as here in the United States.[1] We do so for several reasons: (1) We find his general approach attractive because he desires to hold to the plain meaning and significance of Jeremiah 31:31-34 while affirming its fulfillment in Jesus. (2) His views regarding Jesus and the new covenant prophecy have found a positive response among many clergy and scholars. (3) Our discussion with him will demonstrate the tensions that exist between "depth" interpretation and the original sense of the Old Testament text.

This interaction will not result in assured solutions, but it may help us find ways of speaking so that we do not say too much or too little about Jesus and the new covenant. Although at various points we take issue with him, Norbert Lohfink is one who exemplifies the subtitle of our volume: *Embracing Change — Maintaining Christian Identity.*

The New Covenant: Fulfilled in Israel and in Jesus

Jeremiah's announcement of a "new covenant" is to be seen in the context of Israel in the seventh and sixth centuries B.C.E. This covenant, whose fulfillment has to do with the "house of Israel and Judah," is not completely new. Its content is that of the covenant made at Sinai through Moses.[2]

Lohfink holds that the new covenant spoken of by Jeremiah "was very soon fulfilled in its primary sense in the return from the exile."[3] However, he says, as time went on Jeremiah 31:31-34 took on a "depth dimension." The "primary" or plain meaning began to fade away as people of a later time interpreted this passage in the light of their own day. Both the Jews at Qumran and in the early Christian movement interpreted this prophetic text at its "depth,"[4] and in so doing were able to relate the text to their communities. Regarding the later history of this famous Jeremian passage, Lohfink says: "Like most prophetic oracles of this type, it takes on a perspective and envisages an eschatological sort of fulfillment. This depth dimension of many prophetic procla-

1. We are concentrating on Norbert Lohfink's recent volume: *The Covenant Never Revoked: Biblical Reflections on Christian-Jewish Dialogue*, trans. J. J. Scullion (New York: Paulist, 1991).
2. See Lohfink, pp. 45-47, as well as our discussion in the preceding chapter.
3. Lohfink, p. 53.
4. See our discussion of "depth" interpretation in chapters 2 and 3.

mations only found its way into consciousness in the centuries that followed."[5] Jeremiah 31:31-34 is an alive text which took on a new dimension when viewed through the eyes of those following Jesus Christ. At its "depth," Christians held that this new covenant announcement had its complete fulfillment in Jesus.

Together with others, Lohfink finds Jeremiah 31:31-34 to be a difficult text. He is aware of elements in the text that appear to set the new covenant over against the one made at Sinai (e.g., "not like" the covenant with the ancestors). He refuses, however, to literalize these statements. He notes "the rhetorical counterpoint" present in the oracle but declares that this is not intended to characterize the Sinai covenant as "completely different" or "utterly outmoded." Rather, he holds that the new covenant is "the fuller and more lasting actualization of what was given of old."[6]

But the basic content of this new covenant is the same as that of the Sinai covenant; both center, for example, on Torah.[7] But if the content of this new covenant is essentially that of Sinai, what gives it a "more lasting actualization"? What is new about the new covenant? The *newness has nothing to do with the content* of the covenant; it has to do, Lohfink says, with *how* it is given. He believes that the new covenant is a unique creative act of God. When the text declares that God will write the Torah (law) on the heart, Lohfink believes this means that God will do something completely different from what he did in the past at Sinai: At some time in the future, God will set his law within the heart in such a way that it cannot be disobeyed. At the thinking, willing center of one's life, declares Lohfink, there will be a natural inclination to say "yes" to God's teaching: "The earlier 'covenant' was in fact broken. Hence, it must have been given to Israel in such a way that it could be broken. The 'new covenant' will be given in a new way; it will be something within, with a torah written on the heart, it not being necessary to teach it from without."[8]

5. Lohfink, p. 53.
6. Lohfink, p. 48. On the same page, he says, using the imagery of Paul, "the new covenant is but the earlier one, now brilliant and radiant."
7. Lohfink, pp. 45-47.
8. Lohfink, p. 47. As he approaches Jer. 31:31-34, Lohfink, on the one hand (p. 48), refuses to literalize the "rhetorical counterpoint" of the text (i.e., the "not like" comparison of the covenants), but on the other hand he subjects the "God alone" aspect of this text (i.e., God writing the law on the heart) to a near literalism. We have discussed this view in the previous chapter and do not believe that the text

Assuming that Jeremiah's teaching of the law written on the heart has reference to a heart created free of sin, he asks if in all of human history there existed such a heart. There was *one* such heart, he affirms, namely, the heart of Jesus of Nazareth — whose heart was "entirely one with torah." In his heart "we see a fulfillment of the promise of the 'new covenant' which surpasses all that preceded it, *the* fulfillment of itself." Those who "bind themselves to this heart in faith," declares Lohfink, "even when they themselves fail continually and must obtain pardon again, share in the strength of its fidelity to the torah."9

At this point we take issue with Lohfink. If Jesus is the only person whose heart is completely given over to Torah, what significance does this have? Did Jeremiah have one person in mind as the fulfillment of his announcement of a new covenant? Can one person be a new covenant community? May the Christian community, which "fails continually" and is ever in need of pardon, declare: we are frail and given to evil, but we have Jesus and *he* has a heart completely loyal to the divine teaching? Such declarations sound very similar to what Jews were supposed to have said, that is: "We have Abraham as our ancestor" — a claim that appeared empty and invalid to the Gospel writer (Matt. 3:9). Lohfink's view in its stated form is difficult to accept, because the fulfillment of the "new covenant" is limited to one person, Jesus.10

---

is calling for such a literalistic interpretation, even though this view is widespread among biblical scholars. Although we disagree with this understanding of the text, we wish to pursue Lohfink's discussion because of his important comments concerning the significance of Jesus for Christians and Jews.

9. For the various citations above, see Lohfink, p. 54. Further, p. 57: "The 'new covenant' was only fulfilled in its definitive, eschatological fullness in Jesus of Nazareth."

10. Hans-Jürgen Hermisson approaches the matter in the following manner ("Jeremiah 31,31-34," *Göttinger Predigtmeditationen* 83, no. 5 [1994]: 137-43): he holds also that the Jeremiah text "speaks of an eschatological act of God which the Christian community knows has already happened in Jesus Christ. This event, however, has historical implications: it calls for belief and it creates a new community which *already now* lives from this act of God" (p. 241). But Hermisson declares that if we measure fulfillment in terms of Christian behavior, then this text has not found fulfillment. For Christians as well as for Jeremiah, the fulfillment lies still in the future. He thinks Jeremiah's oracle is in the process of fulfillment. When the complete fulfillment comes, then forgiveness will no longer be necessary because everyone will naturally carry out the divine teaching (pp. 238-42). However, for the time being, because of our sins, we need forgiveness.

The community of Jesus continues to share the same proneness to evil that characterized the Israelite community.[11] It is this solidarity in sin, shared by both communities, that enables Christian ministers to preach sermons based on both the severe and the comforting passages from the Prophets. True, the world has been blessed when the heart of Christ has been extended into the hearts of Christians; but, at the same time, it is clearly the case that the world has received blessing from Jews whose hearts and lives have reflected the tenderness of Torah.

The New Covenant in Jesus Does Not Exclude Jews

In spite of the above declarations that the heart of Jesus is the only heart at one with the law, Lohfink speaks appreciatively of Israelite and Jewish faith that arises from the heart. To declare that Jesus is the only one who had the Torah written fully on the heart does not mean, says Lohfink, that Jewish faith, representing "partial fulfillment," consisted only of outward acts. He comments:

> We should never do them [i.e., Jews] the injustice of thinking that the partial fulfillment in their favor was merely material and external, that it never touched their heart. That would be to deny the scope of the Jeremian oracle of the "new covenant" and would above all do scant justice to Ps 51, the "Miserere."[12]

But if what Lohfink says is true — and few would deny it — why are Psalm 51 and expressions of faith of this character ignored in the New Testament? This is especially remarkable when one notices that the above psalm has a prominent place in later Christian liturgies.

The absence of reference to Psalm 51 in the New Testament points up the manner in which the New Testament uses the Old Testament. The former scripture cites many passages and relates them to Jesus, but fails to underscore texts that speak of this scripture's emphasis on heart religion, forgiveness, or the law as a gift of life. When Paul, a Jew, speaks about

---

11. Hermisson, p. 241, emphasizes strongly the long period of evil in Israel (see, however, our discussion in chap. 1), but he also acknowledges the continuing sinfulness within the church that has caused immeasurable hurt. Regarding the latter, see also Lohfink, p. 80.

12. Lohfink, pp. 54-55.

Christ, the law, and forgiveness, for example, one could expect that he would refer to such positive passages as Psalms 19, 51, 103, and 119. But he does not. Why? Speaking of Psalm 51 (and the returned exiles), Lohfink attempts a response. He indicates that this psalm and the return of the exiles stand at the beginning of the fulfillment of the new covenant prophecy which found its culmination in Jesus. Psalm 51, therefore, represents a "partial fulfillment."[13] For that reason neither Psalm 51 nor the return of the exiles is "touched" by Paul because "Paul, captivated entirely by the Christ event, does not at all have it in view."[14] Paul is not a neutral observer. He has experienced newness in Christ, and this experience is ever before his eyes. In emphasizing this newness he fails to mention those aspects of Jewish tradition that are similar to Christian proclamation. Christian "depth" interpretation has set aside the "plain" meaning and significance of Old Testament texts. But Lohfink knows that in order to have good balance in approaching the Old Testament, one must do what the New Testament itself does not do: one must recognize the newness experienced by those who followed the God of Sinai. He declares: "It must be acknowledged that this fulfillment [in Jesus] did not have its beginning in Jesus. Jer 31 speaks of something that penetrates to the very depth of the heart, granted to a Jewish people which does not yet look into the countenance of its promised messiah."[15] Here, as elsewhere, Lohfink agrees that the "new covenant" is not completely "new"; it has its roots in Israelite faith. Further, as noted above, he believes that the fulfillment of the Jeremiah 31 oracle had its *primary* fulfillment in the return of the exiles and affirms that the God of grace and forgiveness is present among Israelites and Jews. This God is not restricted to the church community.

Finding the Right Words Leads to Paradox

In his attempt to articulate the relationship existing between Jews and Christians, Lohfink attempts to see the whole of the biblical tradition. In doing so he wishes to affirm the Christian witness ("depth" interpre-

13. Lohfink, pp. 54-55.
14. Lohfink, p. 74. See also Michael Wyschogrod, "The Impact of Dialogue with Christianity on My Self-Understanding as a Jew," in *Die Hebräische Bibel und ihre zweifache Nachgeschichte*, ed. E. Blum et al. (Neukirchen: Neukirchener Verlag, 1990), p. 731.
15. Lohfink, p. 57. For similar expressions, see pp. 54 and 57. Cf. p. 76.

tation) while honoring still the "plain" meaning of Israelite texts. One senses that, faced with this task, Lohfink feels the constraints of language. He is attempting to find language that preserves the core of the Christian tradition while acknowledging that this new covenant is basically the same as the "old" covenant.[16] While rejoicing in Jesus as the fulfillment of the new covenant, he does not wish to claim that God's "newness" is found exclusively within the church.

This conflict of thought leads Lohfink to make paradoxical statements that leave the reader questioning the distinctive differences between Jews who experienced the new covenant before Christ (e.g., Ps. 51), Jews living today, and Christians who have experienced it in Jesus. True, Lohfink has made it clear that the new covenant "was only fulfilled in its definitive eschatological fullness in Jesus of Nazareth," but he cannot bring himself to exclude — at least fully — Jews from an authentic relationship with God. Therefore he can affirm that Jeremiah 31 was fulfilled "positively and in a true sense" in Jewish history. This oracle, he says, "speaks of something that penetrates to the very depths of the heart granted to the Jewish people" who do not accept Jesus as the Messiah.[17] Further, on the basis of "reality" rather than on the ground of "biblical linguistic imagery," Lohfink concludes that "the Jews, who do not accept the message of Jesus, are nevertheless always and for all time 'the people of the old covenant which God has never revoked.'"[18] Although he declares that Jews who do not "believe in Jesus . . . are *not* in the 'new covenant'," he can also affirm that they are "loved by God because of the patriarchs." Further, he insists that the exiles and their descendants "are not to be regarded just as a group that has become blind. God is likewise *effecting in them his 'new covenant'* promised by Jeremiah." Finally, Lohfink urges Christians to recognize "the jewishness in Christianity . . . because perhaps today Jews are in many ways more aware of the 'covenant' than Christians. In their own way they stand within it just as do Christians."

The above paradoxical statements regarding Jeremiah 31:31-34 and the theme of the "new covenant" underscore the difficulty of the discussion. It is clear that Jews and Christians are members of different communities. This difference is, on the one hand, plain to the eye:

16. Lohfink, pp. 47-48, 77, 83-84.
17. Lohfink, pp. 54 and 57. See also similar statements on pp. 54, 56-57.
18. For this citation and those immediately following, see Lohfink, pp. 72, 73-74, 79, and 80.

Christians "believe" in Jesus and Jews do not. But, on the other hand, when it comes to drawing the distinction between Jews and Christians on the basis of the "new covenant" oracle recorded in Jeremiah 31:31-34, the *clear and obvious* difference is not easily arrived at. Jews and Christians are different, but they share, generally, the Hebrew Bible/Old Testament and, except for Jesus, hold similar views concerning the human-divine relationship and hopes for our world.

Lohfink is not the first to have difficulty in describing the relationship of Jews and Christians to each other and to God. In chapter 4 we observed that Paul has this very same difficulty in Romans 9–11. If the relationship between Jews and Christians regarding the "new covenant" were uncomplicated, neither Paul nor Lohfink would offer up these paradoxical statements. Regarding the complexity of relationship between Jews and Christians, Lohfink makes some comments concerning Paul's words in Romans 9–11. He declares that Paul wrote these chapters "out of an impossible situation under which he suffered severely."[19] But Paul's situation would not have been an "impossible" one if the division between Jews and Christians had been clear and definite — one side absolutely right and the other side completely wrong. But such was not and is not the case.

Discovering Jesus in the Depth of Jeremiah 31:31-34

Lohfink's insistence that only Jesus fulfills the oracle in Jeremiah 31:31-34 does not rest on the plain sense of the text in Jeremiah.[20] He does not believe that Jeremiah 31:31-34 points *directly* to Jesus. Jesus is found in the "depth dimension" of this ancient oracle. It is well known, as Lohfink observes, that the people at Qumran (the Dead Sea Scroll community) thought of themselves as the fulfillment of this oracle concerning the new covenant.[21] In doing so, however, they did not take over the plain sense of the biblical text, but "looked deep inside" the text to discover a "depth dimension" that enabled them to relate this biblical text to their community. As the Qumran community read Jeremiah's oracle at its "depth," so also, even if in a different manner, did early Christianity.

19. Lohfink, p. 77.
20. Lohfink, pp. 53, 74.
21. Lohfink, p. 7.

It is no surprise that early Christians were drawn to Jeremiah 31:31-34. For Christians who had experienced newness of life in Jesus Christ, this prophecy of a new covenant took on a fuller meaning. The oracle provided the words and imagery which helped them express what Jesus meant to them. Naturally, other words and images, taken out of the general experiences of life, were employed also by the New Testament writers, for example: Christ is light for our darkness, life for our death, water for our thirst, bread for our hunger, a shepherd for our vulnerability and lostness.[22] Other images are known to us also: Jesus is the suffering servant, the second Adam, the second Moses, the Messiah, et al.[23] To these images then we may add that of the "new covenant." All of these images from the Old Testament helped early Christians articulate their experience of Christ while at the same time establishing continuity between the Christian witness and the Old Testament scripture.

The above manner of interpretation by the New Testament authors does not reflect the plain sense of the Old Testament texts. Rather, as in the case of the New Testament's use of Hosea 11:1, Jeremiah 31:15, Psalm 41:9 — and Jeremiah 31:31-34 — we are dealing with a *re*interpretation of these ancient texts. Elsewhere we have characterized this reinterpretation as a "creative" or "depth" interpretation. The New Testament authors were attempting to understand and bring to expression the meaning of Jesus' presence among them. The mystery was not the Old Testament; it was Jesus. They "knew" the blessing of God's presence in him but required the words and images of scripture to bring this knowing to expression.

The New Testament was written to nourish faith, not to transmit the plain meaning of the scripture. In the closing chapter of the Gospel of John, the writer makes clear this faith-focus: "But these [words] are written so that you may come to believe that Jesus is the Messiah, the Son of God, and that through believing you may have life in his name" (20:31).

---

22. See 1 Pet. 2:9; John 8:12; 12:46 (light); John 10:10; 14:6 (life); John 4:14; 7:37-38 (water); John 6:35, 48 (bread); John 10:11; Matt. 9:36 (shepherd).
23. See further our discussion in chapter 9.

CHAPTER 7

The New Testament Proclamation of Jesus

WHAT DOES THE OLD TESTAMENT CONTRIBUTE?

Synopsis

The Old Testament is an equal dialogue partner with the New. In this dialogue one can: (1) hear agreement on some basic issues; (2) notice that the New Testament carries forward and develops some Old Testament themes; (3) recognize that the Old Testament contains themes that are lacking or undeveloped in the New Testament; (4) realize that the New Testament's newness needs the Old Testament to prevent this newness from becoming irresponsible and unreal.

The Old Testament: The Scripture of Early Christians

The only Bible that first-century Christians used was the Jewish scripture, called by the later church the Old Testament. When Christian writings began to assume the status of scripture, the Old Testament continued to be considered a part of the church's canon. But for many Christians, the Old Testament has been viewed as a second-level scripture, heavily marked by age. Expressions such as "the Old Testament God," "Old Testament religion," and "the Old Testament law" serve to underscore the aged and limited character of this scripture.

There are, of course, selected Old Testament passages that have found a home in the church. For example, the Ten Commandments have been valued as a statement of basic human ethics to which Christians should hold fast. Further, certain psalms have found a special place in Christian private and public worship because it is thought that they "anticipate" Christian piety and "breathe the air" of the New Testament. In the main, however, it has been believed that the Old Testament was superseded by the New Testament. The older scripture's special importance, so it was held, existed in its role as a witness that pointed to the New Testament and legitimized the proclamation concerning Jesus. New Testament texts have always dominated in Christian preaching, and that tradition stands intact today.

Discovering the Real Old Testament

Change is taking place. In general, contemporary seminary education presents a very appreciative understanding of the Old Testament. Even though the traditional, negative view of the older scripture continues to find strong representation within the church,[1] the many books and articles written today provide evidence of an emerging new attitude toward it.

At the center of this rediscovery of the Old Testament is the recognition that one cannot simply dismiss it as a second-rank scripture, superseded by the New Testament. It is increasingly being understood that the Old Testament, as expressed by Werner Schmidt, is a scripture that stands alongside of and with the New Testament.[2] Both are the scriptures of the Christian church; *the one without the other cannot be the*

1. Although few today would ask the question that a woman directed to me: "Why do you want to teach about this bloody book?" still there is hesitation within the church in accepting the Old Testament as an equal to the New Testament. Sometimes those who view the Old Testament negatively forget that some passages in the New Testament also appear to be less than compassionate (e.g., Matt. 23; Acts 5:1-11; Matt. 5:22; Gal. 5:12; Rev. 20:8). Although explanations are offered, uneasiness with these and other passages is shown by the fact that they seldom surface in the teaching and preaching of the church. See similar observations by Alden Thompson, *Who's Afraid of the Old Testament God?* (Grand Rapids: Zondervan, 1989), p. 14.

2. See, e.g., Werner Schmidt, "Das Problem des Alten Testaments in der christlichen Theologie," in *Meilenstein: Festgabe für Herbert Donner,* ed. Manfred Görg (Wiesbaden: Harrassowitz, 1995), pp. 248-51.

106

scripture. The church must "listen in" on the conversations taking place between the two scriptures in order to live fully the life of faith. Brevard Childs has demonstrated how texts from both scriptures can assist Christians in approaching present-day issues. In order to understand and give guidance in the area of sexual relationships, Childs suggests that one needs to listen to the dialogue that takes place between Proverbs 7, the Song of Songs, and the writings of Paul. In the following comments he addresses the joint witness of the Song of Songs and Proverbs: "The witness of the Song of Songs ['sex as a joyous possession of the wise'] corrects and opposes the tendency within Proverbs to view the positive value of sex chiefly in its function as an antidote to sexual incontinence. Rather, human love is recognized and acclaimed for itself." But Childs declares also that it is important to read Song of Songs in the light of Proverbs 7, because the Proverbs passage points us to "God's order" which "provides the framework for all human activity. . . . Proverbs places human love within the established order of the world, and relativizes its function by confining its scope in the context of the family and familial responsibilities."[3] Against the background of the important, but different, emphases of Song of Songs and Proverbs, Childs declares: "The Pauline discussion of the role of sex and marriage is a good illustration of the need of the theologian to understand the New Testament in the light of the Old."[4] Proverbs and the Song of Songs provide a balance to Paul's teaching on this theme, a balance that is fully missing in the New Testament itself.

A Gift and a Plus

Herbert Haag speaks of the "plus" that the Old Testament contributes to the New Testament.[5] He observes that the New Testament does not fulfill the whole Old Testament. Many important texts and whole books

---

3. Brevard S. Childs, *Biblical Theology in Crisis* (Philadelphia: Westminster, 1970), p. 194.

4. Childs, p. 199. See also his discussion of the dialogue existing between Psalm 8 and the New Testament (esp. Heb. 2:5-9), as well as the one between Exod. 2:11-22 and Acts 7:23-29, 35 (also Heb. 11:23-28), on pp. 151-83.

5. Herbert Haag, "Das Plus des Alten Testaments," in his *Das Buch des Bundes* (Düsseldorf, 1980), pp. 304f. See also E. S. Gerstenberger, *Warum und Wie Predigen Wir Das Alte Testament* (Giessen, 1989), pp. 38-40.

in the Old Testament do not find representation in the New Testament — texts that we would miss if there were no Old Testament. In addition to Proverbs and the Song of Songs mentioned above, the books of Job, Ecclesiastes, and the psalms of lament lift up the problems of suffering and the varied contradictions of life. In the laments from the Psalms one finds complaints addressed to God which are characterized by a sharp questioning of God's righteousness, love, and power. In the end there is usually an affirmation of faith, but it is a "nevertheless" affirmation voiced by one who still feels the hurt. Often this honest response encourages faith in the reader because it is recognized that in the psalmists one meets people who have experienced real life. They hold to faith without denying the presence of those experiences in life that argue against trust in God.

These Old Testament books guard the Christian community from becoming unreal in its response to life's afflictions. Being a person of faith, in the light of these writings, does not mean denying the "natural" responses of complaint, impatience, accusation, and questioning that come when misfortune arrives. These thoughts are not to be pressed down and hidden within; rather they are to be presented before God. The church with its emphasis on hymns of praise, says Walter Brueggemann, "has missed the action of healing at the margin by neglecting laments."[6] The Christian congregation needs to be a place where the lament, as well as the hymn, is viewed as a part of Christian worship and faith. The lament is an expression that offers the Christian congregation opportunity to bring "real" life and faith together; it has the capacity to open the ear to the human cry outside the walls of the church. Again, Brueggemann: "The shift from an accent of hymns to a practice of laments posits that liturgic activity can aid in the breakup of both the monopoly of heaven which diminishes the earth, and the monopoly of monarchy and temple which diminishes those who are at the social margin."[7] Elsewhere he observes that "Christian interpretation . . . has a deep propensity . . . to arrive as quickly as possible at affirmation." To this affirmative witness, says

6. Walter Brueggemann, "Monopoly and Marginality in Imagination," in *Interpretation and Obedience* (Minneapolis: Fortress, 1991), p. 194. See further (p. 194): "This neglect has not only denied important resources, but by practicing and encouraging a monopoly of imagination through hymns, we have served the interests of the status quo and have been advocates of a *theology of glory.*"

7. Brueggemann, *Interpretation and Obedience*, p. 194.

108

Brueggemann, there is in the Old Testament a counterwitness — to the Yes there is also the No.[8] The New Testament contains little that reflects themes found in the book of Job[9] or the psalms of lament,[10] which voice questions and complaints (as well as praise) to the Almighty. When life gets hard, people of faith turn often to these texts whose realism speaks words of encouragement. The assertiveness of the psalmists and Job in maintaining their right before God speaks a needed message to the reader, who then understands that one can be a person of faith and still, in certain matters, hold one's own with God.[11]

Job and the psalmists are fully aware of the sinful character of humankind, but this recognition does not lead them to believe that when life goes wrong it is ever the fault of the person involved. One has a right to hold true to one's integrity.[12] This is a side of faith and worship that the church frequently overlooks because of its focus on the New Testament, which underscores heavily patience, willing endurance, and joy in response to such contraries. Only seldom within the Christian

8. Walter Brueggemann, "Biblical Theology Appropriately Postmodern," *Biblical Theology Bulletin* 27 (1997): 7.

9. One may think of the passion narratives in the Gospels as resembling the trials of Job. There is, however, a difference. Jesus, according to the Christian tradition, is conceived of as the divine-human One suffering for the sins of the world, whereas Job is merely a human being facing painful trials that are a part of human life. Everyday people can identify with Job; they draw courage from his strength of faith, which did not yield to passivity. He did not give in to the friends and refused to give up on God.

10. See the excellent discussion of lament and its relationship to the Christian community in Claus Westermann, "The Role of the Lament in the Theology of the Old Testament," in *Praise and Lament in the Psalms* (Atlanta: John Knox, 1981), pp. 259-80 (esp. pp. 274-75). Although in the later Christian tradition one may find a few examples of lament, generally speaking the Christian community has not been drawn to this expression of faith. See also Brueggemann, *Interpretation and Obedience*, pp. 190-204 (with references).

11. See Fredrick C. Holmgren, "Holding Your Own against God: Genesis 32:22-32," *Interpretation* 44 (1990): 5-17.

12. The book of Job and some of the Psalms (e.g., Pss. 17 and 26) hold to their integrity over against a widely held view in Israel which affirmed that suffering and misfortune resulted from some form of personal sin. At times, Paul's heavy emphasis on the sinfulness of human beings has inclined Christians to believe that there is some necessary connection between suffering and sin. The above books, as well as Ecclesiastes, which speaks of the mysterious contraries of life, continue to bring good balance to those engaging the issue of suffering.

tradition do we find persons who risk the spiritual courage of the psalmist by proclaiming in the face of misfortune:

> I have walked in my integrity,
>> and I have trusted in the LORD without wavering. . . .
>> and I walk in faithfulness to you.   (Ps. 26:1-3)

One can admit sinfulness and yet declare: *In this matter* I have been a person of faith and have acted responsibly. This manner of relating to God has its dangers; it can easily cross the border to pride and pretense.[13] However, to declare regarding every case of misfortune and suffering that "I am a sinner deserving of all that I have received" is to demean the God-human partnership which assumes that people have worth.[14]

God and Everyday Life

Further, in the Old Testament, God is portrayed as one who takes part in everyday matters. Although this aspect is not absent in the New Testament, the older scripture emphasizes it more strongly. The New Testament, with its focus on Jesus Christ, holds before us the ideal of his life and calls us to rejoice in him. The Old Testament sets before us also a model life (e.g., Exod. 20–23; Ps. 1; and the Prophets) and invites worshipers to sing praise to God. But this latter scripture, more than the New Testament, is in touch with daily life experiences. In the Old Testament one finds not only a spiritual joy in God but also joy in the family, in good fortune, and in good relationships.[15] The Old Testament finds us where we are. We are found, for example, in the narratives of Genesis, Exodus, and Ruth as we read of people relating to each other wisely and foolishly,

13. Paul's strong statements about the character of his own life may be seen as similar to those found in the Psalms: "I have fought the good fight, I have finished the race, I have kept the faith" (2 Tim. 4:7).

14. See Holmgren, "The Pharisee and the Tax Collector: Luke 18:9-14 and Deuteronomy 26:1-15," *Interpretation* 48 (1994): 258-60.

15. See, e.g., Erich Zenger, *Das Erste Testament: Die jüdische Bibel und die Christen* (Düsseldorf: Patmos, 1991), p. 119. Concerning our general discussion in these pages, see also Marvin Wilson's chapter, "Where the Church Went Wrong," in *Our Father Abraham* (Grand Rapids: Wm. B. Eerdmans Publishing Co., 1989), pp. 166-92, and the fine article of Patrick Miller, "The Old Testament and Christian Faith," *Currents in Theology and Mission* 20 (1993): 245-47.

with generosity and hardness of heart. From the pages of this scripture emerge those who are noble and good as well as those who are beyond despair and full of self-doubt, or who are destroying themselves with self-deception. Without ever declaring to the reader "do this" or "don't do that," the narrative engages us and we realize that we are these people.

Often the people with whom we recognize kinship in the Old Testament are those who have made evil or foolish decisions, suffered loss, experienced oppression or undeserved affliction. But this scripture provides images also of persons who have enriched their own day with generosity, expressions of friendship, integrity, and acts of justice and mercy.[16] The story of Boaz in the book of Ruth, for example, makes us aware that people of power do not always take advantage of those who are vulnerable. Although the Old Testament knows that people can commit great evil, it also witnesses of those who extend themselves in doing the good. These narratives help bring some balance to the Christian view of the world. They are reminders that living among us are people who are kind and just. Though people are prone to sinful acts, human society would fall apart were there not those who had a heart for others. The Old Testament more than the New Testament helps us bring into balance the sinfulness and goodness of everyday people. The church's emphasis on the sinfulness of humankind needs the common-sense portrayal of people found in the Old Testament.

Herbert Haag may exaggerate when he says that the New Testament is the "book about Christ" whereas the Old Testament is the "book about God and people," yet his assertion carries substantial truth.[17] In the Old Testament, God is involved with people in a more practical, everyday way than in the New Testament. C. H. Knights's choice words regarding the Old Testament's engagement with everyday life give expression to this "plus" of the Old Testament:

> Now all that for me at any rate, is a great comfort, for it makes it abundantly clear that God is concerned with every single aspect of our human condition, not just with the religious bits of it. It makes clear that my faith is about my whole life and not just about what I do

16. See, e.g., the "human" stories told about Abraham and Lot (Gen. 13); Tamar, the Canaanite (Gen. 38); Joseph and Potiphar's wife (Gen. 39); Joseph, his brothers, and his father (Gen. 42–47); Jacob's friendly visit with the pharaoh (Gen. 47:7-10); Moses and his father-in-law, Jethro (Exod. 18).

17. Haag, pp. 304-5.

in Church or on my knees. And it makes it clear that God wants me to be honest with him about how I feel, even if that means questioning whether he exists at all. . . .[18]

Such comments are not intended to devalue the New Testament but only to underscore how much this scripture needs the Old Testament in order to present a balanced view of people in relationship to God and the world.

God Loves This World

The Old Testament's strong dual emphasis on God's concern for this world and our responsibility in it (see Exodus and the Prophets) is an additional "plus" for the Christian community. It stands as an important check on the church's faith, which is continually tempted to devalue the significance of this world and to focus on personal, spiritual salvation and life after death. The Old Testament reminds the church that, in order to be a people of God, it must be a saving, healing community to flesh-and-blood persons.[19]

No doubt it was inattention to the Old Testament in some wings of the Christian community that contributed to a late response in engaging the social issues of our day. It is exactly this emphasis on social issues, however, that is the number one priority for many Christian communities in the newly emerging nations.[20] The God witnessed to in this part of the Christian canon understands well the cries arising from

---

18. C. H. Knights, "Why Bother with the Old Testament," *Expository Times* (1991): 46. See further Walter Brueggemann's chapter "Christians in 'Jewish Territory,'" in *Praying the Psalms* (Winona, Minn.: Saint Mary's Press, 1982), pp. 58-62. In his comments on the Psalms, he calls attention to the gifts which Israel's scripture offers Christians.

19. Martin Stöhr reminds us that the Holocaust (Shoah) underscores the terrible results brought about by a Christian otherworldliness. See his article, "Learning Step by Step in the Jewish-Christian Dialogue," in *The New Testament and Christian-Jewish Dialogue,* ed. M. Lowe (Jerusalem: Ecumenical Theological Research Fraternity, 1990), pp. 274-76.

20. Hans Ucko, in *People of God, Peoples of God: A Jewish-Christian Conversation in Asia,* ed. Hans Ucko (Geneva: WCC Publications, 1996), p. xx, notes that "Asian, African and Latin American theologians are criticizing traditional theology for being too individualistic." A number of the essays contained in this volume emphasize the importance of human issues for people of faith.

the oppressed (see Exod. 2:24-25). It is the Old Testament's portrayal of the one God as the creator and lover of *this world* that brings restraint to an unhealthy spiritualizing of the ministry of Jesus.[21]

Torah and the Kingdom of God

Norbert Lohfink's comments concerning the kingdom of God carry on further the above remarks regarding the Old Testament's witness of God's concern for this world. He argues that the New Testament assumes many of the basic teachings of the Old Testament regarding this theme. "If one inquires," he says, "concerning the world, this life, matter and society, then the Old and New Testaments possess a rather common perspective."[22] He observes, for example, that Jesus announces the soon-to-arrive kingdom of God (better: the rule of God), but nowhere does he speak in detail about the inner structure, character, or basic concerns of this rule. Never, says Lohfink, does he indicate anything about the "what" of the rule of God. Why not? Because, Lohfink asserts, the Old Testament provided that kind of information. The rule of God, proclaimed by the New Testament, can be nothing other than a society that accepts the vision of God who delivered Hebrew slaves from Egypt to form a countersociety. God's rule is a society whose inner structure and dynamic is the Torah given at Sinai.[23]

This awareness of the Torah context of the rule of God faded as conflict between the followers of Jesus and other Jews sharpened and as

21. The North Park Covenant Church in Chicago has recently erected a sign on its property that underscores this emphasis in the Old Testament. The sign is so constructed that it may be seen only by worshipers as they leave the church. It cites the following passage from Mic. 6:8: "Do justice, love kindness and walk humbly with your God." It is a continuing reminder to the Christian congregation that the God they know through Jesus Christ is the God of Moses and the prophets who calls people of faith to love and care for this world and those who live in it.

22. Norbert Lohfink, *Das Jüdische am Christentum: Die verlorene Dimension* (Freiburg: Herder, 1989), p. 51.

23. See Lohfink, *Das Jüdische am Christentum*, pp. 116, 67-69. See also Lohfink's volume, *The Covenant Never Revoked: Biblical Reflections on Christian-Jewish Dialogue*, trans. J. J. Scullion (New York: Paulist, 1991), pp. 46 and 83, where he declares that the new covenant fulfilled in Jesus is basically the same covenant as the one given at Sinai; both are shaped by Torah.

the Christian community became increasingly a Gentile movement. With this development, declares Lohfink, the societal, this-world context of the rule of God gave way to a religious and spiritual emphasis which concentrated on individual salvation, the soul, and the future life. The church moved away from its early bond with Old Testament/Jewish traditions. But in our day we are witnessing a return home; the church is becoming aware that in separating itself from Torah (law), it is cutting itself off from both the Israelite/Jewish traditions *and* the early Jesus movement.

Grace and Torah

The church's new appreciation of Torah has resulted from several developments: (1) There is a new understanding of the meaning of the Hebrew term "Torah," which has been translated traditionally as "law." A better translation is "teaching" or "instruction." It is so understood in the Jewish tradition. It may be observed, for example, that Jews refer to the Pentateuch as Torah. Included in this designation is the book of Genesis, whose narratives contain little that one could properly call "law." Rather, these texts have been preserved for the inspiration and nourishment of the Israelite community. But even the "law" sections of the Pentateuch (e.g., Exod. 19–23) are not law in our sense of the word; they are teachings intended to help people live a satisfying life in relationship to others. Many of these so-called laws, by the way, appear in Proverbs as wise teachings. A further development that has brought about a new understanding of Torah is (2) a rediscovery of the important contribution that Torah (law) makes to the New Testament. At one time it was thought that Torah belonged only to the Old Testament and Jewish tradition while grace characterized the New Testament. Today we are learning that both parts of the Christian canon speak of Torah (law) and grace.[24] Finally, bringing about a fresh view of Torah is (3) the Christian interaction with postbiblical and modern Judaism. Here Christian clergy are learning that for Jews the Torah has been and continues to be water, bread, wine, oil, and a wall of protection. It is a

---

24. For recent comments on the place of Torah (law) in early Christianity, see Brad Young, *Jesus the Jewish Theologian* (Peabody, Mass.: Hendrickson, 1995), pp. xxi-xxiv.

teaching that gives life to the community. For this reason, it is often called the Torah of life.

Jesus also holds that life is to be found in accepting the "yoke" of Torah. In response to the lawyer, who inquires as to how one may receive eternal life, Jesus *does not say,* "Believe on me"; rather he asks the lawyer, "What is written in the law?" The lawyer responds with what must have been a traditional short summary of the Torah, basically taken from Deuteronomy 6:5 and Leviticus 19:18: "'You shall love the Lord your God with all your heart, and with all your soul, and with all your strength, and with all your mind; and your neighbor as yourself'" (Luke 10:27). Following his statement Jesus says, "'You have given the right answer; do this, and you will live'" (v. 28). Jesus is sharing with the lawyer the divine teaching that every Israelite and Jew knew to be true: "You shall keep my statutes and my ordinances; by doing so one shall live: I am the LORD [the God of the exodus]" (Lev. 18:5). The words spoken by Jesus, as those spoken in Leviticus, are words of encouragement and promise.[25] With this in mind, it is no surprise to hear Jesus declare in Matthew 5:17: "'Do not think that I have come to abolish the law or the prophets; I have come not to abolish but to fulfill.'"[26]

The Torah, therefore, is a path that leads to a full and fulfilling life rather than becoming a heavy burden to be borne. It must be admitted, however, that the Torah was looked upon as a burden by some people, namely, by those who wanted to take advantage of others by taking ethical shortcuts. The Torah restrained their "freedom"! But for people in general, this Torah (1) was grace because it protected the poor and weak from those whose hands were ever open to grasp

25. Paul's interpretation of these words in Leviticus presents them as a teaching that no one can fulfill (so Gal. 3:10-12). But Paul's comments should not be thought of as the contribution of a neutral observer. Rather, his words are part of an attack on opponents, and in this attack he shifted the meaning of the text to support his argument. See our comments in chapter 3 concerning the way in which Paul, at times, changes the intention of Old Testament texts. Can it be believed that the God of the exodus would give a law that leads to life but makes this teaching so difficult that no one can obey it?

26. Some scholars see this statement as one that is at home in the Jewish tradition. For example, Young, p. xxiii, declares: "Hillel could have made the same statement, especially in the context of a proper interpretation of the Ten Commandments. Jesus placed the meaning of Torah on a firmer footing. As Jesus spoke to a Jewish audience, he treated serious issues relating to the proper interpretation of Torah."

what was not theirs; (2) was enjoyment because, with its teaching of basic rights for those created by God, it enabled people to live peacefully in Israelite society; (3) was a divine gift because God, who shared with Israel his Torah, revealed in this manner his love and concern for the Israelites.

The book of Psalms reflects the love and praise of a Torah community. Psalm 1, a psalm of Torah, is the introduction to the whole book of Psalms, in which God's grace, mercy, love, and forgiveness find prominent expression. The God of Torah is the God of grace and love. Similarly, the Jesus who speaks of God's love and kindness is also the one who speaks and acts Torah.[27] To be sure, there were people who distorted Torah and made it something other than it is, but without the Torah teaching there would have been little reason to preserve the Old Testament as scripture. In addition, without the substructure of Torah, Christianity would have had a very different character.

The Old Testament, Jesus, and Newness

In the following paragraphs we will be speaking about two emphases which are found in greater and lesser measure in the Old Testament, Judaism, and the New Testament. The Torah given to Israel is very much focused on Israelite life. At center, Torah is concerned about preserving the wholeness of the Israelite community. However, this teaching reflects a divine humaneness that does not stop at the borders of Israel. Implicitly and explicitly (Lev. 19:34) it urges Israelites to open their hearts to the outsider. While Israelite emphasis on Torah underscores the *preservation of the Israelite community,* the other aspect, *being open to others,* is not absent.[28] This latter theme finds expression in the books of Ruth, Jonah, and Genesis. It is in a discussion of these themes that we

27. See, among many, Young. He identifies Jesus as a "Jewish theologian" who is "inextricably linked to his people and their faith" and who spoke out of a love and respect for Torah (pp. xxii-xxiii, 264-65). Young further notes: "Like other rabbis and teachers, Jesus developed his own approach within the parameters of ancient Jewish faith and practice. Consequently, Jesus cannot be alienated from Judaism or exiled from his people" (p. xxiii).

28. See the discussion of nationalism and universalism by Elliot Dorff, "A Jewish Theology of Jewish Relations to Other Peoples," in *People of God, Peoples of God,* pp. 52-55.

may be able to see the Old Testament's contribution to one aspect in the teaching and life of Jesus.

Frequently, Christians have seen the "newness" of Jesus' teaching and ministry in his reaching out to others — his concern for the outsider. It is a "newness" which appealed to the British Reform rabbi Claude Montefiore. He observed that although the "virtues of repentance" are strongly underscored in the Jewish tradition, "[Jesus'] direct search for, and appeal to, the sinner are new and moving notes of high import and significance."[29] Indeed, Montefiore insists: "To deny the greatness and originality of Jesus in this connection, to deny that he opened a new chapter in men's attitude towards sin and sinners is, I think, to beat the head against a wall."[30]

In this "newness" one may see the influence of the Old Testament. Jesus' concern for the "sinner" stands in continuity with the similar concern of the author of Jonah, who challenged the people of his day to have a heart for the "outsider" — the "sinner" in the eyes of the Jewish community.[31] While Jesus' courageous stance toward the "outsider" is new, it probably should not be seen as completely new. No doubt there must have been others in the Jewish community of his day who shared his views. If in the evil days of Elijah there were still seven thousand Israelites faithful to God (although we do not hear about them), then it is likely that Jesus was not alone in advocating this move to outsiders. Rather he was a leader of a group (large or small)[32] that contin-

---

29. Claude Montefiore, *The Synoptic Gospels, II* (London: Macmillan, 1909), p. 985. Montefiore does not believe, however, that Jesus offers a completely new teaching. It is one, he insists, that develops themes already present in the Old Testament. See my article, "Outsiders Stretching to Understand Insiders: George Foot Moore and Claude Montefiore," *Covenant Quarterly* 56, no. 4 (1998).

30. Montefiore, p. 86.

31. For further comment on this theme, see my "Israel, the Prophets, and the Book of Jonah. The Rest of the Story: The Formation of the Canon," *Currents in Theology and Mission* 21 (1994): 127-32; "Pharisee and the Tax Collector," 254-57.

32. To be sure, members of this movement are not named, but no doubt there are many important figures in the Israelite-Jewish communities who receive little or no mention in the Old and New Testaments. For example, there must have been a number of prophets and priests who shared the views of Jeremiah. If he had been the single prophet of his day calling for reform, he would have quickly disappeared and his ministry forgotten. We are aware of several persons who walked Jeremiah's path (e.g., Uriah and Ahikam, Jer. 26:20-24), but it is

ued the thinking of the authors of Genesis, Ruth, and Jonah. We should not think, however, that those who favored *openness to others* had little or no concern for the *preservation* of traditional community life. Despite Jesus' critique of some aspects of Jewish leadership, one cannot imagine that he would have embraced a "free society" released from the structure of Torah. Although he questioned some traditions concerning Sabbath observance, it is clear that neither he nor his disciples wished to abolish the laws concerning the Sabbath (see, e.g., Luke 4:16; 23:56). Further, regarding marriages, it is likely that he shared the concern of the Jewish leaders that young people not marry outside of the Jewish community. In any case, one may be quite certain that if a young girl were to ask him advice on whom she should marry, he would not reply: Marry whomever you will! Further, his appeal to sinners would not have gone so far that he would have been unconcerned about integrating "sinners" into the faith community. Jesus was open to others but not so open that he would be willing to destroy the community that lived in respect of God's teaching. Within the New Testament itself we see concerns for the preservation of the community. Jesus, for example, is not willing to let the community be destroyed by those who are "stumbling blocks" for other members (Matt. 18:6). Paul also holds that in some cases people should be removed from the congregation (1 Cor. 5:2), and he thinks there are some people with whom one should not associate (1 Cor. 5:9-11; cf. Ps. 1).

Openness to others and preservation of the community are to be held in balance. Those who advocate an openness to the "outsider" would act irresponsibly if they did not inquire as to the effect this openness would have on the community. But preservation of the community which sees the "outsider" only in terms of danger restricts the grace of God. Every healthy faith community needs this dual emphasis.

---

likely that support for Jeremiah extended beyond these few persons. Further, when we look to the New Testament, we usually consider Paul *the* apostle to the Gentiles and forget that he must have been surrounded by a significant community, in addition to Barnabas and others, who supported his mission.

CHAPTER 8

The Old Testament and the "New" in Jesus

IS "OLD TESTAMENT" A SUITABLE TITLE?

Synopsis

From the very early centuries Christians have used the title "Old Testament." Today this usage is being reexamined by a number of scholars because, in the past, it has been an expression supporting the judgment that the older Testament is an antiquated writing, superseded by the "New" Testament. It follows from this view that postbiblical Judaism, which holds to this scripture, is itself deficient and superseded by Christianity.

The following discussion considers the matter of "supersession," the title "Old Testament," as well as a number of suggestions offered as replacements for this title, namely, Hebrew Bible and First Testament. In both the Jewish and Christian communities, however, there is concern that the desire for dialogue by Jews and Christians may overlook the significance of titles that have had a long history in the respective communities, for example, Tanakh for Jews and Old Testament for Christians. This discussion concludes by noting the danger of misunderstanding that attaches to the use of "Old Testament" but affirming its continued use as the *primary* designation within the Christian community.

Old Testament: The First Part
of the Christian Canon

In the previous chapter we called attention to the continuity that exists between the Old and New Testaments. It appears certain that the character of Christianity would have been radically changed had it not been for significant influences exercised by the Old Testament.[1] Without this scripture the New Testament lacks the ability to be fully the Word of God. Nevertheless, though the church has maintained and defended the twofold canon of Old and New Testaments, still the Old Testament is often thought of as standing second rank.

In the light of the above comments, we raise the question about "Old" Testament as a suitable designation for the first part of the Christian canon because "old," when referring to the "Old" Testament, has often been heard by Christians to mean "out of date" and therefore in need of replacement.

The Old Testament Superseded by the New?

The traditional title "Old Testament" has its defenders.[2] R. W. L. Moberly has argued that although it is not necessary always and in every situation to use "Old Testament," this designation relates to the core

---

1. According to D. Moody Smith, "The Use of the Old Testament in the New," in *The Use of the Old Testament in the New and Other Essays,* ed. James Efird (Durham, N.C.: Duke University Press, 1972), p. 4 n. 2, the Hebrew scriptures were first designated "Old Testament" by Melito of Sardis circa 180 C.E. Quite likely this title was suggested by the occurrence of "old covenant" in 2 Cor. 3:14. It may be surprising to learn that this phrase "old covenant" occurs only here in the entire Bible.

2. E.g., R. W. L. Moberly, *The Old Testament of the Old Testament* (Minneapolis: Fortress, 1992), pp. 147-75. See also the comments of Roland E. Murphy, "Old Testament/Tanakh — Canon and Interpretation," in *Hebrew Bible or Old Testament?* ed. Roger Brooks and John Collins (Notre Dame: Notre Dame University Press, 1990), pp. 11-12 n. 1. Murphy has decided to continue using "Old Testament" because it is a traditional expression, which is rooted in the Bible (i.e., related to "old covenant" in 2 Cor. 3:14) and does not refer to some antiquated writing. Christopher Seitz argues also for the traditional title, in "Old Testament or Hebrew Bible? Some Theological Considerations," *Pro Ecclesia* 5, no. 3 (1996): 292-303.

of Christian thinking. To surrender it in favor of some other suggestion, he declares, would amount to a rejection of the Christian witness which declares that with Jesus came something "new." He points out that the words "old" and "new," used to designate the two parts of the Christian canon, are not chronological terms but *theological designations:* "The terms are first and foremost a theological judgment to the effect that the content of the Old Testament belongs to a period and mode of God's dealings with the world that has been in some ways superseded by the coming of Jesus Christ in the New Testament."[3]

While holding to such terms as "Old Testament" and "supersede," Moberly believes that this terminology should in no way reflect negatively on Jews or Judaism even though he insists that it is an "inescapable fact . . . that in some ways there must be a superseding of existing religion if Christianity is to distinguish itself from the Torah-centered religion of the Old Testament. . . ."[4]

Jon Levenson, a Jewish scholar familiar with traditional Christian interpretation of the Old Testament, articulates, from his place within the Jewish community, why Moberly believes it necessary to use the term "supersede." For centuries, he says, Christian theologians have maintained that the Old Testament leads to the New Testament, where one finds the "new." The Old Testament, he continues, according to traditional Christian interpretation, does not possess an independent integrity: "To say that the Hebrew Bible has complete integrity over

---

3. Moberly, p. 156. In the above citation it should be noted that Moberly uses the phrase "in some ways" in connection with the term "supersede." He employs this qualification several times, for example, on pp. 158, 162, and 163. It is clear that included in this "some ways" is the person of Jesus himself.

4. Moberly, pp. 162-63. He comes to this conclusion by comparing the relationship of Judaism and Christianity to the relationship that existed earlier between patriarchal traditions and those of the Mosaic period. He argues that Mosaic religion superseded patriarchal religion, but that this event of supersession did not result in the demeaning of the latter. However, one questions whether it is appropriate to use the contemporary term "supersede" to describe the evolving relationship between patriarchal and Mosaic religion. The analogy, which Moberly admits has "certain weaknesses" and a "looseness," is not convincing. He himself agrees that "there is therefore no biblical parallel to the phenomenon of Judaism and Christianity as rival claimants to a common tradition" (pp. 166-68). As he concedes, this analogy and approach ignores the very negative judgments about the Old Testament/old covenant found both in the New Testament (e.g., Heb. 8:13) and in later Christian history.

against the New Testament is to cast grave doubt upon the unity of the Christian Bible." Further, with regard to the use of "supersede" as a proper term for describing the relationship of the Old Testament to the New Testament, Levenson declares: "The supersession of an Old Testament theologian like Eichrodt (and he is not untypical) is not adventitious. It is an inevitable corollary of his faith in the unity and integrity of the two-volume Bible of the church."[5] Levenson's remarks describe accurately the dominant view within the church — in the past and to a considerable extent in the present. But we question if Levenson is correct in affirming that the church *must* maintain that the New Testament has "superseded" the Old Testament in order for it to maintain a twofold canon. It appears to us that such an affirmation is not "an inevitable corollary" to "the two-volume Bible of the church." Recent thinking about the relationship of the Old Testament to rabbinic Judaism as well as to Christianity provides new insight into this issue. The following paragraphs are given over to this discussion.

Is "Supersession" the Right Word to Use?

Today, as we consider the way in which Christians interpret the Old Testament (see our discussion in chaps. 2 and 3), we must ask whether "supersede" is the right word to use in a discussion of the relationship of the New Testament to the Old Testament. Its use brings a strong reaction from many Christians as well as Jews. To many this term appears to say too much because it implies that, regarding essentials, the New Testament "replaces" the Old Testament.[6] Our discussion in the pre-

---

5. Jon Levenson, "Theological Consensus or Historical Evasion? Jews and Christians in the Hebrew Bible," in his *The Hebrew Bible, the Old Testament, and Historical Criticism: Jews and Christians in Biblical Studies* (Louisville: Westminster/John Knox, 1993), p. 101. Moberly's following comment reveals the truth of Levenson's analysis: "Whatever, therefore, the apparent initial attractiveness of abandoning the language of 'Old Testament,' it is simply not possible for the Christian to do so and still to explain the logic of a Christian, as distinct from a Jewish position." See Moberly, p. 161.

6. See, e.g., John Sawyer, who, while affirming that "the coming of Christ changes things," rejects the idea that the New Testament supersedes the earlier scripture. He points out that many "theological ideas fundamental to Christianity, are already there, for Jewish interpreters like Jesus and Paul to build on. There was much else in Scripture to build on and other contemporary interpreters —

ceding chapter, which speaks of a dialogical/reciprocal interaction between the two Testaments, points away from this kind of relationship. Nevertheless, it is also true that the New Testament proclamation is not fully one with the religion of the Old Testament. In certain aspects it differs from the latter scripture and moves beyond it. But how should we describe this "different from" and "beyond" character of the New Testament?

Both New Testament and Talmud "Go Beyond" the Older Scripture

We meet a similar situation when we encounter Judaism. Judaism, shaped by rabbinic commentaries and the Talmud, is not the same as the religion of the Old Testament. It roots in the Old Testament, as does Christianity, but in its own way it also *goes beyond* this scripture. Moberly agrees that the relationship of Jews to the Hebrew Bible (Tanakh) is "in many ways as indirect and problematic as is the Christian's relationship to the Old Testament," but he argues that "for the Christian the New Testament represents a qualitatively new divine revelation . . . a new dispensation" and therefore relates differently to the Old Testament than does the Talmud which for the Jew assumes the form of "*commentary:* expounding, elaborating, developing, and applying the existing material but in no way superseding it."[7]

Although it is true, says Moberly, that Judaism is not the same as the religion of the Hebrew scriptures, yet he believes that between the Hebrew scriptures and Judaism there exists a "fundamental continuity." For both the Hebrew scripture and postbiblical Jewish literature, the life of Torah is central. In contrast to the continuity between the two literatures that Jews experience, says Moberly, the Christian experiences discontinuity because the Christian's central

---

including Hillel, Rabban Johanan ben Zakkai and Rabbi Akiba, for example — built another religion on it." See his article "Combating Prejudices about the Bible and Judaism," *Theology* 94 (1991): 273-74.

7. Moberly, pp. 157-58. Marvin A. Sweeney, "Tanak versus Old Testament," in *Problems in Biblical Theology*, ed. H. T. C. Sun and K. L. Eades (Grand Rapids: Wm. B. Eerdmans Publishing Co., 1997), p. 365, is supportive of Moberly's view, observing that the Talmud functions "more or less as commentary upon the Tanak like the Midrashim and Targumim."

witness is Jesus Christ, and he does not appear in the Hebrew Bible/
Old Testament.[8]

Hebrew Scriptures Point as Little
to Mishnah as to Jesus

Some Christian Old Testament scholars share Moberly's view without
however accepting his views on supersession.[9] But a number of Jewish
scholars dispute such a sharp distinction; they believe it is not all that simple. William Scott Green would take issue with Moberly's judgment that
the Talmud is to be seen basically as a "form of commentary" on the Old
Testament. He declares: "It is misleading to depict rabbinic Judaism primarily as the consequence of an exegetical process or the organic unfolding of scripture."[10] Jacob Neusner states the issue in a stronger form: "Judaism inherits and makes the Hebrew Scriptures its own, just as does
Christianity. But just as Christianity rereads the entire heritage of ancient
Israel in light of the 'resurrection of Jesus Christ' so Judaism understands
the Hebrew Scriptures as only one part, the written one, of the one whole
Torah of Moses, our rabbi." Neusner continues:

> Ancient Israel no more testified to the oral Torah, now written down
> in the Mishnah and later rabbinic writings, than it did to Jesus as the
> Christ. In both cases, religious circles within Israel of later antiquity
> reread the entire past in the light of their own conscience and convic-

8. Moberly, p. 158.

9. Agreeing with Moberly that there is greater continuity between the Old
Testament and rabbinic Judaism (see, e.g., the focus on Torah) than between this
scripture and Christianity is Erich Zenger, *Das Erste Testament: Die jüdische Bibel
und die Christen* (Düsseldorf: Patmos, 1991), p. 137. Rolf Rendtorff, *Canon and
Theology* (Minneapolis: Fortress, 1993; German ed. 1991), p. 19, also underscores the continuity of rabbinic exegesis with the Jewish (Hebrew) Bible even
though, as he allows, this exegesis did not have the purpose of conveying the original or plain meaning of the biblical text.

10. William S. Green, "Scripture in Rabbinic Judaism," *Horizons in Biblical
Theology* 9, no. 1 (1987): 32; see also pp. 27-31. See also Ernest S. Frerichs's arti-
cle in the above volume ("The Torah Canon of Judaism and the Interpretation of
Hebrew Scripture," esp. pp. 20-21, 24). Levenson, *Hebrew Bible*, p. 105, observes
that "the Hebrew Bible is largely foreign to both traditions [i.e., Christian *and*
Jewish] and precedes them."

tions. . . . they picked and chose as they wished whatever would serve the purposes of the later system they undertook to build.[11]

One more example of Jewish opinion concerning the presence of a significant discontinuity between the Jewish Bible and Judaism is reflected in the following comments by Matitiahu Tsevat: "Sparse and uncertain paths lead from the Old Testament to the Talmud." Further: "The Old Testament does not know the Talmud and does not of its own initiative, proffer interpretation of it." Again, he declares that "the Talmud judaizes the Old Testament" while observing that the road leading from the Old Testament to the Talmud "appears generally unclear, questionable, or completely impassable."[12]

The New Testament Does Not "Supersede" the Old Testament

The above comments by Jewish scholars emphasize the discontinuity between the Jewish Bible and Judaism — a discontinuity that is more similar than dissimilar to the discontinuity present between the Old Testament and Christianity. It is clear that Judaism is not the religion of the Old Testament, nor is it almost the religion of the Old Testament. Even in Judaism's emphasis on Torah, which represents a central theme in the Old Testament (Jewish Bible), one finds, as indicated above, considerable difference between rabbinic Judaism and the scripture. Judaism brings to light something new and different without thereby superseding or replacing the religion of its scripture. In Christianity also something new has come into being — a newness that is both similar to and different from the newness found in Judaism — but it does not supersede, replace, or make obsolete the Old Testament.

Moberly, however, continues to insist that it is important, even necessary, to employ the designation "Old Testament." To his mind it is

---

11. Taken from Neusner's book *Judaism and Scripture* and cited by Frerichs, p. 22. See further the comments of M. H. Goshen-Gottstein, "Tanakh Theology: The Religion of the Old Testament and the Place of Jewish Biblical Theology," in *Ancient Israelite Religion*, ed. Patrick Miller et al. (Philadelphia: Fortress, 1987), pp. 626-27.

12. Matitiahu Tsevat, "Theology of the Old Testament: A Jewish View," *Horizons in Biblical Theology* 8 (1986): 46.

a theological judgment which is made by the Christian community which believes "that the faith centered on Jesus in some ways supersedes the religion of the Old Testament."[13] At one point during his discussion he appears to indicate what he means by "supersession." He observes that no matter how closely related the Old and New Testaments are, it is the New Testament that is normative for the church, and by its existence it represents "the impossibility of continuance in the old [i.e., the old covenant and the Old Testament] as it once was."[14] But, if that is the basic definition of "supersession," then John Sawyer's insistence that Judaism also supersedes the Old Testament has weight. Most Jews hardly imagine the possibility of going back to what "once was" in the Old Testament.

Sawyer agrees with Moberly that "the coming of Christ changes things" but insists that this does not mean that the Old Testament itself has been superseded. He calls our attention to the influential role played by the Old Testament today: "In recent years Exodus and Isaiah have been just as central to some modern movements in the Church, notably liberation theology, as the Gospels, and more so than much of the Pauline literature. Scriptural authority for biblical teaching on social justice and a 'God of the oppressed', for example, comes from Deuteronomy, the Psalms and the eighth-century prophets." He points out that neither Christianity nor rabbinic Judaism "is identical with the religion of ancient Israel. Both are living religions, rooted in the soil of Israel's faith, which took shape in the first century of the Christian era. Both are filled with social, political and theological insights and influences far removed from ancient Israel."[15]

The term "supersede" should be removed from Christian discussion concerning the relationship of the New Testament to the Old Testa-

---

13. Moberly, p. 161.

14. Moberly, p. 161. This statement arises out of a discussion in which Moberly compares the move from patriarchal religion to Mosaic Yahwism with the move of the early Christians from the Old Testament to the New. Both Mosaic Yahwism and the New Testament Christian movement, he observes, although significantly influenced by the former faiths, supersede those expressions of faith that preceded them. These "new religions . . . have normative status for their adherents and relativize the significance of the former dispensation." These new religions (Mosaic Yahwism and New Testament Christianity) presuppose "the normativity of the new perspective and the impossibility of continuance in the old as it once was" (p. 161).

15. Sawyer, p. 274.

ment.[16] It represents an overreach of the church which has resulted in a denigration of this scripture as well as of Judaism. But if "supersede" is an inappropriate word to use when speaking of the relationship between the Testaments, what words are appropriate? Christians believe that they have experienced something new in Jesus Christ and that this newness is reflected in the New Testament. How may one speak of this newness without undervaluing it or being guilty of overreaching? New words and images are needed. For now we find that it is more appropriate to speak of the New Testament as "going beyond" the Old Testament. One could say the same about Judaism and its relationship to the Jewish Bible. Both Judaism and Christianity "go beyond" the older scripture — although *in different ways*. Jews and Christians need to be involved in a substantive discussion about these "different ways" instead of having the discussion thrown off track by the term "supersede."

It is the close association between "Old Testament" and "super-session" (strongly implied by the promise and fulfillment model) that has opened up the present-day discussion about "Old Testament" as a suitable designation for the first part of the Christian canon. A growing number of Christian scholars, convinced that the designation "Old Testament" is too vulnerable to caricature and too tightly bound to a supersessionist view, are calling for the use of alternate designations for this first part of the Christian canon.[17] Although a number of suggestions have been made, the following two proposals are the most prominent of the ones being considered.

"Hebrew Bible" instead of "Old Testament"?

In recent years "Hebrew Bible" has received considerable attention from scholars and clergy as a replacement for the traditional designation "Old Testament." It is often used by Christian leaders and

---

16. Walter Brueggemann, in "Texts That Linger, Words That Explode," *Theology Today* 54 (1997): 191-92, discusses Jer. 31:31-34 and its interpretation in Heb. 8:8-13 and 11:16-17. Brueggemann sees this claim of supersession over the Old Testament and Judaism to be unjustified and observes: "In the Christian reuse of Jeremiah 31, a text of Judaism is turned into a text against Judaism."

17. See, e.g., Sawyer, pp. 69-70, and Clark Williamson and Ronald Allen, *Interpreting Difficult Texts: Anti-Judaism and Christian Preaching* (Philadelphia: Trinity Press International, 1989), pp. 15-16.

scholars at gatherings attended by Jews and Christians. The title "Hebrew Bible" clearly establishes that this scripture comes out of the Jewish tradition and that it possesses an integrity of its own. There is, however, a growing sense within the church that it may not be an accurate designation for Christians to use. Also, as we will mention below, some Jewish scholars think it may not represent a choice title for Jews.

The hesitation concerning the adoption of "Hebrew Bible" rests on several grounds. We mention first an historical reason. Scholars are generally agreed that the early Christian community for most part did *not* use the Hebrew Bible. As we observed in chapter 3 above, the New Testament writers often cited the Septuagint when they wished to demonstrate a relationship between the two Testaments. In the years following the New Testament period, very few of the known church founders were fluent in Hebrew. Jerome, perhaps Origen, and a few others were exceptions in this regard. Up to the time of Martin Luther, the church depended heavily upon the Greek Bible (Septuagint).[18]

A second reason for hesitation in adopting "Hebrew Bible" as the primary designation has to do with structure. Although the Protestant Old Testament contains the same books as the Hebrew Bible, they are arranged differently; this different arrangement takes on the character of a theological statement. One example may suffice. The Hebrew Bible ends with the second book of Chronicles, whose last verse expresses hope that, under Cyrus, the land will be free again. In this concluding book there is no expression of longing for a Messiah as proclaimed in the New Testament.

In contrast to the Hebrew Bible, the Protestant Old Testament concludes with Malachi. To the Christian reader this is a striking conclusion, because Malachi 3:1 proclaims: "See, I am sending my messenger to prepare the way before me. . . ." In a further announcement, Malachi declares: "Lo, I will send you the prophet Elijah before the great and terrible day of the LORD comes" (4:5). When the next several pages are turned, one is reading the words of Matthew about John the Baptist (Matt. 3:1-12), who is identified as Elijah, the prophet who was to appear before the day of the LORD (Matt. 11:7-14). In turning these

18. See, e.g., the discussion of Mogens Müller, *The First Bible of the Church: A Plea for the Septuagint* (Sheffield: Academic Press, 1996), pp. 78-97.

pages it is easy to overlook the fact that in Malachi "LORD" refers to God, whereas in Matthew it has Jesus in mind. The "Christian" Old Testament, which places Malachi as the last book of the Scripture, reflects and fits the Christian confession of Jesus.[19] This seeming natural continuity between the Old and New Testaments, however, is not evident in the Hebrew Bible, which ends with Chronicles.

A further difficulty with the title "Hebrew Bible" has to do with its suitability in the Christian tradition. Although it may be appropriate for Jews to use this designation, it is much the less so for Christians because it gives no indication that this scripture is a part of the Christian canon. It does not convey in any public way the church's conviction that the early Jesus movement had its roots in the Old Testament scripture.

But it is not only Christians who draw back from using "Hebrew Bible"; its use is contested within the Jewish community also. Ernest S. Frerichs calls attention to two recent publications where, apparently, "Jewish Bible" and "Tanakh"[20] have been preferred over "Hebrew Bible." In the one case Frerichs comments: "The choice of the term 'Jewish Bible' then was not only a rejection of the term Old Testament as reflective of a Christian definition, but also an avoidance of the seemingly neutral usage of Hebrew Bible."[21] Frerichs's words suggest that in the present day there is concern within the Jewish community to maintain a *Jewish* identity for their scripture.

Professor Jon Levenson reflects this same concern in a recent article. He points out that Jews and Christians can put aside, for a time, their own peculiar traditions and understandings concerning the scripture and in this manner meet on a neutral ground. For Levenson, "Hebrew Bible" has become the neutral meeting place for Jews and Christians; it is a designation that has replaced the confes-

19. For further discussion of the structure of the Christian Old Testament as opposed to the Jewish (Hebrew) Bible, see Zenger, *Das Erste Testament*, pp. 177-84; Sawyer, pp. 272-73; and Sweeney, p. 359 (a summary of his position).

20. The references are to Jon Levenson's volume, *Sinai and Zion: An Entry into the Jewish Bible* (Chicago: Seabury, 1985), and to the *Tanakh*, a translation of the scripture by the Jewish Publication Society. "TaNaK" is a short way of referring to the three parts of the Jewish canon, namely: Torah, Nebhi'im, and Kethubhim (i.e., the Law, the Prophets, and the Writings).

21. Frerichs, p. 15. See also Zenger's discussion and rejection of the designation "Hebrew Bible" (for Christians) in *Das Erste Testament*, pp. 149-52.

sional designations of "Tanakh" for Jews and "Old Testament" for Christians. However, he says, meeting on neutral ground cannot be the continuing way of life for the two communities because, as a matter of fact, they are different communities who live out of different traditions. He then observes that "most Jews with an active commitment to their tradition will be suspicious of any allegedly common ground [i.e., Hebrew Bible] that requires them to suppress or shed their Jewishness."[22] Levenson's concern is one that should be shared by Christians: if the church were to employ "Hebrew Bible" as a designation for the first part of the Christian canon, it would be adopting a title that is silent concerning its relationship to the New Testament.[23]

"First Testament" instead of "Old Testament"?

Erich Zenger believes that "Old Testament," with certain qualifications, may be a suitable designation for the first part of the Christian canon. For example, he finds it appropriate to use the expression "Old Testament" (1) if it is recognized that "old" has the meaning of "elder" *(anciennität)* and "origin" *(Ursprung);* (2) if one is conscious that "Old Testament" is "a specifically Christian designation"[24] which calls attention to the impossibility of a New Testament without the "Old Testament"; (3) if it is recognized that "Old Testament" does not correspond to the Old Testament's own self-understanding or to the Jewish understanding of this scripture; (4) if one places the expression in quotation marks ("Old Testament") in order to indicate the special character of this expression and thus avoid misunderstanding.[25]

In the final analysis, however, Zenger believes one must look for

22. Levenson, *Hebrew Bible,* p. 105.

23. Christopher R. Seitz finds "Hebrew Bible" to be fully unacceptable, and his article "Old Testament or Hebrew Bible? Some Theological Considerations," *Pro Ecclesia* 5 (1996): 293-303 constitutes a strong argument for the retention of "Old Testament."

24. So also Cristina Grenholm, "Christian Interpretation of the Old Testament in a Pluralistic Context," *Studia Theologica* 48 (1994): 98-99.

25. Zenger, *Das Erste Testament,* pp. 147-48. For his full discussion, see pp. 140-54.

an alternate designation which would not open itself so much to the dangers of misunderstanding. But, he asks, what should be the character of this new designation? It should not be a neutral one, says Zenger. To decide for such a title would be to conceal the difference that exists between Jews and Christians as they read the scripture.[26] A new designation must "express the specifically Christian meaning of these scriptures," therefore designations such as "Jewish Bible" or "Tanakh" should not be the primary titles for Christians.[27] Nevertheless, Zenger indicates also that this new designation should *not* in any sense undercut the common interests that bind Jews and Christians together.

Recently James Sanders suggested that "First Testament" be used as a designation for the first part of the Christian canon and "Second Testament" be employed to designate the "New Testament."[28] The journal *Biblical Theology Bulletin* has adopted the recommendation of Sanders and requires that those authoring articles on its pages refer to the Old and New Testaments as "First Testament" and "Second Testament." These titles are advocated also by Erich Zenger,[29] who believes they have a number of advantages. They hold basically, he affirms, to what is intended by the traditional references: "First" conveys as effectively as "Old" the fact that this scripture is prior to the "Second" or "New" Testament. Additionally, the designation "First Testament" is less vulnerable to misunderstanding than is the expression "Old Testament." It gives little opportunity for one to speak of it as an "antiquated" writing, superseded by the "Second." These new titles, "First"

---

26. Grenholm, p. 99, employs the designation "Old Testament" in her article because she deals "precisely with Christian interpretation of the Hebrew Bible." She continues: "According to my view, no theologian is objective. Theological research is always made from a certain position. Using neutral concepts might even be a way of escaping from the problem of bias. On the other hand, by choosing this perspective of Christian interpretation I do not imply that it is the only one possible or justifiable."

27. Zenger, *Das Erste Testament*, p. 148.

28. James Sanders, "First and Second Testaments," *Biblical Theology Bulletin* 17 (1987): 47-49. These titles are employed also by John Goldingay in a recent book: *Models for Interpretation of Scripture* (Grand Rapids: Wm. B. Eerdmans Publishing Co., 1995).

29. For the following comments supporting the use of this new terminology, see Zenger, *Das Erste Testament*, p. 153. Zenger undertakes a further discussion of this topic in "Überlegungen zu einem neuen christlichen Umgang mit dem sogenannten Alten Testament," *Kirche und Israel* (1995): 137-51.

and "Second" Testaments, speak of continuity and development in the midst of difference. Further, says Zenger, as with "Old" and "New" Testaments, these new designations convey more than a chronological succession; they reflect a theological judgment. For example, "First" Testament makes Christians aware of the covenant that God first made with Israel which through Jesus Christ is extended to the peoples of the world. But, in addition, the expression "First" Testament underscores that this scripture is a *part* of the Christian canon: "First" Testament implies a "Second" Testament.[30]

The above suggestion, "First Testament," is by far the better choice as an alternative designation for what has been called the "Old Testament." The arguments favoring it are substantial; it creates a strong appeal. One can agree that it has its place in the Christian vocabulary. But to employ it as the *primary* designation for the older scripture brings forth questions. For example, will "First" Testament come to mean the most important Testament? Will "Second" Testament be considered a second-level, added-on scripture? A move in this direction may already be seen in Andre LaCocque's suggestions of "Prime Testament" instead of "Old Testament" and "Appendix Saying" instead of "New Testament."[31] Further, the recommendation of Paul van Buren, employing respectively "the Scriptures" and "Apostolic Writings," holds somewhat the same danger.[32] To the Christian ear, "Second Testament" does not have a fully satisfying sound as the *primary* title for this scripture.

30. Over against Zenger, who holds that these new designations have theological depth and witness to one canon but two Testaments, Moberly believes this terminology is an example of "religiously neutral language . . . in that it evades the basic theological issue of different dispensations posed by the biblical text." See Moberly, p. 161.

31. LaCocque, "The 'Old Testament' in the Protestant Traditions," in *Biblical Studies: Meeting Ground of Jews and Christians,* ed. L. Boadt et al. (New York: Paulist, 1980), p. 140.

32. Paul van Buren, *Discerning the Way: A Theology of the Jewish Christian Reality* (New York: Seabury, 1980), pp. 23-24, 122-25.

"Old Testament" and "New Testament" and the "Newness" in Jesus

The long use of "Old Testament" and "New Testament" produces a questioning response to the new titles suggested above.[33] But reluctance in accepting these new suggestions is not due simply to an unwillingness to accept change. It has to do as much or more with a concern to maintain the core of faith. Zenger puts forth persuasive arguments for the acceptance of "First Testament," but the proposed use of this title comes at a time when Christians as well as Jews are becoming increasingly concerned about community identity. There is concern within the church that, in a desire to advance the Jewish-Christian dialogue, these traditional designations may be changed too quickly and too easily.

Some people, with the desire to move at greater speed along the road of dialogue with the Jewish community, may be critical of a church that is so hesitant to adopt new terms. Admittedly, a glance at the history of the church, both Protestant and Catholic, makes one aware that frequently the church has been much too slow in responding to contemporary issues. However, the Christian hesitation concerning a change in religious terminology is not simply a Christian issue; some Jews, as noted above, have expressed similar thoughts. The comments of Professor Jon Levenson concerning the nature of Jewish-Christian dialogue focus this concern. Writing as a Jew who favors the present-day dialogue between Jews and Christians, he issues, as mentioned above, a note of caution to the Jewish and Christian communities. He observes that there are points in this dialogue (e.g., with regard to biblical studies) where Jews and Christians "bracket their religious commitments." When they do so, then these two communities "meet not as Jews and Christians, but as something else." He indicates that the dialogue tends to seek "neutral" ground. In so doing one may lose sight of the distinctive elements of the two faiths. Levenson then observes:

33. Manfred Görg, *In Abrahams Schoss: Christsein ohne Neues Testament* (Düsseldorf: Patmos, 1993), p. 31, is doubtful that "Old Testament," which has been the primary designation for the first part of the Christian canon for close to two thousand years, can ever be replaced by another expression. Some years ago Rolf Rendtorff apologized for using the designation "Old Testament" but observed that at that time no acceptable alternative presented itself (Rendtorff, p. 198).

"Most Jews with an active commitment to their tradition will be suspicious of any allegedly common ground that requires them to suppress or shed their Jewishness."[34] His words call attention to the fact that Jewish-Christian dialogue must not overlook or suppress those distinctive elements represented in the two communities.

"Old Testament" as the Primary Designation

Those advocating the use of "First and Second Testaments" believe that these designations are not neutral terms but do, in fact, affirm the Christian conviction of two Testaments in one scripture. However, as already indicated, these new designations have vulnerabilities that could reflect on the New Testament. This possibility gives us pause when asked to choose them as the primary titles for the scripture. We believe it is good practice to use a variety of designations for the older portion of the canon, because they make the church aware of different aspects of the relationship that exists between the two Testaments.[35] But we are not convinced that these titles should replace "Old Testament" and "New Testament" as *primary* titles.

Our decision for the traditional titles, however, does not rest simply on the fact that other suggested titles are vulnerable to misunderstanding. There is a positive reason which relates to the matter of Christian self-understanding and identity. One image occurring in the New Testament which has been picked up by the Christian community is the image of Jesus as the "new covenant" (e.g., 1 Cor. 11:25). We

34. Levenson, "Theological Consensus or Historicist Evasion?" pp. 82-105. The above citations are taken from pp. 84 and 105.

35. Zenger ("Überlegungen," p. 144) holds that if one cannot agree to replacing "Old Testament" with "First Testament," then the traditional title should at least be supplemented/complemented *(ergänzt)* by another designation (e.g., "First Testament"). Although R. W. L. Moberly has argued that it would be a mistake for the church to replace "Old Testament" and "New Testament" with some other designations, he does not demand that "Old Testament" should be the only designation used. He observes: "It is not the case that Christians must always and only use the terms Old/New Testament. For a good number of practical purposes, such as either Jewish-Christian dialogue or many facets of academic biblical study, it may be preferable to adopt terminology that is common to all parties, terminology such as scripture or Bible, so as to facilitate discussion of common ground." See Moberly, p. 158.

have discussed this image in an earlier chapter where we maintained that the "newness" in the "new covenant" does not mean something brand-new or completely new. The Christian movement that grew out of his life, death, and resurrection stands in continuity with the teachings of the law, the prophets, and the psalmists as well as with traditions in Judaism. But discontinuity also exists; it reveals itself significantly in the image of Jesus as the initiator of "newness" — a "newness" celebrated by early Christians. Without rejecting the earlier Sinai covenant, they nevertheless believed that he represented a "new" way of thinking about God, a new way of living (e.g., 2 Cor. 5:17; Eph. 2:15; 4:24). This early Christian experience of newness in Christ is one reaffirmed by Christians living in the centuries following the time of Christ. It lies at the core of Christian self-understanding and identity. The designation "New Testament," which mirrors "new covenant," underscores this aspect of Christian witness. To replace it with "Second Testament" hides to a significant degree the impress of Jesus on those who followed him.

But this "new" covenant exhibits very definitely the marks of the old or elder Sinai covenant (to which the covenants with David and Abraham for the most part assimilated). Early Christians, mostly Jews at the beginning, looked at Jesus from the point of view of the traditions associated with this older covenant. Reading the texts of Israel's scripture at their "depth," as did the Jews at Qumran and those who created the later rabbinic interpretations, these Christians gained insight into the significance and identity of Jesus. Although there were some in the early Christian movement who thought that the new covenant made the Sinai covenant obsolete (e.g., Heb. 8:13), such appears not to have been the view of Jesus or of other New Testament authors (e.g., Rom. 9–11). Those who adhered to this latter view considered the "new covenant" as one that "carried forward" or "went beyond" the older covenant, but without abolishing its validity.

In recent discussion, Christian scholars of varied theological positions have underscored the Jewish character of Jesus and the teaching of the New Testament. It is clear that the old (or that which is older) contributes to the newness that the first Christians discovered in Jesus. It is a newness not unknown in Israel's life under the older covenant (e.g., Pss. 51 and 103), but, from a Christian point of view, this newness finds its dramatic expression in the life-event of one person, Jesus, and in the community he created.

We find then that the traditional designations of "Old Testament" and "New Testament" are titles that preserve the important dual witness of the Christian movement; that is, (1) a newness inherent in the new covenant brought about by Jesus and (2) a newness shaped by the traditions of the old or older covenant.[36] Much of the "old" (elder) scripture is in the "new" and much of the "new" scripture is in the "old." Scholars today are seeking words and imagery that express this relationship between the Testaments without saying too much or too little.

"Old Testament" and Present-Day Changes in Biblical Interpretation

Christian identity has been underscored in the above paragraphs as an important reason for retaining the designations "Old Testament" and "New Testament," but such an affirmation does not blind us to the vulnerability of these two titles. We believe, however, that steps may be taken to correct the misunderstandings of the past short of excising "Old Testament" and "New Testament" and replacing them with other expressions.[37] In our day, in fact, steps in this direction are already being taken. At no time in recent history have so many Christian scholars, representing both conservative and mainline traditions, come to agreement on the continuing value of the Old Testament for the Christian church. There is a growing recognition that this Testament gives rich gifts to the Christian community. The caricatures which the church in past years accepted as a true evaluation of the Old Testament are recognized for what they in actual fact are, namely, caricatures. Further, to-

36. See, e.g., Seitz's strong defense of the traditional titles: "Israel's Scriptures are constitutive of God's covenant with her, to which the church is related because of the covenant made in Christ. There is thus an Old Testament and a New Testament record of this series of decisive and non-substitutable theological moments. Abandoning the term 'Old Testament' would be to abandon a statement of the relationship of Christians to the literature of Israel and to modern Judaism" (p. 302). The designation "Old Testament" is also affirmed by Donald Juel in "New Testament Reading of the Old: Norm or Nuisance?" *Dialogue* 31 (1992): 187-88.

37. To the mind of Görg, pp. 31-32, it is better to accept the traditional title "Old Testament" and to devote oneself to freeing it from misunderstandings than to replace it with another designation.

```
        COKESBURY DUKE DIV
            403 CHAPEL DR
        WESTBROOK BUILDING 032
           DURHAM, NC  27708
04/25/13   13:16    6      21       4043

Customer Account Record # 0013389473
Charge to Account # CI07391

SMALL ITEM PURCHASES
301 8TH AVE S

NASHVILLE, TN 37203-3921
Telephone # (615) 749-6123

ORDERED BY SMALL ITEM PURCHASES

   1@ 23.50 9780802844538*90$       2.35
              OLD TESTAMENT AND THE SI
SUBTOTAL                        $    2.35
TAX       @ 7.5000%             $    0.18
TOTAL                           $    2.53
TENDERED Cash    0013389473     $    2.53


Your Savings!                   $   21.15


        ALL CLEARANCE SALES ARE FINAL
        NO REFUNDS - NO EXCHANGES
```

gether with a new understanding of the Old Testament which is taking place among clergy, there is a growing knowledge of and appreciation for the Jewish tradition. Biblical courses taught in many Christian seminaries play a crucial role in bringing about this new stance toward the Old Testament and Judaism. In this important area, change is taking place at too slow a pace, but it is a process that promises to be steady and continuing.

Suggestions for Improving Perception of "Old Testament" in the Church

There are practical steps that clergy can take to bring about a better understanding of the Old Testament within the church. For example, in presenting the Old Testament as the elder rather than the antiquated scripture, one needs to address the Christian use of B.C. ("before Christ") and A.D. ("in the year of our Lord"). These abbreviations represent an expression of faith concerning the significance of Christ for the Christian church; they speak as a witness about the "new" in Jesus. Because these symbols represent a statement of faith, Christians in the worshiping community will continue to employ them, just as Jews in their worship will continue to hold to their ancient count of years dating from creation. The employment of these symbols, however, tends to underscore the traditional Christian understanding of the "Old" Testament as out-of-date, because it is viewed as belonging to the "old" era (B.C.). This tendency takes on greater strength when Christians forget that these symbols are expressions of Christian witness and believe, as is often the case, that they are the factual divisions of time for the world at large.

A current practice among leaders in the two communities, however, offers an alternative to the measuring of time. This practice is the use of B.C.E. ("before the common era," i.e., of Jews and Christians) instead of B.C. and C.E. ("the common era") instead of the traditional A.D. designation. Their use, from time to time, checks a false perception of the Old Testament and underscores the continuing presence of the Jewish community.

Another issue that needs further discussion within the church is the manner in which early Christians "found" Jesus in Old Testament texts (see our discussion in chaps. 2-3). When congregations become aware that the New Testament authors moved from Jesus to the Old Testament, employing a "depth" or "believer" approach to this scripture, then one can expect that Christian worshipers themselves will gain a new understanding of the Old Testament. This approach calls upon the church to be serious about Christian education which involves the discussion of foundational issues about the Bible, Judaism, and the church. In the past, many churches have avoided such issues because it was thought that they were too controversial. As a result, generations have grown up holding caricatured beliefs about the Old Testament and Judaism.

Our present day offers rich resources for open discussion of these issues because many conservative and mainline Christian scholars share similar views concerning them.[38] Not only are these scholars rejecting old caricatures, they are also creating a climate of fairness in which worthwhile examination of these topics can proceed. Churches have a choice opportunity to build on this scholarship which is initiating change but at the same time maintaining the faith.

A moderate change in the format of Christian worship can also contribute to a truer view of the Old Testament. Simple but significant changes in the church bulletin would underscore the church's belief that both the Old Testament and the New Testament are equally scripture. For example, rather than entitling the scriptural readings "Old Testament: Psalm 51" and "New Testament: Luke 15:1-7," why not call them "The Scripture: Psalm 51" and "The Scripture: Luke 15:1-7"? Perhaps also under the heading "Readings from the Scripture" one could simply indicate the individual selections as follows: "Psalm 51" and "Luke 5:17-25." Again, instead of having the reading of the Old Testament scripture preceding that of the New Testament, one could, sometimes, read the New Testament text first and the Old Testament text second. With such a format clergy can break up the worship form which itself expresses the view that the Old Testament always needs to be completed by the New Testament. This change, then, would serve to point to the Old Testament's integrity, which includes its "plus" contributions to the faith community.

Both the Old Testament and New Testament, together, are Christian scripture. The one without the other cannot be the scripture of the church.

38. See, for example, the many scholars cited in this volume.

CHAPTER 9

Jesus: Human and Divine

PART 1
JESUS IN THE NEW TESTAMENT:
IMAGES FROM THE OLD TESTAMENT

Synopsis

The numerous images of Jesus in the New Testament, rooting in the Old Testament and Judaism, depict him as both human and divine. This paradoxical witness puzzles many Christians. In an attempt to understand the affirmation of Jesus' divinity (especially the title "God" ascribed to him), we concentrate, in part 1, on various texts in the Bible and postbiblical Judaism which throw light upon our quest. Part 2 of this chapter concerns the interpretations of Jesus by early Christian councils, predominantly that of Nicaea, and their relationship to the scriptures. In the New Testament, as well as in the early creeds, we find the divinity of Jesus affirmed but not reduced to a literalism as if to declare that Jesus is actually God the Father, the God of Israel.

In both sections of this chapter we underscore the importance of Israelite and Jewish Wisdom traditions and hold that a better appreciation of this kind of thinking can provide insight into the church's witness concerning the divinity of Jesus. Further, the figure of Wisdom continues today as an alive image that can assist the church as it reflects on Jesus and his relationship to God.

Early Christianity: A Jewish Movement

In some of the earlier chapters, we covered areas of continuity that exist between the Old Testament, Judaism, and the teachings of Jesus. So much of what we know of Jesus convinces us that he was not only born a Jew, but lived, taught, and died as a Jew. Although he challenged some traditional interpretations of the law, his teaching did not set him outside of the Jewish community.[1] Even where Jesus appears to have brought about a new emphasis in his teaching,[2] he probably did not move beyond the borders of Judaism.

The Judaism of Jesus' day was multifaceted, as may be seen by its ability to hold within itself such diverse parties as the Pharisees, Sadducees, Zealots, and Essenes. There was room for these very different groups, and undoubtedly there would have remained a place for Jesus also *if* further reflection concerning his identity and significance had not arisen. However, these reflections and affirmations *did* arise, some of which were doubtlessly rooted in Jesus' own self-awareness. Since that time Judaism and Christianity have known two thousand years of painful separation. Schalom ben Chorin focuses the relationship well when he describes Jesus both as a bridge and a chasm. He observes that "the belief *of* Jesus" (i.e., reflected in his teachings) unites Jews and Christians, but "the belief *in* Jesus" (i.e., the divine Jesus) separates the two faiths.[3]

The main difference, therefore, between Judaism and Christianity has to do with Christology, with the identity and significance of Jesus himself. In this chapter, however, we will not attempt to address fully the matter of Christology; we plan only: (1) to speak about the experience and reflection of the earliest followers of Jesus; (2) to indicate the

---

1. See recently Brad H. Young, who titles his book *Jesus the Jewish Theologian* (Peabody, Mass.: Hendrickson, 1995), p. xxxv: "Jesus' theology did not prompt his death. Jesus was killed as a devout Jew loyal to the heritage of his faith."

2. David Flusser, "Jesus and His Ancestry and Commandment of Love," in *Jesus' Jewishness,* ed. James H. Charlesworth (New York: Crossroad, 1991), p. 165, declares that Jesus built on "attitudes already established before his time," but he also speaks of the "revolutionary germ in Jesus' preaching" which had to do "with the radical commandment of love." Further, he comments: "He [Jesus] was closest to the Pharisees of the school of Hillel, who preached love, but he pointed the way further to unconditional love — even of one's enemies and of sinners" (p. 173).

3. Schalom Ben-Chorin, *Bruder Jesus: Der Nazarener in Jüdischer Sicht* (München: List Verlag, 1972), p. 12

crucial role played by the Old Testament and postbiblical Jewish literature in helping the early Christian community discover the identity of Jesus; (3) to examine the church's creedal statements (especially that of Nicaea) and their relationship to the biblical witness. The latter discussion will take place in part 2 of this chapter.

Who Is Jesus? Old Testament Images

In an attempt to understand Jesus, let us look at some images of him in the New Testament. In chapters 2 and 3 of this volume, we saw that early Christians attempted to *understand their experience* of him by "looking back" to their scripture, the Old Testament. Those who believed in Jesus were convinced that in his life, death, and resurrection something *extraordinary* had happened. They stood before a Wonder and were persuaded that they had entered into a *"new"* relationship with God.

But to understand fully what had *happened* meant confronting the *identity* of Jesus. Faced with the question, "Who is Jesus?" Jesus' followers turned to the scripture.[4] Here they found words and images that provided clues to his identity. However, the diversity of images taken over by the New Testament makes us aware that early Christians had not fixed their minds on *one true* statement concerning him. As they viewed Jesus through the eyes of faith, this image or that image came to mind.[5] These

---

4. Consult the fine study of Peter Müller, *"Wer ist dieser?": Jesus im Markusevangelium. Markus als Erzähler, Verkündiger und Lehrer,* Biblisch-Theologische Studien 27 (Neukirchen-Vluyn: Neukirchener Verlag, 1995). He demonstrates that the leading theme of the Gospel of Mark may be focused in the question: "Who is Jesus?" This question is repeatedly asked and answered by various persons mentioned in the Gospel (asked: 1:27; 4:41; 6:2f., 14-16; 8:27ff.; 14:61f.; answered: 4:41; 6:3, 16; 9:7; 10:47; 15:39). See Müller's discussion on pp. 9ff. and 139ff.

5. R. T. France is no doubt correct in understanding these designations (see the list below) as having rootage in early Christian worship rather than in speculative thinking. See, e.g., his article "Development in New Testament Christology," *Themelios* 18 (1992): 7. Of a similar view is Jürgen Habermann, *Präexistenzaussagen im Neuen Testament* (Frankfurt: Peter Lang, 1990), p. 429. Speaking of the christological expressions of the New Testament community, including those affirming preexistence, he observes that these declarations do not employ the precise terminology of philosophical, dogmatic speech. They reflect, rather, adoration rising from the worship life of the Christian community.

varied images were those that were alive in the first century. Nils Dahl comments that early Christians "had something to say about him [Jesus]" and very naturally used the language of their time to speak of their faith in him. Dahl visualizes the sources of these images as "springs from which people draw water."[6]

Jesus Is . . .

The following list (by no means complete) exhibits some prominent images of Jesus. He is:

— a man through whom God works (Acts 2:22 and 10:36-38)
— the second Moses (Acts 3:19-22)
— the second Adam (Rom. 5:14; 1 Cor. 15:22, 45)
— the source of a better hope, covenant, etc. (Heb. 7:19, 22; 8:6)
— greater than the temple, Jonah, and Solomon (Matt. 12:6, 41, 42)
— the son of Abraham (Matt. 1:1)
— the son of David (Matt. 1:1; 15:22)
— looked to by Moses and the prophets (John 1:45)
— the Messiah (John 1:41)
— before Abraham (John 8:58)
— the Son of God (Matt 2:15; 3:17; Luke 1:35; 1 John 4:15; 5:5)
— the Son of Man (Matt. 11:19; 12:40)
— the Wisdom of God (1 Cor. 1:24, 30)
— God (John 1:1-11, 18)

Biblical scholars agree that diverse images of Jesus are present in the New Testament, but they are *not* in agreement concerning the meaning of some of these images nor the significance of this diversity. The following paragraphs touch on this difference of opinion.

6. Nils Dahl, "Sources of Christological Language," in his book *Jesus the Christ: The Historical Origins of Christological Doctrine,* ed. D. H. Juel (Minneapolis: Fortress, 1991), p. 116.

Jesus: Human and Divine

Many of the images referred to in the above list (e.g., the first eight) mark Jesus as a most distinguished figure but do not, in any explicit sense, attribute to him a "divine" status. Even the view of Jesus as the Messiah may not have, at first, set Jesus apart from the Jewish tradition in which the Messiah was considered to be a human being — even if one highly exalted.[7] However, at some time in the first century (perhaps early),[8] "divine" aspects regarding Jesus began to surface more frequently and messianic hope took on a very different character. Jesus was thought to be a divine Messiah, a savior of the world who came to forgive sin and establish a spiritual kingdom. Nils Dahl observes: "What is amazing is the degree to which the image of Jesus the Christ diverges from all known variants of 'messianic' expectations."[9] This divergent view of the Messiah, which is seen in words spoken about or attributed to Jesus, no doubt resulted from a loss of contact with the Jewish context. Raymond Brown observes that members of the developing Christian community reflected on the identity and significance of Jesus and in so doing moved away from Jewish views of the Messiah who was expected to transform Jewish society. Christian reflection, says Brown, focused on a Messiah who would establish a spiritual kingdom.[10] "It is inaccurate and unjust to say that

7. See, however, David Flusser, "The Concept of the Messiah," in *Jewish Sources in Early Christianity* (New York: Adam Books, 1987), pp. 55-60. He observes that among the variety of conceptions concerning the Messiah is the view of a "superhuman" figure: "In the Midrashic literature, the ways of the Messiah acquire a dimension which is beyond everyday life and passes human understanding" (p. 56). Further, he views the New Testament as a source for understanding the Jewish tradition(s) of its day: "Since Jesus was regarded as Messiah and Son of God and was literally identified with God, the New Testament has preserved expressions and views current in Judaism at the time of Jesus and ascribed to him" (p. 58). See also Flusser, *Judaism and the Origins of Christianity* (Jerusalem: Magnes Press, 1988), p. xii.

8. See Dahl, *Jesus the Christ*, p. 129, who thinks that the ascribing of preexistence to Jesus could have happened early. In any case he holds that there is no "trajectory that led from a 'low' to a 'high' Christology" (p. 130; cf. also p. 128).

9. Dahl, *Jesus the Christ*, p. 118. One example may be noted. Nowhere in the Old Testament or in Jewish literature does the Messiah forgive sin or come to establish a spiritual kingdom.

10. Raymond Brown, *An Introduction to New Testament Christology* (New York: Paulist, 1994), pp. 145-46.

the Jews of Jesus' time had corrupted the idea of the Messiah as a spiritual savior by making it secular and nationalistic and that Jesus restored the concept to its pristine meaning." Continuing, Brown declares: "The Christian understanding of a spiritual Messiah with a kingdom not of this world represented a change rather than a restoration — a change that Christians believe brought the development of the messianic expectation to a rich fruition, but a change nevertheless."[11] But not only did the Christian view of the Messiah distance itself from the Old Testament and Judaism in representing Jesus as a "spiritual" Messiah, it stretched the Hebrew-Jewish traditions to their outer limits with its prominent use of terminology that pointed to Jesus' divine status. Few scholars agree with David Flusser concerning the existence of a "superhuman" Messiah concept in Judaism. However, even if one should agree with Professor Flusser that one can discover some trace of a "superhuman" Messiah in these traditions, this view was decidedly in the minority and achieved little visibility in the Jewish tradition. In Christianity, on the other hand, it is the "divinity" of Jesus that has come to be the predominant theme. The following paragraphs will sum up briefly the thought of contemporary scholarly discussion concerning Jesus' divinity in the New Testament.

A Divine Jesus: Evolution or Development?

As may be seen in some of the images and titles listed above, Jesus is affirmed to be basically a man through whom God works, but in other images he is looked upon as a divine figure to whom is ascribed even the title "God." It is generally agreed among scholars that the Christian ascription of divinity to Jesus represents a view that moved the Christian movement beyond the borders of traditional Jewish interpretation. But how are we to understand the rise of this view? Scholars disagree. Some hold that these images of divinity, especially the attribution of "God" to Jesus, are examples of *evolutionary thinking* on the part of early Christians — an evolution from the earliest (authentic) view of Je-

11. Brown, *Christology*, p. 160 n. 220. In agreement is Barry L. Bandstra, *Reading the Old Testament* (Belmont, Calif.: Wadsworth, 1995), p. 516: "Jesus did not fit that mold [of the Old Testament and Judaism], yet his followers still proclaimed him Messiah. They could do this only by redefining the nature of the Kingdom of God to be a spiritual and moral kingdom."

sus as basically a man to a view (influenced by Hellenistic thinking) which "deifies" him.[12]

Other scholars, however, look at the diversity of images and divine titles and come to a different conclusion. One should not speak, they say, about evolution of thought but of a *valid development* of something that was already there in Jesus himself. R. T. France, for example, addresses the amazing variety of imagery in the New Testament and declares that in the beginning of the Jesus movement "mainly Jewish categories" were used. But later, he says, as Christianity spread among Gentiles, "Greek philosophical categories came to be adopted."[13] He agrees, however, with the view expressed some twenty years ago by C. F. D. Moule, that these later images depicting Jesus as divine are founded in the reality of Jesus himself and not in sources alien to him.[14] Holding the same position is Martin Hengel: "The unfolding of New Testament christology . . . was not idle speculation or haphazard mythological 'wild growth'. We find rather an amazing inner consistency from the oldest Christian confession to the Prologue of the Fourth Gospel."[15] David Flusser gives — within limits — some support for this view. He thinks that the higher, divine, designations attributed to Jesus may have had their roots in Jesus' own "exalted self awareness," that is, in his "personal experience of divine sonship."[16]

12. See recently P. M. Casey, *From Jewish Prophet to Gentile God: The Origins and Development of New Testament Christology* (Cambridge: James Clarke, 1991).

13. France, "Development in New Testament Christology," p. 4.

14. C. F. D. Moule, *The Origins of Christology* (Cambridge: Cambridge University Press, 1977), pp. 2-3. See also Peter Stuhlmacher, *Jesus of Nazareth — Christ of Faith* (Peabody, Mass.: Hendrickson, 1993), p. 7. A similar opinion has been expressed most recently by H. Douglas Buckwalter, who summarizes and expounds the views of Hengel, Moule, Howard Marshall, and others in "The Origin of Christology: Evolution or Explosion?" *Evangelical Journal* 14 (1996): 9-24.

15. Martin Hengel, *Studies in Early Christology* (Edinburgh: T. & T. Clark, 1995), p. 389. See also his comments on p. 383, where he discusses the prologue in the Gospel of John, Hebrews, and Phil. 2:6-11: "Christological thinking between 50 and 100 CE was much more unified in its basic structure than New Testament research, in part at least, has maintained. Basically, the later developments are already there in a nutshell in the Philippian hymn. This means, however, with regard to the development of all the early Church's christology, that more happened in the first twenty-years than in the entire later, centuries long development of dogma."

16. Flusser, *Judaism*, pp. 619, xxi. This manner of Jesus' self-awareness is not surprising, suggests Flusser, because Jewish texts indicate that Hillel, the great

New Testament: Jesus Is Divine

The question persists: Do the divine titles represent an *evolution* of the Christian witness, one not grounded in early Christianity, or do they represent a *development* of a reality that was present at the beginning?[17] The truth concerning these two positions can never be demonstrated to the satisfaction of everyone because of questions relating to the texts involved (e.g., dating, meaning, and translation). The view of James Dunn appeals to us. He rejects the idea that the divine titles represent *simply* an evolution of thought concerning Jesus, but he questions also the view of Moule, France, and others which affirms that these titles are *simply* the unfolding of what was already there in Jesus. Finding neither of the two views fully satisfying, Dunn declares that the use of these divine images "involved an inner dynamic (the inner dynamic of religious experience and worship) and that it was *understood* by the participants as an unfolding of the truth of Christ. . . ."[18]

The divinity of Jesus, affirmed by early Christians, was not created out of nothing. It had its origin in the Wonder that they experienced through him. In meeting Jesus, Christians believed that they were, in some manner, in the presence of God. Such an experience excited thought concerning the significance of Jesus himself. Any reading of the present text of the New Testament makes one aware that the Christian witness of Jesus extends beyond the praise given to "ordi-

---

Jewish teacher who lived shortly before Jesus, had expressed "high consciousness about himself." Flusser notes that Hillel's "self-esteem was . . . so exceptionally high that in later rabbinical tradition it was often denied that he really spoke about himself . . . but it was assumed that he was referring to God" (p. 510). But the parallel with Jesus is not as strong as it may first appear because, as Flusser observes, Hillel's "high self-awareness is not limited to his person, but is paradigmatic for everyone" (p. 513).

17. The complete issue of the *Lexington Theological Quarterly* 31 (1996) contains a lively discussion of this subject. See especially the contribution of Ben Witherington III, who addresses numerous questions of the "minimalists" (i.e., the Jesus Seminar), and over against them holds "that there was some Christological content either explicit or implicit in Jesus' life, words and teachings, . . . that his followers later understood and amplified . . ." (p. 160; cp. p. 165).

18. James Dunn, "The Making of Christology — Evolution or Unfolding?" in *Jesus of Nazareth: Lord and Christ,* ed. J. B. Green and M. Turner (Grand Rapids: Wm. B. Eerdmans Publishing Co., 1994), p. 452, emphasis mine.

nary" great figures. A number of titles, images, and narratives point to his intimate relationship with God. How intimate this relationship was is a matter over which there is a difference of opinion. But we believe that all of these references to the divinity of Jesus represent the truth of the early church's reflection on its experience with him.[19] Declares Martin Hengel: "It is just the diverse and numerous titles and names that express Jesus' unique 'worthiness' which at the same time demonstrates the intensity of the early Christian experience of salvation."[20]

But this confession of Jesus' divinity, arising out of the early community's experience of God's presence with them, has created persistent puzzlement (not to speak of controversy) within the church. For this reason, therefore, we concentrate on this aspect of Jesus in the pages that follow. Although a number of images and titles place Jesus in the divine realm, it is the use of the title "God" in some New Testament texts that expresses this claim most forcefully and therefore surfaces as the most questionable.

Jesus Addressed as "God"

Scholars, representing a wide span of theological opinion, are generally agreed that the title "God" does not occur often in the New Testament and that it represents a further (later) development of theological reflection about Jesus. R. T. France, for example, concedes that the use of the title "God" for Jesus is "very rare in the NT, and occurs almost exclusively . . . in the later writings." He points to the disputed passage in Romans 9:5 as an exception to the late dating of this title's use.[21] Else-

19. In similar fashion one can say that the Jewish interpretations of Torah, even those that ascribe to it "preexistence," reflect the truth of the *Jewish experience* with the Torah.

20. Hengel, p. 370. Similarly, Gerald O'Collins, *Christology: A Biblical, Historical, and Systematic Study of Jesus Christ* (Oxford: Oxford University Press, 1995), p. 154.

21. France, "Development in New Testament Christology," p. 4. See also his earlier essay, "The Worship of Jesus: A Neglected Factor in Christological Debate?" in *Christ the Lord: Studies in Christology Presented to Donald Guthrie,* ed. H. H. Rowdon (Downers Grove, Ill.: InterVarsity, 1982), p. 23. Regarding the ascription of "God" to Jesus, he says: "We will find ourselves disappointed that in many cases the apparent direct attribution of divinity to Jesus melts away in the light of uncertainty about either the text, or the punctuation, or the syntax, leav-

where, however, he argues that divine aspects of Jesus are reflected already in early stages of the Christian movement and that the use of the title "God" for Jesus is an outgrowth of an already established insight into his identity.[22] Without debating how the title "God" relates to views of Jesus in early Christianity, we accept the fact that these texts *are* a part of the witness of the New Testament authors to Christ.

Raymond Brown's middle-of-the-road comments concerning the occurrence of "God" in the New Testament would find acceptance among numerous scholars. He holds that five New Testament texts "probably" refer to Jesus as "God," and three appear to do so with clarity.[23] Concerning these passages, he declares:

> As far as I can see, none of the eight instances we have discussed attempts to define Jesus metaphysically. The acclamation of Jesus as God is a response of prayer and worship to the God revealed in Jesus. . . . Thus, even though we have seen that there is a solid biblical precedent for calling Jesus God, we must be cautious to evaluate this usage in terms of the NT ambiance.[24]

---

ing us with no undisputed (or almost undisputed!) direct attribution of divinity to Jesus outside the opening and closing declarations of the Gospel of John (Jn. 1:1; 1:18; 20:28)." However, he finds that other texts in the New Testament point in this direction (see pp. 29-36).

22. France, "The Worship of Jesus," pp. 26-35. See also the observation on p. 25: "The wonder is not that the New Testament so seldom describes Jesus as God, but that in such a milieu [i.e., Jewish monotheism] it does at all. There must have been a very strong compulsion behind such a radical conversion of language." This comment has weight, but one needs to inquire what the New Testament writers intended when they spoke of Jesus as "God." See our further discussion.

23. E.g., John 1:18; Titus 2:13; Rom. 9:5; 1 John 5:20; 2 Pet. 1:1 (probably); and Heb. 1:8-9; John 1:1; 20:28 (clearly). In addition there are passages similar to John 10:30, "'The Father and I are one.'" However, such passages should not be interpreted to mean that there is some kind of ontological identity existing between Jesus and God. Gerhard Forde, *Theology Is for Proclamation* (Minneapolis: Fortress, 1990), p. 111, comments: "Precisely by being not God the Father, Jesus demonstrates his personal unity with the Father. By being precisely the truly human one he shows who the Father is. Thus in obedience to the Father the Johannine Jesus can rightly say, 'I [as one who is not the Father] and the Father are one' (John 10:30). As the human he is, he is perfectly in accord with the will of God. 'My food is to do the will of him who sent me, and to accomplish his work' (John 4:34)."

24. Brown, *Christology*, p. 195.

Brown's statement that New Testament texts which refer to Jesus as God should be interpreted "in terms of the NT ambiance" is an important caution — one that he heeds himself. Thus, for example, when Brown speaks of Jesus as "true God of true God," he does so firmly but carefully in the *relational language* of the New Testament: "Only if Jesus is truly *of God* do we know what God is like, for in Jesus we see God *translated* into terms that we can understand. . . . Only if Jesus is truly *of God* do we know that God's love reached the point of personal self-giving."[25] Klaus Berger approaches the issue of Jesus as "God" in a manner similar to that of Brown. He comments that when Jesus is named God, as for example in the Gospel of John, this should *not* be understood as if he is considered " 'the God', namely, 'the only God and Father'. He is and remains the 'Son'." To be called God means "that the Father has put his 'Word' in him and therefore is present *(anwesend)* in him. . . . it does not mean that the Son is the Father."[26]

Hebrews 1:8: "Your Throne, O God [Jesus]"

The above important text from Hebrews helps us to understand and appreciate the views expressed by Brown and Berger. Hebrews 1:8-9 cites the Greek (Septuagint) version of Psalm 44:7-8 (Heb. Ps. 45:7-8) as if it were addressed to Christ:

> But of the Son he says,
> "Your throne, *O God* [Jesus], is forever and ever, . . .
> You have loved righteousness and hated wickedness;
> therefore *[O] God* [Jesus], *your God,* has anointed you. . . ."[27]

25. Brown, *Christology,* pp. 150-51, emphasis mine.

26. Klaus Berger, *Wer war Jesus Wirklich?* (Stuttgart: Quell, 1995), p. 126. See also Brown, *Christology,* p. 149, who, as Berger, uses the word "present" to represent a high Christology: "Already in Jesus' lifetime there were many indications that God was not only acting in Jesus but was present in him." Donald Frisk, *This We Believe* (Chicago: Covenant Press, 1981), p. 81, speaking of the "true deity" of Jesus, chooses the same kind of expression: "With remarkable unanimity the New Testament writers witness to the conviction that in Jesus God was uniquely present." Such phrasing emphasizes the unique relationship of Jesus to God without opening the church to the danger of literalism.

27. Although there is some dispute concerning the translation of these

Psalm 45, cited above by the author of Hebrews, concerns the king of Israel. In Hebrew thought an aura of divinity surrounded the king because God exercised rule through him. But the king was not himself divine even though he could be addressed as "God."[28] For the translators of the Septuagint, this title did *not* have the literalistic meaning that the king was a divine being. When we consider what this title means for Jesus, we must be aware that even this title, "God," in the context of biblical language, has some flexibility. To be sure, in attributing the title "God" to Jesus, it appears that early Christians conceived of Jesus as greater than the "divinely anointed" king (e.g., Jesus is greater than Solomon, Matt. 12:42), but this is not immediately to conclude that Jesus is considered to be *the* God, the God of Israel. The context of the usage in Hebrews alerts us that the author of Hebrews is not attempting to proclaim Jesus as "the God" because he continues the citation which affirms that Jesus ("O God") is *anointed by God* "with the oil of gladness."[29]

---

verses, the above translation, in which "God" stands in the vocative (i.e., "O God"), represents the view of most commentators. For a thorough discussion of the evidence concerning the two views both in Hebrews as well as in Psalm 45, see Dale F. Leschert, *Hermeneutical Foundations of Hebrews: A Study in the Validity of the Epistle's Interpretation of Some Core Citations from the Psalms,* Dissertation Series, no. 10, National Association of Baptist Professors of Religion (Lewiston: Mellen, 1995), pp. 24-78. Among scholars favoring the above translation are: Harold W. Attridge, *The Epistle to the Hebrews,* Hermeneia (Philadelphia: Fortress, 1989), pp. 58-59 and n. 95; Murray Harris, "The Translation and Significance of *ho theos* in Hebrews 1:6-9," *Tyndale Bulletin* 36 (1985): 129-62 (esp. pp. 142, 149-50; see references); Brown, *Christology,* pp. 185-87; Leslie C. Allen, "Psalm 45:7-8 (6-7) in Old and New Testament Settings," in *Christ the Lord,* p. 235; F. F. Bruce, *The Epistle to the Hebrews* (Grand Rapids: Eerdmans, 1964), p. 19.

28. See, e.g., Murray Harris, "Elohim in Psalm 45," *Tyndale Bulletin* 35 (1984): 65-89 (esp. pp. 83-85; see references to other works).

29. Attridge, p. 60, comments that "the author [of Hebrews] does not simply assimilate Christ as God to the Father." Further, in n. 108 on the same page he observes that the author attributes "*some* divine status to the Son, but makes clear that he is distinct from the Father." See also the careful discussion of Joseph Fitzmyer, *A Christological Catechism: New Testament Answers* (New York: Paulist, 1980), pp. 82-91 (esp. pp. 90-91), who shares, in general, the opinion of Attridge regarding the New Testament witness.

"God": An "Upper Limit" Title

Martin Hengel, writing concerning the use of the title "God" in Judaism and Christianity, observes that Judaism of the first century "was reluctant to transfer the term 'God' directly to a heavenly mediator figure, although it did not rule it out completely. It was expressed as a kind of *'upper limit' statement. . . .*" He comments further: "Even rabbinic mysticism knew godlike mediators such as Metatron, who was named 'the little Yahweh',[30] and the Essenes of Qumran dared to refer a passage such as Isa. 52:7, 'Your God has become King', to the heavenly redeemer of the Sons of Light, Michael — Melchizedek."[31] Such examples as the above make the interpreter aware that the term "God" as it occurred in postbiblical Jewish texts had a more flexible meaning than the term may have in contemporary Western languages.[32]

Usually the title was reserved for the One who created the universe, but at times it could be used of beings that were thought to be intimately related to God. Though the title could stretch to include such

---

30. Compare Justin Martyr (second century), who referred to Jesus as a "second God."

31. Hengel, pp. 367-68, emphasis mine. For further discussion of the above title for Melchizedek at Qumran, see Allen, pp. 241-42. See also John 10:33-36, where Jesus is accused of presenting himself as God. In his reply Jesus uses the title "God's Son" and defends himself by referring to Ps. 82:6, where the Israelites are called "gods ['*elohim*]."

32. Some recent studies of the nature of Jewish monotheism have pointed out that Jews in *worship* may have held to a strict monotheism — worshiping only the one God. However, at another level Jewish monotheism appeared able to allow reference to beings who bore divine titles (see, e.g., above). Larry W. Hurtado, "What Do We Mean by 'First-Century Jewish Monotheism'?" in *Seminary Papers,* ed. E. H. Lovering, Jr. (Atlanta: Scholars Press, 1993), p. 367, summarizes his view: "This commitment to the one God of Israel accommodated a large retinue of heavenly beings distinguished from God more in degree than kind as to their attributes, some of these beings portrayed as in fact sharing quite directly in God's powers and even his name." See also p. 364. An earlier and fuller discussion of the subject may be found in Hurtado's book: *One God, One Lord: Early Christian Devotion and Ancient Jewish Monotheism* (Philadelphia: Fortress, 1988). In substantial agreement with Hurtado is Marinus De Jonge, "Monotheism and Christology," in *Early Christian Thought in Its Jewish Context,* ed. J. Barclay and J. Sweet (Cambridge: Cambridge University Press, 1996), pp. 225-37. See esp. p. 226. Dale Leschert's discussion of Heb. 1:8-10 (Leschert, pp. 65-78) offers examples of the flexibility of meaning in '*elohim* and similar terms within the Old Testament itself.

personages, few people would have been confused as to its main refer-
ent. It was a title that belonged with fullest right to the Divine One worshiped by Moses and the prophets. Against this background then, we
can understand the use of the title "God" in the New Testament. In this
scripture "God" is a title that first and foremost belongs to the Father,
the God of Israel, but on occasion it could be used of Jesus. This divine
title, attributed to Jesus, however, does not arise out of a probing philosophical inquiry concerning the being of Jesus but, rather, out of the
wonder and devotion that resulted from the community's experience
with him.[33] Possibly Leslie Houlden's description of what happened
gives expression to the manner in which Christians crossed the bound-
ary and appropriated the title "God" for Jesus: "From the perspective
of Christian devotion to Jesus, it was probably crossed without full
awareness of what had been done. . . ."[34]

Nevertheless, Christian familiarity with Judaism's ability to affirm
one God while making room for other "divine" beings no doubt played
an important role in ascribing divinity to Jesus. References to these figures in Jewish writings provided the vocabulary and imagery that as-
sisted early Christians in understanding and articulating the meaning of
the exalted, resurrected Christ.[35] However, this does not mean that the
honor given Christ in the early Christian community was exactly that
given to divine agents within Judaism. The similarities are arresting, but
Hurtado maintains that the devotion and honor offered Jesus went significantly beyond that which was given divine agents in Judaism. He believes therefore that early Christian devotion to Jesus was a "modifica-
tion" or "innovation" of the monotheistic belief found in the Jewish
tradition.[36] Early Christians continued to hold to the monotheistic be-

33. So also Hurtado, *One God, One Lord,* p. 122.
34. Leslie Houlden, *JESUS, A Question of Identity* (London: SPCK, 1992),
p. 65.
35. See Hurtado, *One God, One Lord,* pp. 17-92, regarding divine agents in
Jewish monotheism.
36. Hurtado, *One God, One Lord,* pp. 93-124. James Dunn, "Was Christianity a Monotheistic Faith from the Beginning?" *Scottish Journal of Theology* 35
(1982): 336, declares: "But because it was the one God of Jewish faith whom
those first Christians recognized in and through this Jesus it was a redefinition
and not an abandoning of that monotheism." See also Michael Theobald, "Gott,
Logos und Pneuma. 'Trinitarische' Rede von Gott im Johannesevangelium," in
*Monotheismus und Christologie: Zur Gottesfrage im Hellenistischen Judentum und im
UrChristentum,* ed. Hans-Josef Klauck (Freiburg: Herder, 1992), pp. 42-43, who

lief inherited from Israel and postbiblical Judaism even though their exaltation of the divinity of Christ was without real parallel in Judaism. Nevertheless, Hurtado holds back from asserting that Jesus is conceived of as *the* God in the New Testament. Commenting on Philippians 2:5-11, Hurtado says:

> This stunning description of the exalted Christ is clearly not intended to make him a rival to God. Christ's unparalleled status has been given to him by God (v. 9), and the universal acclamation of Jesus in v. 11 is "to the glory of God the Father." That is, Christ holds his exalted heavenly status by the pleasure of God the Father, and the acclamation of Christ which is mandated by God is thus an affirmation of God's supremacy and sovereignty.[37]

Although from a Christian point of view exaltation of Christ constituted no rejection of monotheism, one can well understand the reservations of non-Christian Jews regarding this development. Jews came to view Christian devotion to Christ as inconsistent with the confession and worship of the one God. For this reason they opposed the new Christian movement which began as a development within Judaism. The controversy reflected in the Gospel of John, the latest of the Gospels, may reflect the strong disapproval that many Jews had to affirmations of divinity.[38]

---

holds that the Christian proclamation concerning Jesus assumed without question the uniqueness or singularity of God, affirmed in the Shema. In the Christian exaltation of Jesus, he says, this confession of the oneness of God "became only newly assessed" *(wurde nur neu gewichtet)*. It did not represent a basic compromise of the monotheism inherited from Judaism.

37. Hurtado, *One God, One Lord,* p. 97.

38. In the Gospel of John one can see an example of opposition to the "divinity" of Jesus (5:18; 10:31-33). However, it may be also that the Gospel of John illustrates a Christian response to Jewish accusations of blasphemy. In this Gospel, which underscores the divinity of Christ more than any other Gospel, one finds strong affirmations of the priority of the God of Israel (5:19: "'the Son can do nothing on his own'" [also 5:30]). See the comments of Theobald, pp. 62-63. For a listing of other similar passages in John, see Raymond Brown, *The Gospel according to John, 1–12,* Anchor Bible (Garden City, N.Y.: Doubleday, 1966), p. 407.

The New Testament Refrains
from Saying "Jesus Is God"

The New Testament's commitment to the Jewish traditional emphasis on the oneness of God would have made first-century Christians cautious in using the title "God." As we have noted, this title is not often employed of Jesus, but when it is used of him (usually in the later writings of the New Testament) it should not be seen as a renunciation of Jewish monotheism. The New Testament authors stand with non-Christian Jews in the worship of the one God.

It may be observed that the direct, simple statement, "Jesus is God," is missing from the New Testament.[39] Such a declaration would have said more than early Christians wanted to say.[40] Even John 1:1 lacks this clear declaration, because it states that "the *Word (logos)* — not Jesus — was with God and the *Word* was God." True, the Gospel writer declares that this "*Word became* flesh and lived among us" *in* Jesus, but this is not the same as declaring: "Jesus is God."[41]

Observing this hesitancy of New Testament writers, many biblical

39. This is the conclusion of Murray J. Harris, *Jesus as God: The New Testament Use of Theos in Reference to Jesus* (Grand Rapids: Baker, 1992), pp. 271 and 297, even though he cites passages in the New Testament where *theos* (God) is *applied* to Jesus by New Testament writers.

40. To be sure, there are words and titles that walk along the edge of such an assertion, as for example the title "LORD (= Yahweh)." But the use of this title does not have the same weight as the simple declaration "Jesus is God." See the study of this title in David B. Capes, *Old Testament Yahweh Texts in Paul's Christology* (Tübingen: J. C. B. Mohr, 1992), who undertakes a full study of *kurios* in Paul's Christology. On p. 164, under the heading "Jesus Is Yahweh," he states: "It [i.e., the title, LORD = Yahweh] implies that he [Paul] considered Jesus to be more than a man. It suggests that he believed that Christ was *in some manner* Yahweh manifest as the Messiah" (emphasis mine). Of a similar mind is Fitzmyer, p. 90.

41. See the informative discussion of Richard L. Sturch, "Can One Say 'Jesus Is God'?" in *Christ the Lord,* pp. 326-40. Sturch observes that while the New Testament holds to the divinity of Jesus, neither in the New Testament nor for that matter in the early church councils (Nicaea and Chalcedon) is it declared outright that "Jesus is God." He comments, for example, that Chalcedon's double declaration that Jesus is "fully God and fully man" contains within itself a sophisticated ambiguity that keeps one from shortening the statement to a declaration that "Jesus is God." In no way, however, says Sturch, are these observations an argument against an incarnational theology. See esp. pp. 326-29.

scholars exercise care in their choice of words when speaking of the divinity of Jesus; they do not wish to proclaim that which the New Testament itself does not affirm. We have seen such care exercised by scholars already discussed (e.g., Raymond Brown, Klaus Berger), and it is also evidenced by others. For example, Leslie Houlden addresses this issue in a section of his book entitled "Jesus Is God." He demonstrates that such affirmations were made or implied in the post–New Testament church and holds that such a belief has roots in Judaism. Further, he is convinced that the New Testament points to an extraordinary intimacy between the God of Israel and Jesus, but draws back from the literalism, "Jesus (really) *is* God." Rather, he indicates the character of "is" by setting it in apposition with "shows," as in the following statement: "Jesus 'shows', 'is', God to us." Further, he affirms: "The basic Christian sense was, 'God has drawn near in Jesus — no longer does he speak to us from the other side.' Divine transcendence was overcome yet not negated."[42] The New Testament texts do not provide an extended discussion of the meaning of the title "God" when applied to Jesus, but it is clear that they hold him to stand in "intimacy" with God and are convinced that God's presence dwells in him as in no other.[43] But to move beyond some such general terminology in understanding the ascription of "God" to Jesus places one in danger of wringing from an expression of adoration a significance that it did not have within the Jewish and Christian traditions.

The fact that Hebrews 1 can call Jesus "God" while still affirming that he is anointed by God, gives ample indication that the author was not employing this title in any literalistic fashion. At the same time, however, he did not satisfy our yearning for greater analysis and precision by elaborating on what *exactly* was intended. Perhaps he understood that the power of imagery is frequently destroyed when it is explained!

---

42. Houlden, pp. 65-66. See pp. 58-66 for the fuller discussion. Consult further Sturch, p. 327.

43. Martin Hengel, focusing on John 1 and 1 John 1–2, comments: "In the Son who has become human, God's love, his very nature, has become manifest for humankind; God himself comes to them. The *incarnation of the love* of God, *not* the deification of Christ, is the main theme of Johannine theology." See Hengel, p. 368, emphasis mine.

Wisdom and the Divinity of Jesus

In our day there is a great deal of scholarly activity attempting to interpret and restate a high Christology while listening to the New Testament and the historic church confessions.[44] One approach that has shown increasing fruitfulness is viewing Jesus in the light of the Wisdom tradition. Today there is wide agreement among biblical scholars that Wisdom thinking, represented in the Old Testament and post-biblical Judaism, had a strong influence on the New Testament's portrayal of Jesus. This influence is easily discovered in the *teachings* of Jesus,[45] and it has left a discernible mark on the New Testament's *interpretation of his identity*.[46] The Wisdom tradition is not, of course, the only source for New Testament Christology.[47] It is, however, an important and embracing tradition which provided words and imagery by which Christians were able to articulate better their experience of Jesus Christ. The following texts from the Old and New Testaments as well as from postbiblical Jewish literature demonstrate the extent to which New Testament Christology is indebted to Wisdom thinking.

44. Gerd Theissen, "Zur Entstehung des Christentum aus dem Judentum," *Kirche und Israel* (1988): 186-87, understands that some Christian scholars have difficulty affirming a "high Christology" because it has too often inspired anti-Judaism and anti-Semitism in Christianity. Nevertheless, he counsels Christians not to restrict their faith to some form of "historical Jesus" in an attempt to escape the danger of a negative stance toward Judaism. Rather, he says, because Christian identity is bound up with a "high Christology," the church must hold to it and interpret it in a manner that no longer becomes a source for anti-Semitism.

45. See recently Hengel, pp. 73-93 ("Jesus as Messianic Teacher of Wisdom and the Beginnings of Christology"); Ben Witherington III, *Jesus the Sage: The Pilgrimage of Wisdom* (Minneapolis: Fortress, 1994); Celia M. Deutsch, *Lady Wisdom, Jesus, and the Sages* (Valley Forge, Pa.: Trinity Press International, 1996), pp. 81-110.

46. See, e.g., James Reese, "Christ as Wisdom Incarnate," *Biblical Theology Bulletin* 11 (1981): 44-47; Herman von Lips, "Christus als Sophia? Weisheitliche Traditionen in der urchristlichen Christologie," in *Anfänge der Christologie*, ed. C. Braytenbach and H. Paulsen (Göttingen: Vandenhoeck & Ruprecht, 1991), pp. 93ff.; Habermann, pp. 425-30; Witherington, *Jesus the Sage*, pp. 201-8; Deutsch, pp. 42-80 and 144-47.

47. For other sources see, e.g., the priestly tradition and the traditions associated with creation (e.g., Jesus as the new Adam and Jesus bringing about a new creation).

Jesus as Wisdom Incarnate

In the comparison of biblical texts listed below, we are not affirming that the New Testament texts correspond exactly to those out of the Old Testament or Jewish literature. It is clear that there are differences in some of the details. We wish to demonstrate only that there are remarkable *similarities* between these texts, which indicate that Wisdom thinking is the thought world out of which the "high" Christology of the New Testament is born.

1. Wisdom: With God at creation (Prov. 8:27-30; Wis. 9:9; Sir. 1:1)
   Jesus: With God at creation (John 1:8)
2. Wisdom: God created humanity by Wisdom (Wis. 7:22; 9:1-2; Prov. 8:27ff.)
   Jesus: God created the world by the Word (Jesus) (John 1:3)[48]
3. Wisdom: The "pure emanation of the glory of God" (Wis. 7:25-26)
   Jesus: "Reflection of God's glory and the exact imprint of God's very being" (Heb. 1:3; cf. Col. 1:15ff.)
4. Wisdom: Wisdom has its dwelling place in Israel (Sir. 34:8; Wis. 9:10; Prov. 8:31)
   Jesus: Jesus has come from God into this world (John 1:1, 9-11)
5. Wisdom: Invitation to draw near, bear Wisdom's yoke and learn (Sir. 51:23ff.)
   Jesus: Invitation to draw near, take "my yoke . . . and learn from me" (Matt. 11:28ff.)
6. Wisdom: Whoever finds Wisdom, finds life (Prov. 8:35; Bar. 4:1)
   Jesus: Jesus is the giver of life (John 6:33-35; 10:10)
7. Wisdom: People reject Wisdom and find ruin (Prov. 1:24-31; 8:36; Sir. 15:7)
   Jesus: People who reject Jesus are "lost" (John 3:16-21)

---

48. In some texts Word and Wisdom are closely allied (e.g., Wis. 9:1-2). See Raymond Brown's discussion in *The Gospel according to John*, I, pp. 521-22.

In addition to the above comparisons, one should consider some other passages in the New Testament which speak specifically of Jesus as the Wisdom of God, for example:

— Luke 11:49 (referring to Jesus): "'Therefore also the Wisdom of God said.'"[49]
— 1 Corinthians 1:24: "Christ . . . the wisdom of God" (cf. 1 Cor. 2:6ff.).
— 1 Corinthians 1:30: "Christ Jesus, who became for us wisdom from God."

David Flusser believes that behind New Testament Christology stands what he calls hypostatic entities, by which he means such figures as Wisdom, Word, and Shechinah.[50] These personifications are well known in rabbinic Judaism,[51] and one can readily agree that they played an important role in the christological thought of the early church. The last named personification, Shechinah, speaks of God's presence among his people and calls to mind John's declaration (1:14) that the "Word became flesh and dwelt among us."[52]

49. A comparison of this Lukan text with Matt. 23:34 demonstrates that Jesus is referring to himself with these words.
50. David Flusser, "The Jewish-Christian Schism, I," in *Judaism and the Origins of Christianity* (Jerusalem: Magnes Press, 1988), p. 623. To speak of a hypostasis is to refer to something that has almost individual existence apart from God. We believe that there is no true hypostasis in the Old Testament or in early Judaism. Such images constitute highly colored poetic speech and do not have a separate existence of their own. Therefore we prefer to use the term "personification" when speaking of these entities. Of similar thought is James Dunn, "Why 'Incarnation'?" in *Crossing the Boundaries,* ed. S. E. Porter et al. (Leiden: Brill, 1994), p. 248, and H. Jaeger, "The Patristic Conception of Wisdom in the Light of Biblical and Rabbinical Research," in *Studia Patristica,* IV, ed. F. L. Cross (Berlin: Akademie-Verlag, 1961), pp. 93-94.
51. See, e.g., J. Abelson, *The Immanence of God in Rabbinical Literature* (London, 1912).
52. The Christian incarnation theology, which is anchored in this text from John, is the point of separation between Jews and Christians. Nevertheless, several Jewish scholars have recently pointed to passages in the Hebrew Bible as well as in postbiblical Jewish literature that provide "some" contact with such thinking. See, e.g., Jacob Neusner, *The Incarnation of God: The Character of Divinity in Formative Judaism* (Philadelphia: Fortress, 1988), pp. 1-21 and 165-230. Consult also the contributions of Michael Wyschogrod in "A Jewish View of Christianity," in *To-*

Early Christians Experienced Jesus as the Wisdom of God

Few today would deny the influence that these personifications (especially "Wisdom") had on New Testament thinking about Jesus. Martin Hengel's arresting words sum up the thought of many biblical scholars:

> Early Christian thought was faced with the task of expressing the unique and surpassing worth of the revelation of God in his Christ, Jesus of Nazareth, in such a way that all previous Jewish exaltation and mediator conceptions of men of God, teachers, prophets and angels paled beside it. The linguistic means to express this worth was supplied out of hand by Jewish Wisdom teaching alone. To paraphrase Ernst Käsemann, one might describe it as the "mother of high christology."[53]

This does not mean that one can move without a ripple from Wisdom thinking to the belief that *Jesus* is "divine" or "God." Nevertheless, in the Hebrew-Jewish traditions, Wisdom is an exceptional figure — one who inhabits the divine realm. Identifying Jesus with Wisdom, however, involved taking a step never before taken. Up to the time of the Christian movement, Wisdom had never been identified with an

---

ward a Theological Encounter: Jewish Understandings of Christianity, ed. Leon Klenicki (Mahwah, N.J.: Paulist, 1991), pp. 114-15, as well as in "Incarnation," *Pro Ecclesia* 2 (1993): 208-11, and in *The Body of Faith* (New York: Seabury, 1983), pp. xv, 113, 212. Of a similar opinion is Ernst Hanspeter, "Rabbinische Traditionen über Gottes Nähe und Gottes Leid," in *Das Reden vom einen Gott bei Juden und Christen,* ed. C. Thoma and M. Wyschogrod (Frankfurt: Peter Lang, 1984), pp. 157-77. Some Christian scholars point in the same direction; e.g., Isaac Rottenberg, "'Comparative Theology' and 'Reactive Theology,'" *Pro Ecclesia* 3 (1994): pp. 413-14, and "Christian-Jewish Dialogue," *Journal of Ecumenical Studies* 29, no. 1 (1992): 89-90. W. F. Howard's discussion of *logos* in John, against the background of rabbinic literature and Philo (*Christianity according to St. John* [Philadelphia: Westminster, 1946], pp. 34-56), reflects a similar viewpoint.

53. Hengel, p. 116. Further (p. 117), regarding "the continuity between Jesus and the Son of God and Logos of early church christology," he declares that "the decisive link" has to do with "messianic Wisdom of Jesus and the influence of Wisdom motifs." See Witherington, *Jesus the Sage,* pp. 204 and 208, who holds that Jesus identified himself as a wisdom teacher *and* Wisdom itself.

historical individual.[54] But as early Christians experienced the redemptive work of God in the full event of Jesus (no doubt prompted, as Flusser said, by Jesus' own self-consciousness), they began to view him as one who was "greater than Solomon" (Matt. 12:42), Israel's wisest king. In their experience of Jesus, Christians believed that they met more than a wisdom teacher; they were in the presence of Wisdom itself.[55] James Dunn declares: "The first Christians found themselves compelled by their memory of Jesus and continuing spiritual experience to conclude that Jesus provided not just the pattern of humankind (Adam christology) but also the paradigm for God's self-revelation (Wisdom christology), the image of God in this twofold sense."[56] To early Christians then, who experienced the grace and truth of God in Jesus and who were looking to scripture for understanding of this extraordinary person, Wisdom theology provided an answer: He is the Wisdom of God (cf., e.g., 1 Cor. 1:24, 30).

In the following section (part 2), we intend to examine briefly the character of the post–New Testament creedal statements which speak to the identity and significance of Jesus, especially the creeds of Nicaea (321 C.E.) and Chalcedon (451 C.E.). In so doing we will listen in on the discussion of recent scholars as they attempt to understand the meaning of these creedal declarations and their relation to the New Testament witness. Further, we will indicate the important contributions of the Old Testament (especially regarding Wisdom) to a modern Christian view of Jesus.

54. Some postbiblical Jewish texts did, however, identify Wisdom with the Torah (e.g., Sir. 24:23 and Bar. 4:1). By means of this kind of comparison they were able to indicate the intimate relationship that existed between the Torah and God: the Torah represented God's very own teaching for his people.

55. No doubt we are to read Matt. 2:1-12 in the same manner: the wise men from the east, guided by a star (!) and bringing gifts of great value, *did not come* to welcome the birth of a wise teacher but rather of Wisdom itself.

56. J. Dunn, "Why 'Incarnation'?" in *Crossing the Boundaries,* p. 255. Geoffrey Wainwright, "The Doctrine of the Trinity: Where the Church Stands or Falls," *Interpretation* 45 (1991): 129 n. 25, counsels against using the expression "the triune God" because this abstracts a witness that arises out of the experience of faith.

160

PART 2
JESUS IN THE CREEDS:
WISDOM THEOLOGY IN GREEK DRESS

The Early Church: Knowing and
Not Knowing Who Jesus Is

In the first part of our discussion we noted the existence within the New Testament of diverse titles and images regarding Jesus Christ. The diversity represents the attempt of early Christians to find appropriate words to describe this One in whom they had a "meeting" with God — one which created for them a new way of life. In the post–New Testament period, the identity of Jesus continued to be an issue. Christians felt the need of interpreting the biblical witness but were not in full agreement as to how the texts of scripture should be interpreted. Some believed that the Bible identified Jesus, basically, as a human figure; they held that he was created by God and therefore not fully divine. To others the Bible supported an opposite view; namely, that Jesus was fully God and only appeared to be human. Although both of these views were rejected by the church, it is still a surprise to find two such opposite views of Jesus affirmed by Christians who were dedicated to interpreting the Bible. But such diverse interpretations could be held because of two factors relating to the scripture, namely: (1) the way the Bible was (and is still) used to support views of Christ that had been arrived at, for the most part, on other grounds;[57] (2) the charac-

---

57. See, e.g., the interpretation of Prov. 8:22 and 25 by some early church scholars who wished to support their belief that Jesus was human or that he was divine (cited by Manlio Simonetti, in *Biblical Interpretation in the Early Church: An Historical Introduction to Patristic Exegesis* (Edinburgh: T. & T. Clark, 1994), p. 128. Prov. 8:22 declares (LXX): "The Lord *created me* at the beginning of his ways for his works," while Prov. 8:25 states, "I was brought forth. . . ." The former verse was considered a reference to Jesus' human birth, whereas the latter was regarded as proof of his "divine generation by the Father." Simonetti's fuller discussion (pp. 121-32) gives rich insight into the manner in which early Christians handled scripture. John Calvin was at times very critical of the way in which the church founders used scripture. With regard to John 10:30 ("'The Father and I are one'"), Calvin observes (see his commentary on John): "The ancients misused this passage to prove that Christ is *homoousios* with the Father." Cited by Philip W. Butin, *Calvin, the Trinity, and the Divine-Human Relationship* (Ann Arbor: University Micro-films, 1991), p. 167 n. 66.

161

ter of the Bible itself; that is, the texts of scripture do not exhibit a "systematic theology," and therefore scriptural texts could (can) be cited against each other.[58]

It was only at the Council of Nicaea (325 C.E.) that one can see the beginning of the formation of a doctrine that has become the traditional form of Christian witness regarding Christ; Jesus is both divine (the second member of the Trinity) and human ("became incarnate and was made man, suffered . . .").[59] Although the Nicene Creed proclaims Jesus to be both human and divine, his humanity is not emphasized as strongly as his divinity. At a later meeting of the church in 451 (the Council of Chalcedon), a more balanced statement was arrived at; it underscored his humanity as well as his divinity: "our Lord Jesus Christ . . . the same perfect in Godhead, the same perfect in manhood, truly God and truly man. . . ."[60] On the following pages we will look at the biblical roots of these declarations and inquire as to their character.

Nicaea and Chalcedon: What Are They Saying?

The declarations of Nicaea and Chalcedon,[61] seemingly so direct and clear, did not silence difference of opinion in the early church, nor have they done so in the whole range of church history up to our own day.

---

58. One the one hand passages were employed to stress the full divinity of Christ — for example, such texts as John 1:1: "In the beginning was the Word, and the Word was with God, and the Word was God." But, on the other hand, there were passages cited in order to indicate a subordination of Christ the Son to God the Father, e.g., John 14:28: "'The Father is greater than I.'" See further Simonetti, pp. 126-30.

59. The Nicene formulation of 325 was recast by the Council of Constantinople in 381. This latter declaration is the one that has come down to us today.

60. For a full statement of both creeds (of Nicaea and Chalcedon), see Henry Bettenson, *Documents of the Christian Church*, 2nd ed. (Oxford: Oxford University Press, 1963), pp. 26 and 51-52, and Leo D. Davis, *The First Seven Ecumenical Councils (325-787): Their History and Theology* (Wilmington: Michael Glazier, 1987), pp. 60 and 186.

61. For further information concerning Nicaea and Chalcedon and the contexts in which the respective creeds were formed, see the following volumes: William G. Busch, ed., *The Trinitarian Controversy* (Philadelphia: Fortress, 1980), and Richard A. Norris, ed., *The Christological Controversy* (Philadelphia: Fortress, 1980).

These statements which attempted to interpret the biblical witness need themselves to be interpreted.

A literalistic interpretation of the creeds has had great popular appeal in all ages. But the declaration that Jesus is fully God and fully human, taken in its plain sense, does not appear to correspond to any kind of commonsense logic. In the light of everyday speech, for example, to be "fully" God means that one cannot be "partly," let alone "fully," human. Further, Jesus is not presented as fully God in the Gospel narratives. He appears to be a human being — even if his humanity has a "different" aspect to it. He was born from the womb of a woman (a real womb even if of a virgin), grew in wisdom as other humans do, and used human speech to communicate with the people of his day. Jesus, therefore, is very much a part of human society. On the other hand, however, the Gospels clearly do *not* portray him as fully human. He is born of a woman, but he is not born into this world as other people are. He is different — greatly different. The Gospel of Matthew declares that he is born of a "virgin" (1:23). But if his birth, however explained, is different from that of other people, one can hardly affirm that he is "fully" human.

Sometimes Christians are urged to believe a literalistic interpretation of the creeds even if they do not understand it — one must take it on faith, it is said. But, if those who shaped the creeds had been content to take it on faith, they would never have involved themselves in years of discussion in order to create the Nicene and Chalcedonian formulas. It seems certain that these declarations had meaning for the theologians who framed them. Undoubtedly they had given consideration to the kind of comments we have made above and, as we will maintain further on in this chapter, did not intend their declarations to be considered in a literalistic fashion.

However, many Christians hold to a literalistic understanding of Jesus' divinity. They affirm "Jesus is God" *as if* this declaration had the meaning that he was *literally* identical with God the Father, the God of Israel.[62] Not only does this literalism misrepresent the thinking of the

62. In the Jewish community also, a literalistic view of Nicaea and Chalcedon is often taken as *the* Christian understanding of Jesus' divinity. For example, Wyschogrod, "Incarnation," p. 208, declares: "Disagreement about whether a particular person is or is not the Messiah is a very important issue but it is hardly comparable to the issue of whether we can point at a specific human being [i.e., Jesus] and say, 'Here is God'."

creeds (whose very language, "fully God and fully human!" discourages such a belief), it has anchored an anti-Judaistic/anti-Semitic stance within the Christian tradition. Jews have felt the pain of such an interpretation because the Jewish rejection of Jesus (considered "God" by Christians) was viewed as the rejection of God. Further, Jewish involvement in the death of Jesus was seen as their attempt to kill God.[63] Until the time of the Vatican Council in 1965, Jews had endured this accusation of deicide. A people so evil, it was thought, deserved to be punished and rejected by God. Only in 1965 — almost two thousand years after the death of Jesus! — were Jews "absolved" from this accusation of being God killers.

A High Christology:
Not Bound to a Literalistic Interpretation

Holding to a "high Christology" does not necessarily deliver one over to literalism and anti-Semitism. Even those whose theology is characterized by a "biblicism" do not necessarily follow the path to anti-Semitism. There are those, according to the judgment of the noted Jewish scholar Eugene Borowitz, who hold to a traditional high Christology without displaying anti-Semitic views. Such a scholar, says Borowitz, is G. C. Berkouwer, a representative of a conservative, Christian position. Speaking of Berkouwer's interpretation of the Bible, he declares: "Because of G. C. Berkouwer's biblicism we might expect him to be the most explicit anti-Semite of the group studied here. In fact, however, Berkouwer seems almost devoid of anti-Jewish sentiment." Borowitz does hold, however, that in Berkouwer's thinking he detects "remnants of prejudice against the Jews," but, he continues, "I am very much more impressed by the example he sets of what a thoughtful, humanly responsive exegete can do in interpreting Christianity from a scriptural base so as to transcend the old anti-

63. See, e.g., the words of Hippolytus: "Why was the temple made desolate? Was it on account of the ancient fabrication of the calf? Or was it on account of the idolatry of the people? . . . By no means, for in all these transgressions they always found pardon open to them. But it was because they killed the Son of their Benefactor [i.e., God], for He is coeternal with the Father." This citation is taken from Rosemary R. Ruether, *Faith and Fratricide: The Theological Roots of Anti-Semitism* (New York: Seabury, 1974), p. 128.

Semitic Christian traditions."[64] No doubt there are a number of biblical scholars, pastors, and laypersons whom these words of Borowitz would fit.[65] But the tragic truth is that persecution of Jews by Christians has been strongly linked to a high Christology which frequently was interpreted to mean that Jesus — *actually, literally* — was God. Such a Christology, when *logically* pursued, makes the Jewish refusal to become followers of Christ a crime against God.

It must be said, however, that many Christians did not pursue *logically* the implications of *this* understanding of Christology. Such logic may seem inescapable to some theologians or to those who are theologically minded, but many Christians (even if they admitted the logic) did not have the heart to press it. Anyone who has served as pastor knows something of the worshiper's independence in carrying out the logic of church doctrine or traditional teaching. For example, although numerous evangelical Christians affirm that those without faith in Jesus will go to hell, few appear to take it seriously, and even fewer go public about it. Some may defend the doctrine, but far fewer will propagate it.[66]

Martin Marty's words on a related matter reflect a similar point of view. Speaking about the charge that Jews killed Jesus or that the Chris-

64. Eugene Borowitz, *Contemporary Christologies: A Jewish Response* (New York: Paulist, 1980), pp. 179-80.

65. Such persons would include clergy such as Billy Graham and Cardinal Joseph Bernardin, whose church, while holding to a high Christology, has renounced judgment on Jews for the death of Christ and has brought to an end missions to the Jews. Both Graham and Bernardin have earned the respect and friendship of many Jews, even though the foundational differences regarding the person of Christ remain.

66. As I remember my earlier years in a church congregation, when someone died "outside the faith" both pastor and people always found some reason to believe that God would care for this person. See also the article by Alan M. Linfield, "Sheep and Goats: Current Evangelical Thought on the Nature of Hell and the Scope of Salvation," *Vox Evangelica* 24 (1994): 63-75. While conservative scholars still hold to the reality of hell, there are those who distance themselves from the traditional view of hell as a place of torment. Further, Linfield calls attention to "a number of evangelicals [who] are arguing that final salvation can be possible without the need for explicit acceptance or knowledge of the Christian revelation" (p. 63). This citation should not be interpreted to mean that conservative scholars are on the verge of rejecting the existence of hell. That such discussion is taking place, however, indicates that there is an uneasiness about traditional teaching in this area.

tian church has replaced Jews as the people of God, he declares: "Most Christians have a simple faith in simple stories. Like most people of faith, they are locked into subcommunities that dig in, no matter what the scholars have to say. They have their lives to live and don't create for themselves enlarged problems where they experience problems hardly at all." Further, Marty continues:

> They [i.e., Christians] may be college graduates, but on this theme they may well be content with the "Jesus loves me, this I know" level of story they hear from their Sunday School children. They may say, feel, and know that "Jesus died for me," and that not Romans or Jews but *I* put him on the cross — without thinking through all the implications of atonement and sacrifice.[67]

Nevertheless, though many Christians do not follow out the implications of a literalistic interpretation of a high Christology, still the fact remains that Jews have been persecuted by the church. Their refusal to believe in Jesus has been interpreted as a full rejection of God. For this reason, as well as others (e.g., the philosophical language of the creeds is little understood in our day),[68] the decisions at Nicaea and Chalcedon are in need of further study and restatement. We must continue to inquire as to the identity and significance of Jesus Christ — specifically the *character* of his divinity.[69]

Jesus: Avoiding Extremes — Finding the Right Words

The many thousands of books, articles, lectures, and debates devoted to the identity of Jesus, in the last hundred years alone, testify to the difficulty the Christian community has had in interpreting the Bible as well

67. Martin Marty, "Removing Anti-Judaism from the Christian Pulpit," in *Removing Anti-Judaism from the Pulpit*, ed. H. C. Kee and I. J. Borowsky (New York: Continuum, 1996), p. 20. My own experiences in four churches — two as pastor and two as a member of the congregation — give assent to Marty's observations.

68. See our discussion below.

69. See the excellent article of John Macquarrie, "Pluralism in Christology," in *Radical Pluralism and Truth*, ed. W. G. Jeanrond and J. L. Rike (New York: Crossroad, 1991), pp. 176-86, in which he pursues Bonhoeffer's question: Who is Christ for us today?

as the creeds. The difficulty, however, does *not* stem from the fact that Christians were or are in the dark as to Jesus' identity. No, for the most part Christians "know" who Jesus is but have great difficulty finding the right words and images to use in articulating his identity. They know the frustration of attempting to give language to the mystery of experience. Church history reveals that, in various periods, the church has gone from one extreme (Jesus is human) to the other (Jesus is divine). But the Christian community has not been able to live with these extremes. It seeks ever to find words and images that reflect more truly the community's experience of Jesus — an experience that led to the conviction that in "meeting" the man Jesus the community had also "met" with God.

Saying Today What Nicaea and Chalcedon Wanted to Say

Today, scholars are looking at the scriptures, as did those who framed the statements of faith at Nicaea and Chalcedon. At the early councils, the church attempted to interpret the biblical texts for their time amidst the *limitations* of their culture, historical understanding, and philosophy. Today, with the same limitations, Christian scholars are attempting again to understand the biblical message. Every century, every generation, must do its own theological work. God does not change, but theology changes. It is the nature of theology to change because it is a human undertaking performed by people living in changing cultures and subject to the inadequacies of human language. However, looking anew at scripture does not mean the rejection of Nicaea and Chalcedon. John Macquarrie speaks to this point when he declares:

> We have to find a way of speaking [about Christ and God] that will reach the hearts and minds of modern men and women, yet we will not do this by reducing Christianity to something so inoffensive that no one will care very much whether it is accepted or rejected. We must say something that is not less than what the fathers of the church said at Nicea and Chalcedon, but we must say it in the language of today.[70]

70. Macquarrie, "Pluralism in Christology," p. 185. See also the comments

Contemporary reflection is not done in isolation; it takes place against the background of Christian thinking that has gone on before. Today's scholars are neither more intelligent nor more faithful than those preceding our time. In our day, however, we are more informed about the character of the Old and New Testaments and more knowledgeable about postbiblical Jewish traditions, both of which help us better understand what lies behind the New Testament and the creedal declarations. Present-day Christian interpreters, representing both the mainline and conservative wings of the church, are giving more attention to Jewish traditions that impinge on the rise of Christianity. More than ever before, for example, scholars recognize that New Testament thinking concerning Jesus *reflects* and *develops* the Israelite and Jewish thought world regarding the figure of Wisdom. It may be, also, that the image of Wisdom lies behind early Christian creedal formulations concerning Jesus. At the very least, the daring personification of Wisdom in the Old Testament and Jewish literature provided the possibility of such philosophical expressions as those found in the creeds.

The Council of Nicaea: Wisdom Theology in Greek Dress

In the thought context of their day, namely, Greek speculative philosophy, early Christian scholars attempted to articulate the significance and identity of Jesus. Nils Dahl holds that the early church's reflection on Jesus, such as took place at Nicaea, was very much influenced by Wisdom theology: "I hardly need add that this type of language [i.e., wisdom language] was of special importance for the later formulation of the dogma about Jesus as the eternal Son and Logos, the second divine person or hypostasis."[71] Jürgen Habermann agrees that Wisdom

---

on p. 186: "If there is a sense in which God was in Christ, this is something so stupendous that we could only destroy it by trying to package it too neatly. But we do have a duty to come clean about what faith in Christ means today and to find a way of expressing it that is both adequate to the reality and honest toward those with whom we communicate."

71. Dahl, *Jesus the Christ*, p. 120. Helmut Gese in *Alttestamentliche Studien* (Tübingen: Mohr, 1991), p. 247, believes also that one can discover traces of Wisdom theology in the Nicene Creed. Larry Hurtado in *One God, One Lord*

reflection (especially regarding preexistence) was transferred to Jesus and that this Christology was "an important pre-requisite for the future confessional development." The figure of preexistent Wisdom gave to the New Testament authors as well as to the framers of the Nicene Creed the imagery that "fit" the figure of Jesus. It is unfortunate, however, as Habermann indicates, that the church received this gift of language and imagery but forgot its Jewish roots.[72]

The following passages from Jewish Wisdom texts,[73] together with a selection from the Nicene Creed, provide support for the above judgment of Dahl that Jewish Wisdom reflection influenced the Nicene formulation. The citation of the various Wisdom texts is *not* an attempt to prove that one moves naturally, without seam, from these texts to the Nicene Creed. Rather, we wish to show that these texts reflect a thought world which, given another context (Christian) and culture (Greek), could be transformed into a declaration such as the one from Nicaea. Of Wisdom it is said:

> The LORD created me at the beginning of his work,
>   the first of his acts of long ago.
> Ages ago I was set up,
>   at the first, before the beginning of the earth. . . .
> When he [the LORD] marked out the foundations of the earth,
>   then I was beside him. . . .   (Prov. 8:22-23, 29-30)

She [Wisdom] glorifies her noble birth by living with God, and the Lord of all loves her. For she is an initiate in the knowledge of God, and an associate in his works. (Wis. 8:3-4)

(Philadelphia: Fortress, 1988), p. 127, cautions against overlooking the distinctions between later Christian confessions and the New Testament, but he affirms: "It would . . . be simplistic to ignore the fact that the intricate and often heated doctrinal discussion leading to these later formulations was set in motion quite early in the Christian movement by the appropriation of the divine agency category of ancient Judaism [which included Wisdom] and was fueled in large part by the devotional practice of Christians which took shape so early." Concerning the acquaintance of the church founders with the concept of Wisdom in both the Jewish and Greek traditions, see the discussion in Jaeger, pp. 100-106.

72. Habermann, p. 430.

73. For a fuller listing of Wisdom texts from the Old Testament and later Jewish literature — compared with some New Testament texts which speak of Jesus — see part 1 of this chapter.

For she [Wisdom] is a breath of the power of God, and a pure emanation of the glory of the Almighty. . . . For she is reflection of eternal light, a spotless mirror of the working of God, and an image of his goodness. (Wis. 7:25-26)

Scholars are nearly unanimous that the latter text stands behind Hebrews 1:3, which declares: "He [i.e., Jesus] is the reflection of God's glory and the exact imprint of God's very being, and he sustains all things by his powerful word." It may be also that Colossians 1:15-17 reflects Old Testament and Jewish Wisdom teaching in its praise of Christ: "He is the image of the invisible God, the firstborn of all creation. . . ." A selection from the Nicene Creed follows:

We believe in one God the Father All-sovereign, maker of heaven and earth, and of all things visible and invisible; And in one Lord Jesus Christ, the only-begotten Son of God, Begotten of the Father before all the ages, Light of Light, true God of true God, begotten not made, of one substance with the Father, through whom all things were made; who for us men and our salvation came down from the heavens. . . .[74]

Although the Nicene Creed nowhere refers specifically to the figure of Wisdom, the general tone of the creed is that of the Wisdom texts cited above. But, as we observed earlier, even as the church took over the imagery of Hebrew Wisdom, its Hebrew roots and character were forgotten. Wisdom, which was colorfully personified in the Hebrew-Jewish traditions, now, under the joint influence of Greek speculative philosophy and Christian doctrinal formulation, was transformed into statements that addressed the being and substance of Jesus Christ. Therefore, though one can understand how the figure of Wisdom may have influenced the declarations at Nicaea, it appears that the creed itself (certainly as discussed through the centuries) transformed the Wisdom imagery into something foreign to the thought of the Bible.

74. Cited by Bettenson, p. 26. For further information concerning this creed, see W. H. C. Frend, *The Rise of Christianity* (Philadelphia: Fortress, 1984), pp. 474-505 and 616-42, and Davis, pp. 33-130.

Insight from Hindsight

In its use of language and imagery, the New Testament differs greatly from the pronouncements of Nicaea. Whereas, for example, the biblical descriptions of Jesus underscore the functional aspect of his identity (i.e., what God did through him), the Nicene formulation emphasizes the *ontological* aspect of Jesus (i.e., his "being" or "is-ness" in relationship to God). To travel from the New Testament to these early church councils is to make a long journey which finally comes to an end at a place where people not only speak another language but express the God-human relationship in a quite different manner. Raymond Brown speaks to this distance between the New Testament and Nicaea when he observes: "A development from the Scriptures to Nicea, at least in formulation and thought patterns, must be recognized by all. Indeed the council Fathers at Nicea were troubled over the fact that they could not answer Arius [who believed that Christ was created by God] in purely biblical categories."[75] Nevertheless, Brown, together with many other scholars, while recognizing the Hellenistic, philosophical shaping of the language at Nicaea, believes these confessions "root in," "stem from," and are "faithful to" New Testament thinking.[76] One may agree that this is so, *if* it is agreed that the rootedness of these conciliar confessions in the New Testament comes to light through hindsight. This *hindsight*, which is insight that does not surface from foresight, opened the eyes of both the New Testament authors (with regard to the Old Testament) and those who formulated the creeds (with regard to the New Testament).

The author of Hosea 11:1 could hardly have imagined that hundreds of years later a New Testament author (Matthew) would use this text to speak of the child Jesus. No less in the dark would have been New Testament authors attempting to conceive of Nicaea and Chalcedon. *Looking back* from these early church declarations, one may find themes in the Bible that support in some fashion the

---

75. Brown, *Christology*, p. 171.

76. E.g., Brown, *Christology*, pp. 142-52, esp. pp. 142 (n. 208), 148, 150. Similar opinions are expressed by Basil Studer, "Das Christusdogma der Alten Kirche und das neutestamentliche Christusbild," *Münchener Theologische Zeitschrift* 44 (1993): 20.

church's christological statements, but for New Testament authors, Nicaea and Chalcedon would have been a complete astonishment and possibly a disappointment.[77] Had they been given the opportunity to read the fourth- and fifth-century creeds of Nicaea and Chalcedon, they would have been amazed at how complex and abstract their experiential, descriptive witness had become.[78] In fashioning the church's confession of faith in philosophical language, the creeds set the Christian community at a distance from the New Testament witness.

Nicene Creed in Need of Interpretation and Restatement

The above comments are not intended to indicate that these early creeds are to be rejected; rather, they are to affirm that they should be appreciated as *attempts* by earlier Christians *to interpret scripture in*

---

77. Houlden, p. 120: "It does, however, need to be recognized how strange and blasphemous the first Christians would have found the ascription to Jesus of divinity as later conceived. Their concentration on him, and the exclusivity they ascribe to him, derive not from formal beliefs along those lines, but from his filling their horizons from end to end. . . ." The judgment of Bas van Iersel, "'Son of God' in the New Testament," in *Jesus, Son of God?* ed. E. Schillebeeckx and J.-B. Metz (New York: Seabury, 1982), p. 47, reflects similar thought: "The language used is miles away from anything that has to do with living experience. The abstract words (godhead, humanity, rational soul, consubstantial, inseparable, person, hypostasis) make clear that this was an attempt to reach a kind of philosophical exactitude and clarity of concepts."

78. A Jewish legend which appears in the Babylonian Talmud (Menahot 29b) may reflect something of what New Testament authors would have experienced if they had been able to jump forward several hundred years and read the Nicene and Chalcedonian formulas. The great lawgiver Moses is transported hundreds of years ahead in time to listen to Rabbi Akiba as he discusses the law of Moses with his disciples. Moses listens to the teaching of Akiba but is unable to understand it. However, he does feel "affirmed" when Akiba declares that the authority for his teaching was Moses! Moses returns from his transport to the future and questions God as to why he, Moses, was given the law when God had such a gifted person as Akiba available. One may question whether the New Testament authors' final evaluation of Nicaea and Chalcedon would be as positive as was Moses' supposed response to Akiba's teaching.

terms of their day, and in this way *to establish dialogue* with a society that was more influenced by Hellenistic philosophy than by Israelite-Jewish traditions.[79]

It must be emphasized, however, that the Nicene declaration is not scripture. It is an interpretation of scripture,[80] several hundred years in the making, stemming out of Greek philosophical thinking. "It is evident to everyone who knows the New Testament," says Klaus Runia, "that it nowhere offers a full-scale Christology a la Nicea and Chalcedon. Nowhere does it speak of a union of two natures, a divine and a human nature, in one divine Person."[81] This view is echoed by Roger Haight, who emphasizes that the doctrine of the Trinity "is a product of historical development . . . developed by stages over a long period of time through reflection and debate."[82]

Today, giving full attention to the scripture and the early councils, we need to state the faith in the language of our day and in terms that can be appreciated by Christians representing a variety of cul-

79. See the comments of Jürgen Seim, "Der Gott Israels und der dreieinige Gott," *Kirche und Israel* 1 (1995): 46-47.

80. F. F. Bruce, *Jesus: Lord and Savior* (Downers Grove, Ill.: InterVarsity, 1986), p. 156, declares: "The Nicene Creed, like other ancient formulae in which Christians have traditionally confessed their faith, is couched in an idiom of its own, which is different from that of the New Testament. Its affirmations, though distinctive, are based on the witness of the New Testament; they have no independent validity apart from that witness."

81. Klaus Runia, *The Present-Day Christological Debate* (Leicester: Inter-Varsity Press, 1984), p. 89. See also James L. Garrett, Jr., *Systematic Theology: Biblical, Historical, and Evangelical,* vol. 1 (Grand Rapids: Wm. B. Eerdmans Publishing Co., 1990), p. 271: "The New Testament writings did bear witness to a relationship involving Father, Son, and Holy Spirit, but they did not define or elaborate on the precise nature of that relationship." Despite these comments, however, both of the above authors believe that Nicaea and Chalcedon are valid developments of the New Testament witness.

82. R. Haight, "The Point of Trinitarian Theology," *Toronto Journal of Theology* 4 (1988): 192. Haight uses the word "debate," but "fierce controversy" might better describe what took place in the early years of the church — controversy that did not come to an end with the final form of the creeds. The following words of Jaroslav Pelikan, *The Christian Tradition: A History of the Development of Doctrine,* vol. 1 (Chicago: University of Chicago Press, 1971), p. 173, are not intended to suggest that theological integrity was missing in the discussion of doctrine (e.g., regarding the Trinity), but those who know the history will admit the truth of his words: "Doctrine often seemed to be the victim — or the product — of church politics and of conflicts of personality."

tures.[83] This means that the creeds, which interpreted scripture, must themselves be interpreted and restated for our day. The creeds should not be privileged above scripture![84]

As mentioned above, Raymond Brown recognizes the philosophical character of the Nicene and Chalcedonian creeds, but holds that "Nicene affirmations are truly in the direction of the NT."[85] Nevertheless, he issues a caution to the Christian community. Although setting high value on the creedal confessions of the church, he reminds Christians today that *neither* the declarations of the New Testament *nor* those of Nicaea and Chalcedon "solve all the problems."[86] Past declarations which speak to the identity of Jesus have employed the human language of a certain time and culture and therefore fall short of being the final and absolute statements concerning Jesus. They are, as Brown states, "limited christological formulations"; he observes that human language is always inadequate "to do justice to what God has done in Christ. That insight should allow constructive reformulation in the face of new and deeper perceptions about Christ."[87] Klaus Runia also points out that Nicaea and Chalcedon should not be thought of as "the last word" or "terminal point" in discussion about Jesus. He, as Brown, points to the "limited nature of the definition of Chalcedon" and issues a call back to the scriptures, for he says, "the witness of Scripture to Jesus

83. Hans Ucko lifts up the lament of Asian Christians who believe that "the early mission enterprise placed an equal-sign between Christianity and Western civilization" and required Asian Christians "to become what they were not and never could be — Western Christians." Western thought structures have taken on almost canonical authority in the christological discussions. See Ucko, "Jews and Asian Christians," in *People of God, Peoples of God,* ed. Hans Ucko (Geneva: WCC Publications, 1996), p. viii; cf. pp. ix-xiv.

84. See also A. N. S. Lane, "Christology beyond Chalcedon," in *Christ the Lord,* p. 274: "Chalcedon is a document of the fifth century. As such it is, like all documents, including the Bible, culturally relative inasmuch as it is expressed in the language and concepts of a particular age. Like the Bible, it needs to be translated into contemporary terms if it is not to be misunderstood." The interesting comment of Leslie Houlden deserves notice (Houlden, p. 125): "There is no reason to suppose that the range of images forming belief about Jesus will not continue to extend in unimaginable ways. If they do not, it will be the sign that at long last Jesus has ceased to play a vital part in religious thought or indeed in reflection on life under the aura of the Christian tradition. . . ."

85. Brown, *Christology,* p. 143.

86. Brown, *Christology,* p. 147.

87. Brown, *Christology,* pp. 148 and 146.

Christ is so rich and so profound that it cannot possibly be exhausted by any one dogmatical formulation."[88]

Contemporary Discussion:
The Intention of Nicaea Must Remain

There is general recognition today that the philosophical language of the early creeds makes little sense to the average Christian worshiper. Millard Erickson echoes the thought of many Christian scholars when he suggests that today we must find new ways of articulating the identity of Christ because the language of Nicaea has little meaning for modern believers.

> We have also observed that the specific metaphysical vehicle used to express the classical doctrine of the Trinity as originally formulated was a Greek metaphysics that was viable in that time but no longer makes a great deal of sense to most persons today. Consequently, we must now attempt to find a contemporary set of categories that can be used to express this crucial doctrine.[89]

---

88. Runia, p. 105. Cf. also p. 108. However, in so saying, Runia is unwilling to oppose a functional Christology in scripture to an ontological one present in the Nicene and Chalcedonian declarations. A. N. S. Lane, "Christology beyond Chalcedon," p. 258, asks what should be the stance of an evangelical toward the christological definition of Chalcedon. He comments: "To be committed to the biblical doctrine of the incarnation is not necessarily to be totally committed to the Chalcedonian exposition of it. Simply to identify the two is to confuse text with commentary. . . . It will be the thesis of this essay that, valuable though the Chalcedonian Definition may be, it is neither necessary nor desirable nor possible to accept it unreservedly." See also Tarsicius van Bavel, "Chalcedon, Then and Now," in *Jesus, Son of God?* pp. 60-61 ("The Significance of Chalcedon Today").

89. M. J. Erickson, *God in Three Persons: A Contemporary Interpretation of the Trinity* (Grand Rapids: Baker, 1995), p. 211. Roger Haight, "The Situation of Christology Today," *Ephemerides Theologicae Lovanienses* 69 (1993): 315-34, surveys the contemporary situation with regard to the christological doctrines of Nicaea and Chalcedon and concludes that many theologians recognize that these doctrines, while important to the church, need to be made "intelligible" for our day. See also Brown, *Christology*, p. 148, who speaks of the need "to reach answers to new dilemmas in fidelity to God's revelation in Christ." The response of Studer, pp. 20 and 22, holds with Brown that the Nicene declarations root in the New Testament, but affirms that Christians today must respond to the mystery of Christ out of contemporary life.

In mainstream Christian churches, theologians, for the most part, are not suggesting that the declarations of Nicaea or Chalcedon are in error and to be rejected. Chalcedon, for example, as John Macquarrie has said, represents "what the church in a solemn ecumenical council summoned at a critical juncture in its history confessed as the summary of its faith in Jesus Christ. We could hardly reject it without rejecting our identity as Christians."[90] Though scholars are not of one mind on *how exactly* and with what language the church should articulate its conviction concerning the identity of Christ or the nature of the Trinity, there is wide agreement that Christians today need to build on the foundational labors of those who lived in the early centuries. Douglas Hare reflects this view when he declares: "Although the *language* of Chalcedon [and one might say also, of Nicaea] no longer satisfies, *its intention* persists in modern statements that affirm that God was in Christ in a unique way."[91]

John Calvin: The Nicene Creed — a Song to Be Sung

Numerous scholars have called attention to the difficulties involved in attempting to articulate the divinity of Jesus in philosophical terminology. For example, Jaroslav Pelikan declares:

---

90. John Macquarrie, *Jesus Christ in Modern Thought* (London: SCM Press, 1990), p. 383. Earl Richard in *Jesus: One and Many: The Christological Concept of New Testament Authors* (Wilmington: Michael Glazier, 1988), p. 485, voices a similar view, while noting that "acknowledgement of a past need not be uncritical." Further, he declares that one must "ask questions that could not be framed prior to the rise of modern scholarship. In grappling with answers to these questions the church comes to the awareness of itself as an ongoing community of intepretation."

91. Douglas Hare, review of *From Jewish Prophet to Gentile God*, by P. M. Casey (Cambridge: Clarke, 1991), in *Horizons in Biblical Theology* 15 (1993): 97, emphasis mine. Macquarrie, *Jesus Christ in Modern Thought*, p. 383, agrees with Hare. He calls for a restatement of Christian thinking about Jesus but believes that Chalcedon, for example, has still a "normative status." He declares: "But what has to be retained does not lie in the words, but in what is sometimes called the 'governing intention,' something that can never be expressed apart from words, yet may be capable of expression in many verbal formulations." For a similar statement see Frisk, p. 86.

This puzzling, indeed frustrating, combination of philosophical terminology for the relation of One and Three with a refusal to go all the way toward a genuinely speculative solution was simultaneously typical of the theology of the Cappadocians and normative for the subsequent history of trinitarian doctrine. Formulas such as *homoousios*, three hypostases in one *ousia*, and mode of origin were metaphysically tantalizing; but the adjudication of their meaning was in many ways a defiance not only of logical consistency, but of metaphysical coherence.[92]

John Calvin's comments on the Nicene Creed are in agreement with the above judgment. He does not appear to take the language of the Nicene declaration, with its superfluity of words, to be a serious example of philosophical logic. Calvin declares: "You see therefore that it is more a song that is suitable for singing than a confessional formula. . . ."[93] Many Calvin scholars point out that the Genevan Reformer had little interest in the Trinity as a philosophical statement about the actual *being* of God. Rather, for him, as for many scholars today, the doctrine of the Trinity had to do with God's work of redemption. Calvin therefore opposed the rationalism of those who fought against the trinitarian declaration of Nicaea, but also stood against those who supported the Nicene declaration, because they exhibited the "scholastic . . . tendency to concentrate Trinitarian doctrine upon elaborate discussions about the 'being of God'

92. Pelikan, *The Christian Tradition*, p. 223. Dietrich Neuhaus, "Ist das trinitarische und christologische Dogma in der Alten Kirche antijudaistisch?" in *"Mit unsrer Macht ist nichts getan . . . ,"* ed. Jörg Mertin et al. (Frankfurt: Haag & Herchen Verlag, 1993), p. 264, comments that the declarations of Nicaea and Chalcedon must have sounded odd to the ears of Greek philosophers — bringing them even to laughter — because such affirmations set aside all the rules of metaphysics. Houlden, p. 80, makes a similar comment regarding the creed established at Chalcedon. He notes that it "was more successful at the verbal level than in terms of religious understanding, or strict logic. . . ."

93. Cited by Jans Koopmans, *Das altkirchliche Dogma in der Reformation* (Munich, 1955), p. 46. Cf. also p. 48. I am indebted to Seim, p. 45 n. 5, for my knowledge of Koopmans's important volume. The comments of Frisk (p. 85) make a similar point: "A careful reading of the [Chalcedonian] Creed makes it clear that the Church did not intend it to be a rational explanation of how Jesus could be both divine and human. It is rather the affirmation of the mystery before which the Church kneels in reverence. The Creed's mood is worship and adoration; it directs attention to the mystery of God's presence in Christ which can only be spoken of in terms of paradox."

which relied heavily on extra-biblical philosophical method and catego-ries."[94] The Nicene Creed is not a law to be obeyed, but a witness to God's revelation of himself in Jesus Christ over which one should rejoice.

Nicaea: Not Intended to Say That Jesus Is the God of Israel

Calvin's description of the Nicene declaration as a song to be sung is a caution for Christians against a flat reading of this creed, as if it could be understood as a logical, forthright statement: "Jesus is God."[95] The framers of the creed, apparently, did not intend to affirm that Jesus and the God of Israel are one and the same. Jesus is not the Father God, the God of Israel, walking on earth, an image that resides often in the minds of laypersons. Both the creeds of Nicaea and Chalcedon re-frained from making that simple, direct statement.[96] Had this been the intention of these early church leaders, then the creeds could have been shortened significantly.

At Nicaea and Chalcedon, declares Dietrich Neuhaus, scholars were attempting a sophisticated confession of faith that dealt with a

94. Butin, p. 132. See also Koopmans, pp. 93, 96-97. Modern-day scholars carry on this emphasis of Calvin, for example: Catherine M. LaCugna, *God for Us: The Trinity and Christian Life* (San Francisco: Harper, 1991), p. 380: "The purpose of the doctrine of the Trinity is to affirm that God who comes to us and saves us in Christ and remains with us as Spirit is the true living God." Further, see Wainwright, p. 130: "My implicit trust has been that the doctrine arose from, and corresponds to, the self-revelation of God in the work of human salvation."

95. One can, of course, use the expression "Jesus is God" without being committed to a literalistic understanding of it. See Houlden, p. 126: "Jesus 'shows', 'is', God to us." See also p. 65. One remembers the controversy between Zwingli and Luther concerning the words of Jesus at the supper: "This is my body." Zwingli interpreted it to mean, "This signifies my body." Luther insisted on the word "is." But for Luther "is" did not mean "This is [actually, literally] my body." Luther is not equating the substance of Jesus' fleshly body with that of the bread. While insisting on the "real presence" in the sacrament, which Luther con-sidered to be a matter of faith, he was careful not to identify "body" as "flesh." The discussion of Jaroslav Pelikan is informative: *Luther's Works. Companion Vol-ume: Luther the Expositor* (Saint Louis: Concordia, 1959), pp. 137-56.

96. See Dietrich Neuhaus, "Ist das trinitarische und christologische Dogma in der Alten Kirche antijudaistisch?" in *"Mit unsrer Macht ist nichts getan . . . ,"* ed. J. Mertin et al. (Frankfort: Haag & Herchen, 1993), p. 259; and Seim, p. 46.

continuing problem for Christians, that is, the relationship of Father and Son — *the issue of oneness and difference.*[97] John Macquarrie shares a similar observation in his comments on the "subtlety" of the language in the Gospel of John, especially regarding John 1:1: "The Word was *with* God, and the Word *was* God" (emphasis mine). He declares:

> He [i.e., John] is a master of paradox, saying things that appear to be contradictory, yet point to something that we cannot say directly. . . . If the Word was *with* God, then it must have been distinct from God; if the Word *was* God, then it must have been identical with God. *John's meaning hovers between distinctness and identity.*[98]

Macquarrie's comments remind us that experience often stands beyond the ability of language description. The early Christian community as well as those who later framed the declarations of Nicaea and Chalcedon struggled to articulate rightly the experience of being acted upon by God in their meeting with Jesus. In meeting him they experienced both humanity and divinity — distinctness and identity. It is the language of paradox. Such an approach does not satisfy the mind's desire for flat-out answers, but, thankfully, the paradoxical response of John and others preserves the reality of experience.

It is not our task in this chapter to develop a full discussion on the Trinity; we desire only to point out that the Greek philosophical undergirding of the Nicene Creed has brought about extensive discussion by both conservative and mainline scholars. There is wide agreement in the church today that the metaphysical language of Nicaea needs restatement, but restatement that retains the *intention* of Nicaea, which is to affirm, according to an above citation by Douglas Hare, "that God was in Christ in a unique way." Sometimes these restatements and interpretations take the form of further philosophical formulations, but in recent years one can see a growing appreciation for the character of the

---

97. Neuhaus, *Das christologische Dogma*, p. 259.

98. Macquarrie, "Pluralism in Christology," p. 181, emphasis mine. See also the discussion of Neuhaus, "Ist das trinitarische und christologische Dogma in der Alten Kirche antijudaistisch?" p. 259, as well as that of Tarsicius van Bavel, p. 60. Something similar is probably intended by two comments made by Harris, *Jesus as God*. He says Jesus "is all that God is without being all there is of God" (p. 293). Elsewhere he expresses this sameness and difference in another way: "While Jesus is God, it is not true that God is Jesus. . . . The person we call Jesus does not exhaust the category of Deity" (p. 297).

biblical witness. The witness of scripture is older than the early creeds, but it may be that its imagery will prove more appealing to modern readers than the language of the later creeds.[99] In large measure this is true because in the New Testament, in contrast to the intellectual statements of the creeds, we see Jesus' "humanity" and "divinity" reflected in his relationship to people.[100]

Wisdom and Jesus

In recent years, as indicated in part 1 of this chapter, biblical scholars have turned their attention increasingly to Wisdom reflection in the Old Testament and postbiblical Jewish literature. On the following pages, we are suggesting that these texts offer Christians contact with one very important approach to the understanding of the identity of Jesus. Interestingly, John Calvin, in attempting to describe the significance of Jesus in his Catechism of Geneva (1542), speaks of him as the Wisdom of God. The Father is represented as the creator and source of all that is, and the Son is spoken of simply as the Father's "eternal Wisdom."[101]

Jesus viewed as the Wisdom of God sets him in the context of the Hebrew-Jewish traditions, traditions out of which the New Testament came into being. Wisdom is a striking image whose varied ex-

99. Increasingly biblical scholars are questioning the traditional importance given to Nicaea and Chalcedon in determining the shape of Christian theology. Houlden, p. 121, reflects the thought of many. Although he recognizes that the Bible and Nicaea are marked by their own place in time, still he has questions regarding the creeds and their relationship to the New Testament: "But it is hard to see why those first responders to Jesus should dance to Chalcedon's tune or be somehow constrained to affirm propositions that never occurred to them. At least, in that Jesus himself is the one about whom we seek to express belief, they bring us, however elusively, and with whatever degree of indirectness, within range of the fount of the tradition." Further, see the comment on p. 123: "It is odd, to say the least, to assert the unique importance of this particular punctuation mark [i.e., Chalcedon] in history."

100. Although the comments of Davis, p. 69, may be too strong, they still carry a degree of truth. He declares: "Objectively, the Gospels and the apostolic writings teach the truth about Christ but in a way that appeals to all human powers [e.g., the imagination, affections, the heart, eyes, and will]. However, the creedal statements of Nicaea declare the truth but bypass senses, feelings and will to appeal only to the intellect."

101. Koopmans, p. 133.

pressions convey the wonder of the early Christian response to Jesus. This figure offered Christians exalted language with which they could express their conviction that in meeting Jesus they had met God. A look at only one portrayal of Wisdom from the postbiblical book of Wisdom (7:25-26) will demonstrate the appeal this image must have had for Christians.

> For she [Wisdom] is a breath of the power of God, and a pure emanation of the glory of the Almighty. . . . For she is reflection of eternal light, a spotless mirror of the working of God, and an image of his goodness.

It is this familiar image of Wisdom that comes very naturally to the Christian mind when searching for language that would express the significance and identity of Jesus: "He is the reflection of God's glory and the exact imprint of God's very being, and he sustains all things by his powerful word" (Heb. 1:3). "He is the image of the invisible God, the firstborn of all creation" (Col. 1:15). Here is the language of devotion and worship; it affirms in dramatic fashion the presence of God in Jesus Christ. This "picture language" crosses easily the borders of the past into our present time.

Wisdom Interpretation: Christology Is Theology

Wisdom provides the imagery that affirms the divinity of Jesus while avoiding the danger of literalizing Jesus' relationship to God. Nicaea was vulnerable at this point. The language of Nicaea which speaks of Jesus as of one substance with the Father has tended to merge Jesus and the Father, the God of Israel. In so doing, Christians have frequently used "Jesus" and "God" as if they were interchangeable terms. In fact, in some wings of the church there is a tendency to speak more about Jesus than about God. A woman in the first congregation I served upon graduation from seminary sensed a wrong emphasis in the proclamation of our church. She asked: "Why do you speak so much about Jesus and so little about God?" The reproach which I heard in her question hit home. It brought about change!

One of the present dangers of the church to the mind of Raymond Brown is "the current tendency . . . to emphasize the Son at the expense of the Father and Holy Spirit."[102] But this danger is not a modern one; it has existed from ancient time. Living within the church community, whose existence is bound to the figure of Christ (e.g., the church is the "body" of Christ), tempts Christians to focus their faith on Christ rather than on the God who sent him.

Probably most people who speak with great emphasis on the divinity of Jesus would agree, if questioned, that it is the God of Israel who has acted in the life and ministry of Jesus. But, though this may be true, the church's proclamation accents often the wrong syllable(s). The true accent is always and forever on God. In the preaching and teaching of the church, Jesus is not to be given the place which belongs only to God the Father. The image of divine Wisdom serves the church well here. Jesus portrayed as the Wisdom of God affirms his oneness with and difference from the God of Israel. Wisdom thinking maintains his intimacy with God but, because Wisdom cannot be literalized, also allows place for images which proclaim his humanity. Jesus is therefore not a rival of God the Father, the God of Israel. In short, Wisdom thinking allows one to confess the divinity of Jesus while at the same time holding to the worship of one God. This is the remarkable character of the New Testament witness. It affirms a high Christology while holding firmly to monotheism. *Christology is expressed in terms of theology:* "In the New Testament, Christology functions within theology, the divine significance of Christ is actually a subcategory of the doctrine of God, the divine identity of Jesus Christ is held firmly within the frame of the Christian (as well as Jewish) axiom that God is one."[103] In so much of what the New Testament teaches, it assumes the Old Testament. That appears to be true also with regard to its witness concerning God. God is the central figure here, as he is in the Old Testament. Al-

102. Brown, *Christology,* p. 173 n. 242. See also Nils Dahl, "The Neglected Factor in New Testament Theology," *Reflection* 73 (1975): 5-8. The neglected factor Dahl writes on is God. Writing out of the perspective of 1975, Dahl comments (p. 5): "For more than a generation the majority of New Testament scholars have not only eliminated direct reference to God from their works but also neglected detailed and comprehensive investigation of statements about God." Brown's comments above appear to indicate that Dahl's observation has validity still today.

103. J. Dunn, "Christology as an Aspect of Theology," in *The Future of Christology,* ed. A. J. Malherbe and W. A. Meeks (Minneapolis: Fortress, 1993), p. 203. Cf. p. 212.

though the New Testament's enthusiasm for Jesus is not to be missed, still, even in the Gospel of John where Jesus is highly exalted, he is depicted as one sent by God to do God's will.[104] The focus of Jesus' preaching is God. While it is true that, at times, Jesus called upon people to make decisions concerning his identity, a dominant theme in his teaching was the kingdom of God, the rule of the God of Israel.

In the period following the New Testament, the church moved steadily away from the Old Testament as well as from the Jewish context of the New Testament. Increasingly emphasis concentrated on Jesus and his divinity, an emphasis that has continued on into our day. In such proclamation, the God of Israel stands in the background; the full biblical context for the New Testament witness is missing. As a result, therefore, Christian proclamation concerning Jesus at times actually conflicts with the declaration of the New Testament. For example, a common bit of "theological shorthand" is to hear salvation spoken of *as if* Jesus is its source. Although the New Testament is lyric in its praise of Jesus, early Christians glorified God as the one who brought salvation to pass (see, e.g., Rom. 1:16-17). Further, not seldom, at Easter time, the God who created the world and brought Israel into existence is shunted aside and first place is given over to Jesus. In many pulpits one can hear the resurrection proclaimed *as if* Jesus raised himself from the dead when, in truth, it was the God of Israel who raised him (e.g., Rom. 4:20-25; 1 Cor. 6:14; 15:4).[105]

Nicaea: Focus on Christology — Being over Act

The New Testament, then, places the emphasis where it belongs — on the God of Israel. It is this God who acts in and through Jesus Christ whom he has sent. In the Nicene Creed, however, this perspective is not so clearly maintained. This may be due to its brief creedal form as well

104. So Brown, *The Gospel according to John*, p. 407, who has gathered together numerous texts from the Fourth Gospel in which Jesus is shown to be acted upon by God. See also De Jonge, pp. 225-37, who in his remarks on the Gospel of John (pp. 234-36) argues that while the Gospel writer emphasizes the "uniqueness" of Jesus, he is careful to underscore that "the initiative is with God, from the very beginning to the very end."

105. Further, see: Acts 4:10; 5:30; Rom. 4:24; 8:11; 10:9; 2 Cor. 1:9; 4:14; Gal. 1:1; Col. 2:12; Eph. 1:20; 1 Pet. 1:21.

as to the situation in which the later church found itself, that is, finding it necessary to present its witness to a society influenced by Hellenistic philosophical thinking. In any case, the language of the creed reflects a philosophical, mathematical character that places too much emphasis on the figure of Jesus.

Gerhard Forde points out that the creedal teaching which affirms that Jesus is of one substance with God the Father (Nicaea) or that Jesus possesses a human and divine nature (Chalcedon) tends to point us away from the New Testament witness. How so? Forde explains: the "substantialist language tends to convey the idea that Jesus rescues us *because* he is a synthesis, that he is made up of undying substance [Godness] joined in some way with dying substance [humanity]."[106] The result is a much too fine focus on Jesus. We become preoccupied with his divinity and humanity. We want to know *how* this human being can be of one substance with God the Father, the God of Israel; *how* can he possess two natures (human and divine)? When the church begins to concentrate on Jesus being of one substance with the Father, the God of Israel, then Christian proclamation easily becomes focused on proving how Jesus could be human and divine. With such a concentration on Jesus, one can easily overlook an important point of the New Testament witness, that is, that God is acting in Jesus for our sake.

The New Testament:
"God Does Himself to Us in Jesus"

Forde does not wish to set aside fully the substance language of the creeds,[107] but he believes that, for the most part, this language has hidden the action language of the New Testament. In this scripture, he affirms, one sees Jesus, not as one who reflects God's being but as one in whom God acts for us: "Jesus is the repetition of God to us."[108] With such an expression the author is underscoring his belief that the language suitable for expressing the humanity and divinity of Christ is the *language of action:* "Jesus is . . . the true human in whom God does God to us. The point is that we can move forward here only if we realize that

106. Forde, p. 89.
107. Forde, p. 101.
108. Forde, p. 103.

in and through the human, suffering, dying, and resurrected Jesus we come up against God. *God does himself to us in Jesus.*"[109] The creeds, with their preference for the language of substance, underscore the *being* of Jesus in relationship to the God of Israel. They do not portray effectively God acting in Jesus, or as Forde says, God doing God to us in Jesus. Had the creeds more effectively retained the New Testament action imagery regarding the relationship of Jesus to God, then, perhaps, many of the bitter christological disputes in the church could have been avoided.

These differing emphases (i.e., "action" as opposed to "substance") are not small matters. The difference may have something important to say about how Christians relate to each other and to the world about them. To see Jesus as relating to God principally in terms of essence or substance sets us in the arena of philosophical thought where we fight to establish the correct ideas about Jesus. But to see Jesus as relating to God principally in terms of action underscores the character of response which God expects from those who follow him. We do not wish to convey the impression that thinking and ideas are unimportant; nevertheless the beginning and the center of the gospel is the divine Act done for humankind — an Act that looks to find continuation in the lives of Christians.

Christianity is Act more than Idea. Although there may be general agreement with this statement, still the history of the church points in another direction. Christians, too often, have become fixed on an ideational-philosophical Christology. Even when we speak about "doing Christology," we most often mean "christological discussion"! But "doing Christology" points us in the right direction because "it is the crucified man, who does God to us. Any proclamation of this man must therefore seek to do it again. Systematic theology must leave us in the spot where there is nothing left to do but such proclamation."[110]

Our discussion above regarding the unity of Jesus and God as a unity of action gives us a vantage point from which we can view the

109. Forde, p. 100, emphasis mine. Further, Forde observes, the unity of Jesus and God the Father is a "unity of doing." He cites the following passage from John 5:19: "Truly, truly, I say to you, the Son can do nothing of his own accord, but only what he sees the Father doing; for whatever he does, that the Son does likewise." See also his comments on pp. 103-4.

110. Forde, p. 105. Further: "Christ cannot merely be talked about, he must finally be done to us" because he is "the act of God to us."

worship of Jesus. We observed earlier that the tendency to elevate Jesus is a somewhat "natural" one arising out of the Christian community's experience of meeting God in the life and ministry of Jesus. Christians, who were brought to newness of life through God's act in Jesus Christ, spoke often of Jesus and of what he meant to the Christian community. They praised him and addressed prayer to him, but, as we will see, such acts were set in the context of the worship of the God of Israel who acted for us in Jesus.

Prayer to God — Prayer to Jesus

Early Christianity, according to the witness of the New Testament, continued the Old Testament's emphasis on the worship of the one God, the God of Israel (Matt. 6:9-13). It is to this God that prayer is customarily directed — even by Jesus himself (e.g., Luke 22:42). Christians may pray *in the name of* or *through* Jesus (e.g., Eph. 5:20; Heb. 13:15), but prayer or praise, especially in public worship, is normally offered to the God of Israel.[111] There are, however, passages in the New Testament in which we find praise and prayer directed to Jesus (e.g., Rev. 5:9-10, 12-14; Acts 7:59; 2 Cor. 12:8).[112] Similarly, in the early post–New Testament period there are occasions on which prayer or worship is addressed to Jesus by individuals outside of formal, public worship. But "the normal pattern of Christian prayer prior to the fourth century was to God *through* Christ, emphasizing the high priestly role of Christ

---

111. See the foundational study of Josef A. Jungmann, *Die Stellung Christi im Liturgischen Gebet* (Münster: Aschendorffsche Verlagsburchhandlung, 1962), pp. 112-22.

112. France, "The Worship of Jesus," pp. 17-36, has assembled a number of texts from the New Testament which point to the worship of Jesus. Some texts speak of an informal worship ("worship" understood in a "broad" sense) during his lifetime. Such passages, France indicates, do not indicate that Jesus was worshiped as one who was divine. "Formal worship" of Jesus, he notes, with its assumptions of divinity, began after the resurrection. See also Hurtado, *One God, One Lord,* pp. 101-8, who points out that this reverence for Jesus, which arose out "of the fervent religious enthusiasm of the early Christian communities" (p. 102), had no counterpart in Judaism (e.g., with regard to the recognition given divine agents, see pp. 107-8). The devotional practice of singing hymns to Christ and addressing prayer to him, says Hurtado, speaks of Christian innovation regarding Jewish monotheism (p. 108).

who in his humanity intercedes for us on our behalf."[113] However, after the Council of Nicaea (325), prayers addressed to Christ in formal worship became more frequent. No doubt this was due to the wording of the Nicene declaration which, while confessing the humanity of Jesus, emphasized heavily his "divinity." It appears that the Council of Chalcedon (451) attempted to bring the affirmations of Nicaea into better balance by underscoring Jesus' humanity (he is "truly God and truly human"). But in practice the church continued to proclaim the "divinity" of Jesus while softly conceding his humanity.

To many Christian worshipers the separation of Father and Son was lost, and they felt free to merge the two and, without distinction, to offer prayer to God the Father or to Christ. There were those in the church, however, who saw the danger of this development. Two early church councils attempted to stem the tide of popular thought. The Council of Hippo (393) declared: "At the service of the altar, prayer shall always be addressed to the Father."[114] A few years later a similar declaration was made at the Council of Carthage (397): "In prayer one should not put the Father in the place of the Son, nor put the Son in the place of the Father; when standing at the altar one should always address the prayer to God the Father."[115]

No doubt Christians will continue to address both praise and prayer to Jesus because of the conviction that God was *in* him reconciling the world to himself. But this practice in many Christian churches has gone beyond the bounds of both the New Testament and the creeds; it threatens the New Testament's emphasis on God working *through* Jesus Christ. In many Christian churches the name of Jesus (and the titles given to him) dominates the worship. H. Richard Niebuhr warned against this seductive temptation of turning theology into Christology — of investing such "absolute significance" in Jesus that it obscures "his relation to the One beyond" him.[116] This tempta-

---

113. LaCugna, p. 124. See Jungmann, pp. 112-51 (regarding the New Testament and the development to the fourth century).

114. Cited by LaCugna, p. 126.

115. Cited by LaCugna, p. 141 n. 88.

116. H. Richard Niebuhr, *Radical Monotheism and Western Culture* (New York: Harper & Brothers, 1960), pp. 59-60. Writing concerning radical monotheism which Christianity professedly holds in common with Judaism, Niebuhr declares (p. 59) that a "frequent form of the deformation of radical monotheism in Christianity occurs when Jesus Christ is made the absolute center of confidence

tion must be strongly resisted because if the exaltation of Christ hides from view both his humanity and the initiating, continuing activity of God in him (both strongly emphasized in the New Testament), then we have lost two themes that were crucial in defining the early Christian movement.

Jesus the Wisdom of God: An Image for Today

Accepting a New Testament view of Jesus as the Wisdom of God offers an important image that emphasizes the *preeminence of God* the Father but preserves, as we have said already, the *divinity of Jesus*. Further, the image of Jesus as the Wisdom of God resists reduction to literalistic thinking and therefore preserves also the *mystery of his relationship to God*. The latter point, the mystery of that relationship, is one that the New Testament respects. The dual affirmation that Jesus is human and divine rises out of experience and worship and not from a logical, philosophical analysis. The latter approach steps far beyond the confessional, descriptive character of New Testament thinking; it substitutes static terminology for the language of devotion. Further, philosophical analysis is largely reserved for the theologians; it does not function effectively to inform or nourish the worshiper.

Early Christians did not know the "how" of Jesus' relationship to God, but from their experience of listening to and following Jesus they "knew" that in some manner God was present in him.[117] They were convinced that God had worked something "new" through him. They used many and varied images to describe this newness, and *one* important image was that of Jesus as the Wisdom of God. It is an image whose wide us-

and loyalty. The significance of Jesus Christ for the Christian church is so great that high expressions about his centrality to faith are the rule rather than the exception in the language of preaching and of worship." He cautions, however, against substituting "the Lordship of Christ for the Lordship of God" and further asserts: "At various times in history and in many areas of piety and theology Christianity has been transformed not only into a Christ-cult or a Jesus-cult but into a Christ- or Jesus-faith."

117. See the fine article of Elizabeth A. Johnson, "Trinity: To Let the Symbol Sing Again," *Theology Today* 54 (1997): 299-311. She emphasizes that the first Christians were Jews who held to belief in one God. But, she declares, "they came to see that what had happened in their lives through their encounter with Jesus of Nazareth was nothing less than something divine."

188

age in varied contexts before and during the time of Jesus impressed his followers and caused them to say "Amen, so is he." This ancient image can be easily appreciated today as a way of speaking about God's revelation of himself in Jesus Christ. Recently, Leander Keck declared that "it is time to stop telling the Bible what it may mean" (that is, by scientific analysis) and suggested that we let the biblical language "restore imagination to our faith and thought."[118] Jesus as the Wisdom of God touches our imagination. This image enables affirmations of faith while preserving the mystery of God's revelation in Christ.

However . . .

Jesus is "human"! The human aspect of Jesus has not been the focus of this chapter because we wanted to emphasize that his divinity, affirmed in the New Testament, has roots in the Hebrew-Jewish traditions. However, having served as a pastor before taking a post as a professor in a seminary, I believe that for many people it is the humanity (humaneness) of Jesus, reflected in the Gospel narratives, that attracts them to the Christian faith and nourishes them in their living. But for many centuries the church has tended to hold to an ontological interpretation of the divinity of Jesus as the test of a true Christian witness. Often this emphasis has reduced Jesus' humanity to a second level — to a "however" category. Leslie Houlden comments on the danger which the creedal formulations represent for the humanity of Jesus: "Once the belief in Jesus in terms of the personal pre-existent Logos had taken almost universal hold, it was virtually impossible to hold it together with a realistic belief in Jesus' humanity, whatever forms of words were attempted."[119]

The exaggerated emphasis on the divinity of Jesus has at times endangered the Christian community's own sense of humaneness.[120] Those unable to conform to a certain interpretation of his divinity have

118. Leander E. Keck, "The Premodern Bible in the Postmodern World," *Interpretation* 50 (1996): 137. See further his comments on p. 136.

119. Houlden, p. 80.

120. See Mark A. Noll, *The Scandal of the Evangelical Mind* (Grand Rapids: Wm. B. Eerdmans Publishing Co., 1994), pp. 54-55, who warns the church today against embracing a docetic view of Jesus — a view that does not give adequate emphasis to the humanity of Jesus and therefore fails to consider seriously the structures of human society.

been excluded from Christian fellowship.[121] Naturally, legitimate concerns underlie the affirmation of Jesus' divinity. But concentrating too fully on the *divine* Son may cause us to miss the Jesus who bore the sorrows of his day and reached out to those who did not fit in. It is the humanity (humanness) of Jesus that strikes the chord in the human heart. Again, Leslie Houlden says it well: "One may hazard the guess that in a world where substantial bodies of people feel undervalued and oppressed, it will be the human simplicity of Jesus, playing down all human pretension and destined for death, that will occupy centre stage."[122] Grounding the truth of Houlden's comments is the witness of the New Testament which speaks of a human-humane Jesus who has a heart for those on the fringe of society (Matt. 9:10-11; 11:19). It is precisely the human Jesus, sent by God, that witnesses to God's own suffering concern for all sorts and kinds of people. The comments of Gerhard Forde provide food for thought: "Only the Jesus who washes his disciples' feet and is about to be glorified in crucifixion can say, 'He who has seen me has seen the Father' (John 14:9)."[123]

Holding to a Both-And Theology

The above comments may appear to urge the reader to focus entirely on the humanity of Jesus, for with this emphasis the tire seems to hit the road. However, to do so would be to repeat the mistake often made within the church; that is, the underscoring of one aspect of Jesus at the expense of the other. We are not encouraging any view that would suppress the divinity of Jesus. Together with others, we wish to hold to the witness of the New Testament and the creeds that Jesus is human and divine. But we believe also that placing the humanity of Jesus at a secondary, "however" level represents a danger for the church. In so doing we separate ourselves from the witness of scripture *and* that of the creeds, which affirm *both-and* concerning Jesus.

121. A case in point is that of John Calvin. According to some of Calvin's contemporaries, his interpretation of the Bible did not appear to support fully enough the creedal formulas concerning the Trinity. For this perceived lack, he was sharply and publicly attacked. But he returned this favor to others who disagreed with him (Butin, p. 167 n. 66, pp. 87-127).
122. Houlden, p. 125.
123. Forde, p. 106.

A strong affirmation of images of Jesus which underscore him as a human being obedient to God is the needed counterbalance to the affirmation of his divinity; it restrains the tendency of the church to literalize his divinity. Such literalizing views lead to a blurring of distinctions between the Son and the Father, the God of Israel. They tend to create a Jesus piety and a Jesus faith. Although the New Testament community may have arrived fairly early at a view of Jesus as divine, that portrayal of him did not suppress the many images of him as a human being doing the will of his Father. Raymond Brown speaks the truth: "How impoverished would be our understanding of the revelation in Christ had the earlier ways of speaking about the identity of Jesus been erased in favor of the Nicene formulations!"[124] If that had been done, the "divine" Jesus would no longer have had a human face and would hardly have been the one in whom the God of Israel became present in our world.[125]

124. Brown, *Christology*, p. 149.
125. See the excellent articles appearing in the October (1997) issue of *Theology Today* which focus on the Trinity. The essays of Elizabeth Johnson ("Trinity: To Let the Symbol Sing"), Donald Juel ("The Trinity and the New Testament"), Colin Gunton ("The God of Jesus Christ"), Ian A. McFarland ("The Ecstatic God: The Holy Spirit and the Constitution of the Trinity"), James P. Mackey ("The Preacher, the Theologian, and the Trinity"), and Ellen T. Charry ("Spiritual Formation by the Doctrine of the Trinity") all deserve careful attention. I am sorry that this issue arrived too late for me to incorporate the contributions into the present discussion.

191

CHAPTER 10

Final Reflection

IN THE BEGINNING: THE EXPERIENCE

The previous chapters addressed the relationship of the New Testament to the Old Testament, but, as is clear from our discussion, at center this issue has to do with the relationship of Jesus to the Old Testament. It is he, his ministry, death, and resurrection, that has created the New Testament. Except for him there would be only one Testament.

Throughout our discussion in this book, the word "experience" has surfaced frequently because we believe that for early Jewish Christians the experience of meeting and following Jesus was the beginning of a new way of living, worship, and thinking. For them, as for the Christian community ever since, Jesus constituted a new relationship — a "new covenant" — between God and humankind. He was one sent by the God of Israel; in him and in his ministry Christians found God to be "present" in a special manner. This experience of meeting God in Jesus was a personal experience but not a private one. On the contrary, it was a Wonder that a growing community — using a variety of images and expressions — acknowledged and confessed as life-changing.

Early Christians were predominantly Jewish. The beginning Christian movement was, as numerous scholars today agree, a movement inside of Judaism. The "experience" of Jesus therefore was not the only experience that these Jewish believers had. Rather, it was an "experience" inside and alongside of their "experience" of God which was mediated to them through the Old Testament scripture and its interpretation by the Jewish community. The two "experiences" were not seen to be foreign to each other. Jesus' own proclamation that he was

192

sent by the God of Israel — together with the impress of his ministry — created the conviction that these two "experiences" were basically two expressions of one reality; that is, in Jesus Christ the God of Israel had acted once again for the good of humankind. Christians celebrated this revelation in Jesus as a "new" act but were aware that it was not a "brand-new" action; it stood in an analogical relationship with what God had done previously in Israel. When, therefore, Jewish believers encountered Jesus, it was only natural that they would look to the Old Testament scripture for words and images that would help them interpret and articulate this new expression of God's concern for those he created.

The Old Testament texts date hundreds of years before the time of Jesus, but Jewish Christians, looking back from their meeting with him, believed that many passages in this ancient scripture — interpreted in their "depth" — cast a revealing light on the significance of this extraordinary person. Such an interpretation, which represents a "believer" or "faith" understanding, constituted a new reading of scripture.[1] Many years earlier other Jews, members of the Qumran community, had interpreted the scripture by means of a similar method. Further, rabbinic interpreters, living long after the Old Testament text had taken its basic form, discovered in the "depth" of this ancient scripture a divine word for their time.

Just so was it with the Christian community. As Christians viewed the Old Testament against the background of events surrounding Jesus, the scripture came alive with meanings that had never before surfaced. Early Jewish Christians, as Jews generally, did not believe that the scripture was to be interpreted only in terms of its plain or literal meaning. To them, scriptural words were the inspired, intentional expressions of a believing community. These words had a definite meaning for the day in which they originated, but they contained a "more" — a "more" which revealed itself when probed in the light of contemporary events. Intentional words — words originating in a faith community — have depth; they have a plain, historical meaning, but they also have meanings that can only be discovered by a later believing community as it responds to the experiences of its day. For Christians the words of the

---

1. See most recently the contribution of Nikolaus Walter, "Urchristliche Autoren als Leser der 'Schriften Israels,'" *Berliner Theologische Zeitschrift* 14 (1997): 59-77, esp. pp. 64, 67, 71, and 76.

Old Testament scripture crossed the border that separates the "then" from "now" and provided revealing insight into the significance and identity of Jesus. Looking back to the Old Testament from their meeting with Jesus, they "saw" in this holy writing what could never have been seen before, namely, Jesus, his ministry, death, and resurrection. In meeting him they knew that something extraordinary had happened, but they could only come to speech about the significance and meaning of this event by turning to their scripture, the Old Testament.

Today, as in earlier times, Christians turn first and foremost to the New Testament scripture because it is through the proclamation of this scripture that one hears the clear witness concerning Jesus Christ. The church was and is right in its concentration on the New Testament. Without the ringing proclamation of "newness" in Christ, the Christian movement would have died out early. In addition, however, the church in our day is right in recognizing that the Christian community stands in need of the witness of the Old Testament because the New Testament by itself is not adequate to tell the whole story regarding God's act in Jesus. In recognizing the crucial importance of the Old Testament, the church is reflecting kinship with the conviction of the early Christian movement which believed that the new community created in Jesus was the work of the God of Israel who sent him. In the event of Jesus, the God of Abraham, Moses, and the prophets revealed once again his loving concern for humankind. The close relationship that existed between early Christians and the faith of Israel may be seen, as we pointed out earlier, in the fact that this early movement was one that took place within Judaism. It was initiated by the Jewish Jesus and indelibly marked by Israelite and Jewish traditions. If one were to remove, for example, the Israelite-Jewish references/allusions from the New Testament, this scripture would be radically reduced in size. It was due to the Christian conviction that the God and Father of Jesus Christ was also the God of Israel that caused them to turn to the Old Testament as they attempted to understand what had taken place in their meeting with Jesus.

The Old Testament and the New Testament, in dialogue with each other, constitute the Christian scripture. Neither can be the scripture of the church without the other. The Old Testament does not exist simply as the background of the New Testament, nor is it to be viewed as a writing that, in its plain and literal sense, points to the New Testament. It is, rather, an integral part of the character of the New Testament. To become only "New Testament" Christians has serious implications for our contemporary experience of Jesus Christ. Concentrating, for example, only on the "New Testament" character of the New Testament, we overlook significant assumptions, allusions, and references to the Old Testament and tend to embrace a Jesus piety. On the other hand, when we recognize fully the Old Testament as scripture and are alert to its presence in, with, and under the words of the New Testament, then we become aware that it is the God of Israel who worked his will in Jesus. By means of this awareness, our "experience" of the Christ event is the experience of *God* acting in Jesus Christ. It was this surprising breaking-in of divine activity in Christ that excited praise in the early Christian church.

Although this belief that God revealed himself "present" in Jesus Christ placed strain on the early Christian adherence to monotheistic belief, the New Testament witness never surrendered to a Jesus piety. No doubt it was this emphasis on *God* acting and present in Jesus that protected the Christian movement from becoming a sect that would die out in the course of history. It is this same affirmation of *God* acting and present in Christ that will provide the staying power of Christianity today.

Index of Names and Subjects

Index of Scripture References

Old Testament

Genesis
17:7-8	50

Exodus
1:8	77
2:24-25	113
4:22-23	43
15:1	23
15:23-25	31
17:6	31
17:9	22
19	63
19–23	114
20–23	110
21:24	22
34:6-7	61n, 88-89
34:9	89
34:29	63

Leviticus
18:5	61, 115
19:18	77, 115
19:34	77, 116

Numbers
20:9-12	31

21:16-20	31

Deuteronomy
6:5	115
10:16	84, 86
22:8	77
25:4	42
30:6	84, 86
30:11-14	61, 87
31:16	23

Joshua
8	84
11	84
12	84

Judges
1	84
15:13	77

1 Samuel
20:5	77
20:18	77
20:24	77
20:27	77

1 Kings
11:29	77

19:8	63
19:18	4

Ezra
9:6	2, 6n, 89
9:13	4n

Nehemiah
9:6–10:1	57n.1
9:26-30	89
9:31-32	89
9:32-33	81n.4
9:38	86n.11

Job
10:10-11	23

Psalms
1	110, 118
8:5	49-50
19	101
26:1-3	110
32:5	61n
40:3	77n
40:6	48-49
40:6-8	48
40:8	86-87, 92
41:9	38, 45-46, 104

201

CPSIA information can be obtained at www.ICGtesting.com
Printed in the USA
BVOW030859081212

307517BV00003B/12/A